Stop Throwing Cash in the Trash

Your Guidebook to Finding Hidden Treasures and
Transforming Them into Huge Profits

To: Ehren
Parks

Patricia Penke

Patricia J. Penke

Stop Throwing Cash in the Trash.......Your Guidebook to Finding Hidden Treasures and Transforming Them into Huge Profits; is in no way authorized by, endorsed, or affiliated with eBay or its subsidiaries. All references to eBay's website and other trademarked properties, are used in accordance with the "Fair Use Doctrine" and aren't meant to imply this book is an eBay product for advertising, or used for other commercial purposes.

While every care has been taken in the compilation of this guide book, the readers of this book should know online auctioning has certain risks. Readers who participate in selling or buying online, do so at their own risk. The author, editors, publisher, or the books contributors, cannot guarantee financial success, and therefore renounce any liability, loss or risk sustained, either directly or indirectly, by reliance placed on information contained in this book.

The current values, prices and photos in this book should be used only as a guide. They are not intended to set prices, which vary from one section of the country to another or global pricing. Auction prices as well as dealer prices will vary and are affected by condition of the said items as well as current demands. The editors, publisher, or its contributors cannot assume responsibility for any losses that might be incurred as a result of consulting to this guide.

The author of the book have made all reasonable efforts to provide current and accurate information for the readers of this book. The author will not be held liable for any unintentional errors or omissions that may be found. This book contains references to specific brand-name products and/or trade names of products. These brand-name products and/or trade names are trademarks or registered trademarks and are property of their respective owners. Further, references to specific brand-name products, companies, or trade names do not imply that the owners of said products or companies have endorsed this book.

ISBN-13: 978-0692515013

ISBN-10: 0692515011

Cover Design: Joshua Foo

Editor: Gina Foutch

For my parents,

Ray and Ann Mills; Matthew Mills,

and my family,

for teaching me patience and to never give up.

Contents

Introduction

Treasure Hunting! It's the thrill of the hunt and the unmatched joy of finding unknown treasures that keeps the pursuit of antiquing fresh and enticing.

A dumpster placed in front of a home in my neighborhood caught my eye today. Can you imagine the possibilities? Most people would think that it held trash destined for the city landfill, but what is one person's trash, could be another's, "treasure" as I would call it.

Dumpsters are common sights in neighborhoods, dotting the landscapes of older, established areas. Most of the time, the sight of a dumpster placed in front of a home, is evidence of an estate liquidation about ready to take place. Usually overflowing with vintage discarded household items, the possibilities of dumpster diving for undetected cash enters my mind. I have learned numerous times, personal possessions being discarded can literally be turned into substantial revenue just by reselling them on the World Wide Web.

Diamonds in the Rough

For over 16 years, I have been involved in the resale of vintage collectibles. I've spent countless hours at auctions, flea markets, garage-tag sales, rummage -yard sales, and thrift stores looking for those "diamonds in the rough". It's a wonderful feeling to invest a small amount of cash to purchase someone else's cast-offs, with the hope of making a substantial amount of income when reselling them. We love the adventure and the hunt!

I used to get this same feeling during my earlier childhood days when helping Dad and Mom mine for gold when living in Alaska back in the 1960s. My siblings and I would be so excited to get up early on a weekend morning and make the perilous road trip to Crow Creek Mine. The car trip we had to take from Anchorage to Girdwood was via a mountain road, so I was never thrilled about the journey. Once we arrived to our destination, we would gather our gear and put on rubber boots, then walk a mile down a mountain trail to the banks of the creek, all in hopes of finding treasure. My Dad would set up two sluice boxes along the banks of the raging rapids; inspect the area along the creek for perspective hidden gold deposits; and start digging. Once the buckets were filled with dirt and rocks, Mom would carry the buckets over to the boxes where my siblings and I, would sort and wash through the dirt and toss away any non-essential rocks and debris. All this work was in great anticipation of sighting that bright gleam of gold, left behind on the floor of the box. I wouldn't ever trade those marvelous memories. Dad was known for his keen sense of finding great gold digs, and he made a substantial amount of cash by selling some of his gold nuggets.

The subject of reselling vintage merchandise encompasses such a vast amount of information, it would literally take several hundred pages to teach my readers about all the *hidden* wealth waiting to be discovered. It is my hope that the following information will be helpful in clarifying *what* these hidden gems are, *where* to find them, and *how* to make a large profit by reselling these desired items online. We will discuss *why* the item is valuable? Factors, such as genres, colors, textures, makes and models; eras, styles, consumer products and events, are very important when discovering an item's present market value. This book will discuss some of the most important information about these disguised treasures waiting to be discovered and resold for a substantial profit. This book will discuss the current resell values for items being listed for sale on the World Wide Web. What someone will actually pay to own them, *not* for what their appraised values might be.

This is not just another antiquing reference book; this book will disclose specific vintage and some not-so-old items considered quite collectible, thus valuable to their buyer. These certain treasures are just waiting to be discovered and can be....rather easily. Additionally, this book will discuss some important key tips to help in identifying these collectible items and why, they are sought-after?

Keep in mind, not all antiques and vintage items are valuable. For instance, the realm of baseball card and stamp collecting is vast, but only a fraction of them are valuable. More examples: A vintage 1960's lunchbox can be worth $15 or $1,000 - depending on the graphics found on the tin metal boxes, their condition, and the matching thermos is present. A vintage matchbook cover may only sell for a $1 or for $100. Just because a matchbook cover depicts a defunct or obsolete business, doesn't make it valuable.

When searching for authentic vintage collectibles, a person has to be mindful of all the reproductions and replicas that can be mistaken for being an actual vintage piece. This book will help the reader to recognize true-vintage merchandise.

We live in a trend setting, on-demand society, with trends that can change overnight. Today's collectibles may not be popular tomorrow. With that in mind, we will take a look at collectibles that are currently in demand-and those that are *not* in demand.

This book will help readers locate these *one-of-a-kind*-often missed, but valuable items most of us might consider trash or junk. Those discarded items could in fact, be an undetected fortune waited to be discovered. For example, I purchased a vintage doll at a local auction a couple of years ago. At first glance, I had considered the doll to be quite ugly, but unique, so I bid on her. When I arrived home, I was elated to discover it was a hard-to-find vintage 1972 *Kenner*, big-eyed Blythe doll. I sold her online for over $800. The doll had been found in good condition, but not in her original box. Had the doll been found in excellent condition with original accessories and box; she could have brought me in a profit of over $2,000. (Blythe was reintroduced in the 21st century by *Hasbro* so, watch for the original *Kenner* markings found on her back.)

Yet, another example of a unique one-of-a-kind item that can sell on eBay, are specific boxes of original 1970s-1990s disposable diapers by *Pampers*, which can sell for over $500. Seriously!

You will discover in the following pages, examples of the unbelievable secret treasures waiting to be discovered--most of which are often mistaken for being cast-offs, or profitless. Believe me, it's probably not the heirloom china and glassware that

1972 KENNER, Big-Eyed Blythe Doll.
Listing Price-$1,700

has been kept in the china cabinet for safe keeping. Additionally, the book *will* mention antiques and collectibles that the masses will still pay a large sum of cash to possess-versus those that currently have lost popularity or values.

It's not impossible to buy a vintage piece of luggage for $2 and sell it for over

$300. The vintage *Zero Centurion-Halliburton* aluminum suitcases, mid-century - Hartmann belted leather; and tweed-covered travel bags, sell in the hundreds of dollars. Early 1900s' designer, *Louis Vuitton* steamer trunks, can sell for.....over $8,000! (Okay, most of know designer, *Louis Vuitton* anything can be quite valuable, but I definitely will make the effort to make a bee-line for the attics and basements at estate sales, to search for these antique trunks.)

Mid-century Halliburton Zero Aluminum
Suitcase-22" - $125

Vintage Designer Louis Vuitton (LV)
Monogram Steamer Trunk

Vintage Hartmann Tweed Luggage
Bag Label

Vintage Hartmann Tweed Luggage
Bag

 Tip: Research is KEY for discovering those hidden gems!

It would take a substantial amount of research to learn all areas of the current collecting arena, so with this in mind, this book is a summary of several of the collecting arenas in our current society. Its contents will give the reader basic knowledge for learning- how to find, what to buy, and sell- in their quest to making a substantial second income; and some important tips to start selling these items on ecommerce sites. The reader might also want to invest in additional educational antiquing resources, and go at the local library and read-up on some antique collecting reference books. Additionally, read any recent articles published on the Web, or current magazine/newspaper articles about the current popularity of a specific collectible. I have spent hours researching collectibles on the Internet, which has revolutionized the world markets.

Equally important, I've learned a lot from chatting with savvy antique collectors and dealers (local experts). The best antique dealers are also wholehearted teachers. They have a passion for what they collect, and most are happy to share information with people who are sincerely interested in learning. These connoisseurs of vintage wares will usually share some invaluable information about how to recognize and date authentic, vintage merchandise. Additionally, dealers can give you advice on what items you may want to avoid purchasing, due to lack of popularity in the current antique resale market. Study their buying trends at auctions and antique sales. *How much* are they willing to invest for an item?

I have placed internet links throughout this book that can help my readers learn additional information on a particular theme of collecting. Conversely, keep in mind that these are current online sites and can become outdated and disappear with time. This book does not promote any particular reference online or book source over another-they are only used to be of assistance to the reader for educational reasons.

Becoming a retailer of vintage goods or an antique dealer, is a great vocation. You are not only becoming a treasure hunter; but additionally, a detective, a seller, marketer and archaeologist. To be a successful dealer, you will need to have a passionate interest in the items you deal in, and certainly have a knack for being a good negotiator. Most importantly, you'll need good judgment, excellent sales skills, and the ability to spot those low-cost, but highly profitable deals.

Separation Anxiety "No PACK RATS Allowed!"

> **Tip**: When collecting we must learn to swiftly let go of our new found treasures!

The pursuit for treasure is a great hobby, but if cash is what you're looking for, be sure to release your treasure trove before it's too late. Buying trends will constantly change. Items you hold for too long may lose their popularity and decrease in value. If you are looking to make money by finding desired collectibles, you must learn to release your treasure trove in a timely manner. You wouldn't want to end up with storage units, or a garage filled with lots of stuff that may sit for months or even years. Once you decide to sell these hoarded items, they just might be considered *worthless* because their values have plunged due recent economic causes--or loss of popularity.

Through my own experiences when buying items to resell for profit, I have learned that in order to make money it is vitally important to emotionally detach yourself from those "treasures." I have met many eBay sellers who avidly buy, but then, store their new found wares. It's fun to discover, but it requires time and work to list items them for sale online. Just think about the excitement of seeing those items sell, and seeing your profits grow. Personally, I have been guilty of accumulating my own purchases with the intentions of selling them as-soon-as-possible, but let's face it—it is much more entertaining to find these treasures, than it is to prepare, and then list them for sale. I have to remind myself about why I purchased these items originally—definitely not to hoard them!

Tip: Always keep in mind, "Any collectible is only worth what someone is willing to pay for it!"

I have used eBay's online auction website for over 13 years, so I will be quoting prices based on merchandise sold on eBay, and Etsy selling price ranges within the last year, throughout this book. There are various other online marketplaces to sell your items for making that extra income. I have found eBay to be the best when selling items via auction listings.

Now, let's get to work and *"Stop Throwing Cash in the Trash."*

Chapter I

"One Man's Trash, Could be Another Man's Treasure!"

(Some of My Personal Stories of Finding Hidden Household Treasures)

I've been bitten by the vintage collecting and reselling bug; and over the years, the "bite" has gotten worse. The reason is because I've made a significant amount of cash from buying and selling collectibles.

The items I've made money on haven't always been necessarily antiques or vintage, but also newer merchandise that manufacturers have discontinued, called "dead stock". As unbelievable as it may sound, you can easily add $500 to $1,000 a week, working from the comfort of your home, with only a minimal amount of cash invested. Consider how wonderful it would be by selling from the comforts of your own home. No more fighting traffic during rush hours of the morning and later afternoon. Additionally, dare I say it? Yes, "working in my favorite jammies or comfy clothes."

I personally got the fever to sell online some years ago while I helped a local auctioneer sort through a customer's belongings to get ready for an auction. This particular estate was a hoarding situation. The house had not been exposed to outside air for over 18 years. The auctioneer had offered me all the apparel found in the house, which had included vintage clothing, accessories, shoes and hats (most of this apparel had never been worn) for free, if we would assist in cleaning and sorting merchandise for their upcoming auction. The auctioneer wasn't interested in selling the clothing, and it seemed a fair deal since one of my fortes was dabbling in selling vintage clothing.

There was a large price to pay, as most of the clothing was literally buried under years of dust. One swift move and those dust particles were tossed into the air- not good for the lungs.

Another major issue was tackling the mold found in the abandoned house's basement found under the piles of merchandise. Considering the mold and dust, we wore respirators and gloves for protection. The sorting took us over three weeks, but along with receiving the articles for free, we also got a great preview to the upcoming auction.

One piece of apparel I discovered in a closet, was what appeared to be a men's, vintage 1940's Japanese, silk-rayon shirt with an exquisite print of a crouching tiger-the symbol for power-the front and back of the shirt. Although, it had a missing button and a hole in the arm sleeve, I decided to list it on eBay with a starting bid of $38. This seemed to be a fair starting price for such a unique vintage men's shirt.

Lucky for me, it had been kept in a controlled atmosphere in a cedar closet, which had kept away the moths from damaging the cloth (moths often destroy vintage fabric). Within minutes, an interested bidder had inquired if I could change my auction listing to show a "Buy-It-Now" option for his bid of $1,400. Wow, I was so excited and decided to appropriately change the listing and decided to adjust the Buy-It-Now price at $2,400. Within minutes, it sold for that price! It turned out the shirt was a rare 1940s-WWII Era, Hawaiian/Polynesian shirt.

With all the apparel from this house, we made over $23,000 by listing them on *eBay*'s auction website. Not bad for selling vintage clothing cast-offs.

The point I am trying to convey here, is how unfortunate is it that many articles of vintage clothing, vintage plush, stuffed animals and dolls are thrown into the landfill, or tossed into

Vintage 1940's Hawaiian, Japanese 'Crouching Tiger' Silk-Rayon Men's Shirt

dumpsters because they are thought to be of no value. These articles can in fact, bring in an abundance of cash profit even if they need to be cleaned up a bit!

I once purchased a shirt at a local thrift store for $1. The only label on this shirt had stated that it was a *King Kamehameha* brand-Hawaiian men's shirt. This shirt had been manufactured in the 1940's (one the most collectible timelines for vintage clothing), and I sold it online for $1,400. My profit margin was around $1,300, after paying eBay and PayPal's listing fee—not bad!

Tip: A men's shirt with horizontal button holes-no care instructions on the inside of the collar, has the makers label or size tag-is pre-1960s.

My First BARBIE® Doll Auction Experience and Tips for Identifying Mid-century, *Mattel* BARBIE and Her Friends

When I was fairly new to attending auctions, I had heard of an auction that was being held to liquidate a BARBIE collector's collection. Before the sale started, I spotted an original early 1960's BARBIE doll carrying case, which held a

1963 blonde "Bubble Cut" Barbie doll, additional 1960s BARBIE dolls and a selection of original vintage BARBIE® and Friends outfits. I decided to bid no higher than $80 on the case and contents.

This was the only item I had planned on bidding on, so I waited patiently for two hours. Finally, the time to bid had arrived and the auctioneer started the bidding at $10. Within a matter of minutes, the price had already exceeded my pre-determined limit of $80. Ouch! I ended up winning the case and contents for $300.

I won the auction but now, I was faced with figuring out how to explain to my husband why I bid so much on a BARBIE doll carrying case, and *why* the case was worth that much (and hopefully more). I truly felt I had gotten caught up in the auction bidding frenzy, and had made a major mistake.

When I got home, I carefully examined the dolls and the vintage items inside the case, to see if I might even get my initial investment money back. As I sorted out the clothes and vintage BARBIE dolls, I spotted a *Mattel* brand, *Francie* Doll (Barbie's fab cousin). She was in great condition and even had some of her original 1960s' outfits. I now felt safe.

Tip: Early Francie Dolls will have rooted eyelashes, not painted lashes.

1960's *Mattel, Inc.* "Francie" Doll, Wearing Tagged Bathing Suit

A-Hard to find "No Bangs" Francie Doll Wearing Tagged Outfit

I decided to list on eBay one of *Francie's* outfits, which included a pretty pink formal skirt with cute floral matching top, blue shoes, silver loving cup award, crown, white gloves, and a "Miss Teenage Beauty" torso ribbon. I also listed the blonde-haired, Francie Doll with the set, hoping again that I would recuperate at least $140 of the $300 that I had originally spent on the case at the auction.

Much to my pleasant surprise, I started getting bids right away-- and high ones! I then received a question from a potential buyer. Her question was, "Do you have the original spray of roses that came with the outfit as a set?" Yes, this was a clue to identifying that particular outfit that came with its appropriate matching accessories. I found the set to be called "Miss Teenage Beauty" a truly rare find, but it was missing the rose spray unfortunately.

I sold the *Francie* doll and the outfit (without the spray of roses), for $620. Wow! I was pleasantly surprised and happy! Had I obtained that particular accessory, it would have brought the auction listing over $200 more.

Mattel Francie Doll (ca Pre-1973) "Miss Teenage Beauty"- #1284 Ensemble

> ⌬━━ **Tip**: Be watchful for the "must have" attitude at auctions. You could end up spending money on items that won't bring in a desired profit margin when reselling on ecommerce sites.

Another one of my BARBIE treasure stories happened with a simple search on Craigslist website for local garage sales. While searching, I found a listing for a garage sale, which had posted pictures of some *Mattel, Inc.* BARBIE doll cases full of vintage BARBIE outfits and dolls. The photos had revealed a total of three cases for sale along with BARBIE original outfits, and one-1960's-blonde- Bubble-cut BARBIE doll. I immediately got that old treasure hunter's "rush". I rushed out the door to find this garage sale, but by the time

I had arrived, I was told that someone had showed up earlier and bought two of the three cases. Darn it! But, as luck would have it, the largest case was still for sale. I paid $125 for it. The BARBIE case was literally packed full of early mid-century BARBIE doll outfits in pristine condition. I listed all outfits and the doll the following week on eBay, and made a profit of over $1,400.

BARBIE® Doll Case, Dolls and Miscellaneous Original Tagged Outfits

Did You Know?
Limited Edition BARBIE® dolls have been declining significantly in value, in recent years. Many limited edition dolls were initially purchased as investments only- never to be played with. *Mattel, Inc.* has issued hundreds of different LE BARBIE® dolls over the years.

There are exceptions that are quite profitable if purchased for a low cost. Given this statement, here is a partial list of some of the most garnered LE BARBIE® dolls; Faberge Imperial, designer- Bob Mackie's Empress Bride, "The Tango", Victorian Tea (Orange Pekoe), and Prima Ballerina Classic. The "Silkstone" collection, the "I Love Lucy" series, *The Disney Store*-Designer Character Collections; National Convention dolls, *Moschino* BARBIE (*Moschino* fashion show in Milan, Italy); Women of Royalty Series, and the *Platinum* labeled "Karl Lagerfeld" dolls with a selling range of $200 - $1,500. These exclusive BARBIE® dolls are not considered vintage- but highly collectible.

Examples of *LE Mattel,* Inc. BARBIE® Dolls in Never Opened Boxes (i.e. NRFB)

| 1994 "Scarlett O'Hara" BARBIE® Doll "Gone with the Wind" Series | "Goddess of the Moon" BARBIE® Doll, Designer Series by Bob Mackie | 1988 *Mattel* "Happy Holidays" BARBIE® Doll- 1st in the Series |

Original 1950s-1960s BARBIE Dolls

BARBIE dolls dated between 1959 through 1966- in top condition- still fetch in the thousand-dollar range. Because this particular BARBIE production timeline is such a vast arena, I will discuss some of the most valuable dolls manufactured during that timeline.

This is an area where knowledge is essential, before buying to resell for profit. If you have one of the first BARBIE dolls in mint condition with a brunette or blonde ponytail, lightning bolt eyebrows, metal cylinders in her legs, symmetrical holes in feet bottoms that fit on to a black pedestal stand; marked with a number "1" on her buttocks, and in excellent condition-then you may have found quite a treasure! Original BARBIE dolls are currently selling at approximately $2,000. Some of the other earlier BARBIE dolls and her friends when found in their

#1 *Mattel, Inc.* BARBIE Ponytail Doll (ca 1959)

original boxes and in mint condition-can sell for over $2,500.

Did You Know?

The inspiration for the original 1959 *Mattel, Inc.* BARBIE doll came from the shapely German-made adult doll called the *Bild Lili* doll. The characteristics of the *Bild Lili* doll with her signature spit curl; was based on the popular comic strip from the German newspaper Das Bild. Ruth Handler, who was the wife of the cofounder of the *Mattel, Inc.,* had a notion that "little girls wanted to be big girls." Ruth was abroad in the late 1950's, when she noticed the popularity of the shapely, *Bild Lili-* grown up doll, wearing painted on mascara, and lipstick make-up.

When Mrs. Handler returned home to the states, she convinced others at *Mattel, Inc.* to take a gamble on her insight. The idea for the doll's name "Barbie", came from her daughter, Barbara. Smart advertising ensued, and the first BARBIE advertisement aired during "The Mickey Mouse Club," TV program. The rest was BARBIE history.

German Bild Lilli Doll (ca 1955-1964)

Tip: Original *Bild Lilli* dolls are very collectible, but watch for *Bild Lilli* clones (Hong Kong versions) produced during the 1960s. The original *Bild Lilli* doll has *no* markings on her body because she was marked on her stand.

For more information on Bild Lilli doll, here is an informative link:

http://www.dollreference.com/bild_lilli_doll.html

23

Because of the blonde BARBIE dolls popularity during the dolls debut, they were mass-produced. Due to this factor, today's most sought-after original BARBIE isn't the blonde haired doll, but the brunette and redhead. Rarity and condition, is a key factor in collecting dolls.

Here are some tips on identifying the earlier original BARBIE dolls:

- The first BARBIE had featured a blonde or brunette floss hair ponytail (In 1963- BARBIE came out with the "Bubblecut" hairdo.)

- Presence of copper tubing in her legs that exit through holes in the balls of her feet. This tubing allowed her to be secure when placed on the prongs of her accompanying posing stand.

- She will be marked with the words, "Japan" on the arch of her foot. The number two BARBIE did *not* have the holes in her feet. She wore little pearl earrings and stood with the wire stand that ran up and under her arms for support.

- The number three BARBIE has no holes in the feet, but for the first time, BARBIE was given an eye color other than the, black and white eyed doll with prominent black eyeliner.

- She has a vinyl body. Because of the vinyl body, her metal earrings caused a greenish tone on her ear, known as "Green Ear."

- The first dolls were also marked with the words, "Barbie ™ Pats. Pend. © MCMLVIII by, *Mattel Inc.*" (Remember these important markings, because with time-the wording changed).

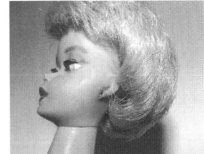

BARBIE® Doll Photo Showing "Green Ear" Defect

- Original 1959 -1960's BARBIE apparel featured black and white, stitched in TM (trademark) labels/tags applied to them.

- All the open-toe pumps were made of hard plastic and are marked "Japan" in capital lettering on the bottom of the arch of one of the shoes. On rare occasions, pairs have been found with both shoes marked "Japan," or no mark at all. However, every pair of open-toed pumps clearly has a left and a right shoe, making them non-interchangeable and easy to identify as correct pairs. The first BARBIE shoes had holes on the soles to fit on the stand that came with the doll's prongs.

BARBIE® Reproductions

In 1994, *Mattel* reintroduced a copy of the first Barbie with the 35th Anniversary BARBIE, which was extremely similar to the original. Keep in mind, the bottoms of an original BARBIE'S feet, will have tiny rod holes with metal tubing in her legs. Her hair is in a longer ponytail, and her bangs loosely curled *not* tightly curled.

1994 35th Anniversary Mattel, Inc. BARBIE doll Reproduction-Note the Differences

For more important BARBIE identifying facts go to the online website:

http://www.dollreference.com/barbie_menu1.html

Other early collectible versions of the *Mattel, Inc.* BARBIE doll can sell from $100 to $800 range.

Here is a list of some of these dolls:

- "Fashion Queen" BARBIE (ca 1963-1964), with a trio of different wigs to wear.

- "Color Magic" BARBIE (ca 1966-1967), with blonde or black hair that could be changed to red.

Fashion Queen, BARBIE Doll (ca 1965)

- Bendable-knee "Twist 'n Turn (TNT)" BARBIE doll (ca 1967-1968); and the mid- '60s *Mattel, Inc.* Francie Doll types- Barbie's mod cousin doll.

Twist 'n Turn BARBIE® Doll, (ca 1967-1968)

Vintage *Mattel* BARBIE® Doll and Friends-Tagged Clothing

The pre-1970s BARBIE doll clothing ensembles can be valuable. The original BARBIE and Ken outfits from the late 1950s and early 1960s, can be identified by a black and white label with the word "Barbie By Mattel", followed by the TM, or copyright symbol found on the inside of the outfit. The fabric was made with vintage prints using snaps, buttons and zippers closures-*not* Velcro. Each outfit was assigned a particular number. In your search for identification information, you will see these numbers. Example: Cruise Stripes #918 (1959-1962)

Early tagged (1959-1964), Mattel
BARBIE Doll Label

Yet, another one of my fabulous BARBIE finds happened while I was preparing to conduct an estate sale for a client. While working in their basement, I found a large trash receptacle that the family had filled with empty shoe boxes and miscellaneous Christmas wrapping paper. As I was emptying out the receptacle I noticed a vintage tiny BARBIE hat and some high-heel shoes stuck to the bottom of the can. This caught my attention and I decided to sift through further. I ended up finding some valuable BARBIE outfits and accessories dating back to the early 1960s. I'm glad I caught this "*Cash in the Trash*", because these items brought an additional $300 to the sale.

Tip: I have discovered three-early *Mattel* BARBIE and Friends-mini, fashion booklets through years of treasure hunting. They are a great resource for putting together original BARBIE outfit sets. These small accessory booklets came when purchasing BARBIE, or other doll collections (e.g. *Vogue, Strawberry Shortcake, Madame Alexander* dolls etc.). They can be found at auctions, buried in boxes.

Small can be Big...Very Big!

Items large or small can be very valuable and tiny treasures other than jewelry are out there, ready to be found. From a practical eBay seller standpoint, I like dealing with smaller collectables because they are so much easier to package properly when shipping.

A great example of a tiny treasure comes from the BARBIE doll collecting area. It is the tiny brass powder compact (10.5mms) that comes from the early "Roman Holiday" (968), BARBIE® set. This piece can sell between $500 -$1550, if found in very good condition. (Make sure that the tiny pink powder puff is inside the compact.)

1959 "Roman Holiday" Mattel BARBIE® Doll Ensemble #968 (without compact).

Tip: Be sure the tiny compact is not a reproduction by checking for the original etched "B" letter on the top, and by noting if it is old, tarnished in appearance?

Informative doll reference online sites can be found at these links:

http://www.collectibledolls.info

http://www.barbiecollector.com

http://www.dollreference.com

Mattel BARBIE Doll "Roman Holiday" Brass Compact Accessory #968 (ca-1959)

These online doll websites encompass a large amount of information for all vintage dolls types.

Tip: BARBIE and other vintage fashion doll defects, will ultimately affect resale prices, and if the doll is being tagging for resale-never apply a sticker to the box.

Avid BARBIE doll collectors are extremely meticulous so the tiniest of defects can take away from BARBIE doll values. Note any of the following defects to the doll as it might hinder your profit margin:

- Chipped paint color from her lips, nail and toes
- Green Ear Syndrome (mentioned earlier)-Green ear stains *can* be removed with regular "Clearasil" pimple medication and patience. Read more on how to get rid of green staining on dolls online at: http:// heresherbie.blogspot.com/2012/10/barbie-green-ear-syndrome.html#.VTWxKiFViko)
- Missing hair plugs and matted or cut hair strands
- Any marks, discolorations or defects to her body. (Some soil and marks, can be removed with Mr. Clean Magic pads, but be careful to not remove original painted-on features).
- Loose joints in arms and legs

A few quick identification tips to tell the difference between the BARBIE reproductions and the originals:

- Original BARBIE dolls didn't come with a "Certificate of Authenticity". Is she wearing original tagged outfits?
- There will always be a number on her buttocks, and the underside of Barbie's right foot should be marked with the word "Japan."

Vintage stuffed animals toys, dolls and vintage clothing (clean or dirty), can be valuable!

As you search for hidden treasures, you will undoubtedly come across a wide variety of toys and dolls, many of which might appear dirty. Take heart-there are a number of ways to either clean, or repair these diamonds in the rough.

Dolls found with tangled hair and soil marks may need repairing, but collector's will buy them in "as is" condition. Collectors will purchase damaged early BARBIE dolls just for their parts even if the doll is not in excellent condition.

Vintage clothes and accessories made for the dolls: *Shirley Temple, Terri Lee, Nancy Lee, Ginny Dolls, Madame Alexander,* and pre-1970s BARBIE-along with her friends-should *never* be tossed in the trash due to age or condition factors.

There are many doll repair sites online with instructions on how to repair most flaws and clean and restore their bodies, as well as, their original clothes. The following online sites can be helpful in restoring vintage hard to find porcelain, bisque, composition, celluloid, hard plastic or vinyl dolls.

http://www.dollinfo.com/caretips.htm

http://adollysworld.com/doll_cleaning_tips.html

I have seen numerous vintage dolls and stuffed animals trashed because they are thought to be full of germs.

> **Tip**: Steaming and spraying alcohol or Vodka on items such as stuffed animals and dolls can kill 99 percent of all bacteria or any lingering germs.

Germs only live on an item for one week. If mildly soiled, they can be washed a damp cloth dipped in one part Clorox to ten parts water, or by placing them in a pillowcase, tying the case and laundering in the washing machine.

Good luck on finding your next valuable BARBIE doll, vintage doll, or stuffed animal!

Bakelite Bonanza!

Not Just…. Another Mini- Garage Sale!

During a weekend junk jaunt, I stopped at a small garage sale. At this sale, there appeared to be only two small tables set up on a driveway. On one of the tables, a gallon-sized baggie caught my eye. Much to my surprise, the baggie was full of vintage costume jewelry, which I had noticed contained two vintage *Bakelite* bracelets. These two bracelets were very similar in style – with the same two colors, made in a "polka dot" pattern, which was intricately inlaid around the bangle bracelets. I had rubbed the bracelets between my fingers, and noted the familiar bakelite-formaldehyde odor.

I bought the bag of jewelry for $15, and listed the bakelite bangle bracelets online. Each one of these rare pieces sold for over $3,000 to buyers in New

York City! They were highly collectible, vintage bakelite bangle bracelets made with a method called "random injected dots." Along with the bracelets, I found a vintage Art Deco choker, which I sold for $75. Not a bad profit for one afternoon of searching for garage sales.

Lot of Vintage Bakelite Bangle Bracelets

Vintage 1950's, Bakelite, Random-Infected-Dot Bangle Bracelet (2.5″ D) list price- $780

Bakelite is a phenol formaldehyde resin with filler fibers, such as wood, rags or asbestos invented by Leo Hendrick Baekeland in 1909 and the *Bakelite Corporation* began in 1922. Bakelite/Catalin, was available in a wide range of colors, such as black, mustard yellow, apple juice (translucent amber), green, cherry red, butterscotch and root beer. You won't find a pure white, pink or blue piece of Bakelite because over time, their color content changed. Bakelite was used extensively in the production of costume jewelry during the early into the mid- 20th century. Additionally, Bakelite was used to create buttons, buckles, and household products (e.g., telephones, radios cases, camera cases and handles on toasters).

The vintage Bakelite/Catalin tile "Mah Jong" games that come with wood carrying cases are favorites to buy currently. These sets can sell in the upper-hundreds range.

Here are some simple tests to help identify an object as Bakelite/Catalin:

1.   If you are at an auction or sale, rub a piece vigorously between your thumb and finger, until hot. It should have a distinct formaldehyde odor.

2.   Dip object in a container of hot water for 15 to 30 seconds. Again, it will have that formaldehyde odor.

3. Cleaner test: Dip a cotton swab into the cleaning product called "409", than rub the swab on the selected piece, for a few seconds. The cotton will leave a distinctive *yellow* stain if it is bakelite plastic.

4. Heat a fine sewing pin over flame or stove burner, while hot touch inside of the object. If it leaves a mark, it is not Bakelite, as the pin will not penetrate into Bakelite. (This is not recommended, unless all other attempts fail.)

5. Bakelite will not have a seam or mold marks.

6. Note: There is no such thing as "white" bakelite.

Tip: When heated up, similar to the bakelite/catalin test using friction or hot water, celluloid plastic will have an odor similar to camphor, a "Vicks Vapor Rub" odor.

For more information I found the following online website educating on the subject of bakelite jewelry:

http://antiques.about.com/od/bakeliteandplastics/tp/aa041506.htm

Don't Donate Those Old Computer Components Yet!

A few years ago, I picked up some outdated, late 1970s and early 1980s *Apple* computers, along with vintage components such as monitors, printers and floppy disc games in their original boxes. I paid the seller $300 for the lot. I figured I could make $700 from a listing on eBay. To our delight, we sold the computers, components and games for $3,350. Original *Apple* computers and there components are highly collectible. If I had sold the same pieces today, they would probably sell for over $5,000.

Early 1977, Apple II Series Computer and Keyboard

The 1970s original *Pong Electronic Games* and *Pacman Tabletop Arcade Game* by Coleco—sell for more than $200 if in very good working condition. How many people have thrown out outdated computers. or taken them to a recycling center not knowing they were more valuable than a gold diamond ring?

1980's Computer with Computer
Programs and Games

1980's Computer Games

Tip: Pay attention to low serial numbers found on the 1970s' *Apple* computers as a quick guide to discover if a computer is valuable.

Pacman Table Arcade Game by Coleco
(ca 1981)

According to an article found in the *Business Insider,* May 2013; one of *Apple's* first computers-the Apple One-a functioning 1976 model, sold for a record 516,000 euros ($668,000 USD), at *Becker Auction House* in Berlin, Germany. Unbelievable!!

Watch current collecting trends to find out what popular items are selling on ecommerce online sites. Trends come and go and change day to day. What might be considered a treasure today, found at an auction, garage or estate sale-could be considered worthless tomorrow. Make sure to always do research on present day garnered items before purchasing and reselling them for profit online.

Chapter II

Learning Where and How to Find These Secret Treasures

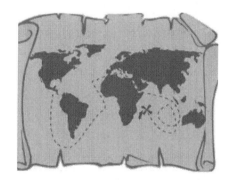

I n this chapter we will take a look at places--other than your home or a relative's estate--where you can find hidden treasures. Each area offers opportunities for finding obscure treasures to resale in search for that much sought –after profit, and we'll examine each one.

Here is a list of the locations that we will discuss:

- Estate Sales and Moving Sales

- Garage, Tag, Yard and Neighborhood Sales

- Church and School Rummage Sales

- Auctions-Storage, Personal and Business

- Thrift Stores

- Flea Markets

- Becoming a Picker and Traveling "Door-to-Door"

- eBay and e-commerce online sites

Estate Sales

I have been a licensed owner of an estate sales and service company for over five years. Estate sale treasure hunting is a vast subject, but I will address some important tips when attending these types of second-hand sales.

Pointers for Conducting you're own Estate Sale

For over five years now, I have been the founder and CEO of an estate sale-liquidation company. So, here are a few pointers I would like to pass on to my readers who might be interested in conducting their own estate sale.

In today's society, estate sale companies are plentiful. A person can either choose to call upon these professionals, or perhaps to conduct their own sale. If you decide to use a professional estate sales company, ask the company what method is used to mark items for sale, and their commission levels. Most estate sale businesses have a set commission level-each is unique to that particular company. I found that most estate sale businesses will set a commission of 25 to 35 percent on average.

Ask them to restrain from marking the sale items extremely high because a potential customer entering the sale the first day may get discouraged with the hefty prices and leave as fast as they entered the door. It is usually on the estate sales "half price day" -- the last day the sale is conducted, that customers may return and purchase articles at a much more affordable rate. The problem with this , is the customer may not come back. Try and entice the customer the first day.

My sole reason for haggling or dealing on the first day, is to avoid having an abundance of merchandise left unsold at the end of the sale. The remainder of the estate, normally goes to thrift stores.

If you end up with a lot of items unsold after the sale; call salvage companies for removal of any metal items, stoves, refrigerators (working condition or not); clothing consignment stores for designer clothing, local carpet companies who purchase second- hand Persian and Oriental rugs in very good condition; piano and musical instrument companies who purchase working keyboard instruments, and local jewelers for buying precious metals and jewelry. Jewelry companies are usually interested in purchasing quality vintage pieces-even odd or broken pieces. Creative individuals can make some wonderful artisan jewelry with vintage jewelry pieces.

When to use terms: Vintage or Antique for selling your merchandise.

Tip: If you have scheduled a sale and the weather turns sour, ask the estate sale company, if they can reschedule for a better day. It will make a huge difference to your profit margin.

An antique is an object of ancient times and at least 50 to 100 years old. The term *vintage* to an antique dealer means that the item is not considered antique, but still has some age to it. This term should be used when speaking about items that fall into the timeline of being at least 20 years old or older.

When conducting estate sales, I have noted attending dealers and collectors are usually on the hunt for these vintage items:

- Vinyl records (e.g. LPs, 45 rpms and 78s)
- Fishing tackle-rods and reels; lures and cleaning knives-Watch for early 19th century and early 20th century split bamboo fly fishing rods that have two or more sections. Names to watch for: Thomas & Thomas (T & T), H. L. Leonard, E. F Payne and W.E Edwards to name a few. These antique rods can sell for over $1,000.

1960s Dublo-Dinky Metal Die-Cast Miniature Vehicles with Original Boxes

- Antique mechanical die-cast metal toys and vehicles (e.g., *John Deere Company* series; Wyandotte, Hot Wheel Redline cars; *Meccano Ltd, Dublo-Dinky; Matchbox Lesney* series, and *J. Chein and Company* tin lithograph mechanical toy vehicles).

Vintage Red-Line Hot
Wheels Toy Car (ca 1968)

- Pottery vessels-*Mccoy, Red Wing, Roseville, Mochaware, Van Briggle*, Native American types etc.
- Vintage electronics (mid-century stereo systems, CB-radios and components, computers, speakers and radios
- Antique and primitive tools
- Advertising Memorabilia- prints and objects with advertising logos applied to them.
- High-end collectible furniture styles by Gustav Stickley, and pieces from the Mission, Arts and Crafts Era. *French Louis XV & XVI, Queen Anne, Rococo* and *Eastlake* furnishings. Mid-century furniture manufactured by *Henredon, Drexel, Heywood Wakefield, Broyhill* and *Ethan Allen* companies; all solid, quality-constructed wood furniture with exquisite taste. These pieces are desirable for their durability and style. (It is amazing how a piece of furniture built 50 years ago is still in like-new condition, but furniture produced in the last 20 years has lost some of its longevity.)
- Antiquarian, signed and first edition books
- Vintage fine jewelry (Additionally-signed Costumer jewelry from the mid-century.)
- Mechanical pens/pencils (with gold content)
- Distressed pieces or primitive pieces used for upcycle purposes (e.g. old metal garage tool cabinets and drawers, weathered, alder-wood ladders), basically vintage furniture that may need a facelift on their appearance.
- War/militia memorabilia--especially uniforms and clothing. Vintage designer clothing (Pre-1990s)
- Antique auto parts and catalogues. Instruction manuals and pamphlets

(early 1900s-1970s) for vehicles, military equipment and farm machinery.

- Antique dolls
- Sterling flatware and serving pieces
- GOLD! Various types.
- Vintage electronics (stereos, radios, turn-tables, stereo-speakers, CB equipment etc.)

Examples of some of those "less-obvious", but valuable items I have discovered through research on the internet to be found at these sales are:

- Vintage Needlepoint Craft Kits: Circa 1960s into the 21st century-selling for over $200

This is one of the newest "must have" trends. Finally a desire for these handmade crafting kits has returned. I remember in my younger years spending hours and days working on projects made from these all-in-one kits. The kits included crewel, embroidery, needlepoint and counted cross-stitch patterns. They were created using stenciled, fabric patterns, or using felt pieces; jeweled sequins, pins, beads, thread, and supplies needed to embellish the item. All that was needed to complete the projects were scissors, glue and a lot of *time*.

Some notable craft kit brands marketed during the 1970s, were *Bucilla, Dimensions, Leewards, Walco Sunset, House of Hatten*, and *Horizon*. To be of optimum value, they need to be intact (mint in package-MIP), complete, and in very good-clean condition.

2 #25-Bucilla Christmas - "Shopping Spree" 18" Maria Stanziani Stocking KIT 2007 NIP

Tip: Watch for vintage discontinued Christmas-related craft kits (e.g., Christmas stockings, Christmas tree skirts and Nativity calendars). Completed craft items, or kits can fetch over $100 if sold during the fall months just before the Christmas holiday season—timing is everything.

Prized are the beaded ornament kits manufactured during the 1970s by the *June Zimonick Studio* and *Cracker Box Inc.* The early unfinished kits (as *Cracker Box Inc.* are still manufacturing kits), are true treasures. These named, unfinished kits sell can for over $700, due to the amount of embellishments used, and its size.

Completed Vintage-Bucilla- Peanuts "Snoopy " Jeweled-Felt Christmas Stocking

- Needlepoint Pillows and mid-century, round tufted, corduroy button pillows from the 1950s and 1960s- sell for over $75

- *Mattel's* 1989, Sparklins-PJ Sparkles, plush stuffed animals

- 1980's *Hallmark*-Playskool "Jammie Pie" dolls selling in the hundreds range based on condition and rarity

- 1970's *Fisher Price*-Plaid Bunny Security Blankets- most of these items can sell between $100 and $200!

1986 Playskool Jammie Pie "Pitty-Pin" Plush Doll in Purple-$250

1979 Fisher Price Bunny Rabbit-Security Blanket Puppet in Original Box

- Vintage particular types of sneakers/shoes (e.g. 1980s *Air Jordan, Adidas, Nike*; and mid-century Chuck Taylor All-Star- *Converse* styles. Example: A pair of 1992 *Nike Air Force 180*, David Robinson shoes, sold for

$3,750…..Yes! Truly hidden gold!

- Certain PBN (paint by number) paintings or painting kits-Watch for old west themes, and animal depictions. A "Star Trek" PBN, recently sold online for over $700!

Vintage Custom Air Jordan Retro 1 Shoes/Sneakers-$335

Vintage 1962 Paint-By-Number Finished Native American Pictures- 11" x 13" with Frames-$198

Vintage PBN Finished "Ballerina Dancer" Picture- 21.5" x 17.5"-$75

- Vintage *RUSHTON* rubber face, stuffed animals.

The line of *RUSHTON*, rubber-faced stuffed animals can sell up to a thousand dollars- based on condition.

Mid-century-RUSHTON Toys, Star Creation Label

Vintage RUSHTON Star Creation Toys Rubber-Face Duck, Stuffed Animal

Vintage RUSHTON Toys-Owl- Rubber Face, Stuffed Animal

Rushton's Star Creation toy line also featured hand painted, rubber faced animals and dolls. They

39

were made from the 1950s through the 1960s. This line is the one of the most collectible from the company.

Rushton rubber-faced, stuffed assorted toy characters included cuddly bears, ducks, kitty cats, cows, *Santa Claus* character, bunnies and lambs.

The *Rushton Company* was founded by Mary Rushton, from Atlanta. Her daughter, Wight Rushton, designed the toys. It was a family owned and operated business from 1917 to 1983. The *At-Play Toys* were one of the most collectible lines produced by Rushton. The toys were made of the finest rayon & plush materials, stuffed with clean top grade cotton, and eyes that were sewed in and did not pull out. They also featured hand embroidered or stitched noses, felt tongues & large bows.

When searching for valuable vintage stuffed animals, it is important to know how to launder them as most found will probably have been used. Here are a few laundering tips for cleaning vintage rubber-faced Rushton and other plush fur stuffed animals.

Always try first, to simply wipe the toy down with a damp (not wet) cloth if the stuffed animal is simply dusty, this can be enough to revive it and get rid of the grime. Spraying with a solution of 50/50 water and Vodka to clean and disinfect and also kill germs. Make sure and dry for a day or two after spraying. This vodka mix is called, "Poor Man's Febreeze" as it also takes away unfavorable odors.

Mr. Clean Magic pads work great for cleaning the rubber faces-if present, but use diligently because too much rubbing will affect the colors and cause fading.

Also, take some warm water and mild dish soap (I use Dawn dish soap). Make suds by vigorously whipping the water back and forth with your hand. Once you have a large amount of suds-take a damp facecloth or sponge and dip into the suds. Rub the items faux fur with the suds-once you are satisfied with your cleaning job- wipe again with the water and sponge-than set out to dry.

- Vintage 1970's macramé maxi-dresses, woven jute & wool wall art, and miscellaneous items can are selling in the $200 range. (I remember making those woven jute dream catchers, hanging macramé tables and owls for cash at local craft sales.)

- 1960's Vanity Fair Underwear….What! Yes, nylon underwear (with lined gussets) can sell for over $200. Of course, in unused or lightly used condition.

- The 1980's Care Bear cousin named "Proud Heart Cat" can sell for over $600!

Vintage Red Vanity Fair Nylon Panties With Pillow-tab and Mushroom Gusset—Unused $80

1980's Kenner Care Bear's Cousin "Proud Heart Cat"

- Margaret M.H Keane signed and dated "Big Eyes" Collection of artwork is selling in the thousands, and her prints selling in the hundreds. (Check out the 2014 biographical movie titled "Big Eyes", which was directed by Tim Burton.)

Framed 1963 Margaret Keane Signed Print "Big Eyes" Artwork (Circe) 34.5" x 22.25"

Ms. Margaret Keane is an American artist who painted "Big Eyes" pictures of women, children and animals.

When attending estate sales remember that with most second-hand sales, there are lots of deals on the last day. It's the last ditch effort to sell the estate belongings. It is definitely worth the extra trip to go back and deal, sometimes 75 percent off from the opening day's original prices.

> **Tip**: Remember to sift through those boxes. Vintage designer scarves (e.g., Hermes, Louis Vuitton, Vera Bradley or Vera Wang), vintage Art Deco hand painted neck-ties (e.g. ties with designs by artist "Salvador Dali"- who is best known for the striking and bizarre images in his surrealist work and Atomic Era patterns), vintage fine silk and lace lingerie; corsets, and vintage ladies nylon panties-can be found in boxes.

Salvador Dali Artwork

> **Tip**: When entering an estate sale, head for the closets (vintage clothes and accessories), rummage through basements-grandma and grandpa's old belongings-and don't forget to locate the attic! Hiding in others areas of garages and sheds are vintage radio and electronic parts, vintage Christmas/holiday items, fishing equipment (vintage rod, reels and wooden lures), primitive furniture and tools.

Moving Sales

Garage and moving sales abound. Moving an entire household costs thousands of dollars. Sometimes it is much easier to sell off the less important, larger and non-essential items-then later-buy them again upon arrival at the new destination. You can find some great bargains on vintage furniture at these sales, especially in upscale, older neighborhoods. Mid-century furniture is currently "on fire" for buying for resell due to current trends in home decor. Sellers will want to make deals with potential buyers just to clear out the home

1940's Salvador Dali, Floral Surreal Designed Silk Tie-$265

quickly. This is considered good news for the buyers.

If you happen to spot a dumpster set up in front of a home with furniture piled up inside of it; stop and take a second look. The house may have been recently sold and its contents are being tossed out by a realtor, family members or construction team. Stop, and *ASK* if you can possibly view inside the container because you are into recycling cast-offs. They usually don't mind. Some people just want to get the house emptied out as-quick-as-possible, and don't care about what is being thrown away. It never hurts to *ASK*. In fact, it clears up more space in the rented container in their endeavors to liquidate the property.

Garage Sales (Also known as Tag, Yard and Rummage Sales)

My personal favorite place to discover hidden treasures is a garage sale. The first and most important thing to remember is to- *DO YOUR HOMEWORK*. By that, I mean, go through the classified ads in your local newspaper or Craigslist (online) on Wednesday night and early Thursday morning. Their posts are the most popular resources available to gain information about upcoming garage sales.

This is the time to plan your strategy or prearranged route. Stick to it, especially if you only have a limited amount of time. Remember to bring along a city map, or car *GPS Navigation System* (most important), a large canvas bag; flashlight for going through dimly lit areas (I once climbed up into a crawl space to get into an attic at a family run estate sale and wished I had brought a source of light.); a magnet, which is used to determine if an item is brass, bronze or gold (the magnet won't stick to these metals), a quality magnifying glass or loupe-- one that can be worn around the neck would be best.

A *Wi-Fi* cell phone is a must for quickly looking up information on a prospective treasure. One of the newest inventions in technology, the Wi-Fi cell phone, definitely helps play an important role in facilitating research to see what an item discovered, may be worth. It's so convenient now to take your computer where ever you travel. Additionally, bring a measuring tape, some newspapers to wrap delicate items, and some boxes. Oh...and don't forget the cash!

I enjoy going into older established neighborhoods -homes built pre-1970s and earlier. Try to arrive at your high-lighted "priority" marked sales fairly early, but not so early as to have the sellers get angry. Please use etiquette and be polite; don't expect to get into the sale two hours before it is set to start. The sellers might allow it, but it can be seen as inconsiderate on your part. I tried this once, and the people got every upset with me. (Coming from their point of view, I understand because I have run several sales, and it's very stressful trying to prepare for the sale when certain attendees are trying to get in before everyone else.) In being polite, you will find that the sellers are much more willing to bargain with you on their already set prices.

If you arrive at a sale early and fellow attendees are there, already going through the boxes, don't be afraid to join in and search for yourself in the same box. Get tough! After all, it's not their property yet.

Always be alert for purchasing damaged items such as glassware that has chips or flea bites, vintage clothing soiled or flawed, records with scratches to their surfaces; and electronics or appliances that are aren't in working order. Paying a high price for damaged purchases could result in losses in *your* pocket.

I love pulling my car up to a disorganized garage sale with the sellers still bringing out boxes. None of the merchandise is marked, and they announce, "Make an offer?" At this point, become what's known as a *"Grouper"*. A *grouper* is a buyer who puts a pile together and asks, "Will you take $20 (or given dollar increment) for the whole pile?" I offer a fair price and if they want more, we haggle a bit until everyone is happy. As I watch the owners continue to bring out boxes-I ask if they have much more in the home that is yet to come out for sale-if the answer is yes? What type of objects will be in those boxes? It doesn't hurt to ask questions. You may even tell the sellers what certain items you are looking for. I have attended sales and asked about any vintage clothing that might possibly be for sale. Unfortunately, most elderly people think vintage clothing is of little value.

Watch for sales that have signs knocked down or turned downward due to wind, and have the tiniest of hand writing applied to them. These hard to find garage sales are beneficial because you may be one of their first customers, which means-the first to discover treasure. When I find these sales, inform the people running the sale about how the signs were hard to read or find, and then suggest they make some changes to help bring in more shoppers.

Learn to distinguish the writing or print written on garage sale signs. Garage sale signs that are made by using big and bold writing with balloons attached usually signify the sellers are a younger crowd. This could mean you probably won't find much for vintage items at that particular location. Rather, you're likely to find infant and toddler clothing and accessories, i.e. strollers, playpens, toys etc.

Likewise, at these particular garage sales there may be other bargain-priced, valuable items. I have been known to come up with new (1990-current) treasures that are not necessarily vintage treasures, at some of these sales.

Newer items, such as designer merchandise (e.g. *Prada, Dooney & Bourke, Kate Spade, Gucci, Louis Vuitton, Marc Jacobs* and *Coach*) handbags, clothing, shoes and accessories (Remember to watch out for knock-offs and reproductions!); 1990's *Super Nintendo* and similar video games, *Fitz and Floyd* Pottery, Disney character LE Pottery, *Pottery Barn* merchandise; and high-end children's clothes and toys.

Authentic *Kate Spade* Handbag

Years ago, my mother-in-law and I had decided to have a garage sale. By the time I had arrived, she had already sold most of her *JUNK* to early-riser garage sale gurus. Her junk had consisted of old stoneware crocks, and a couple of old 1950s chairs from a local bar she had worked at. The bar had closed down, but it once had been a favorite with the locals for years. She had received one dollar for each of the stoneware crocks and three dollars each for the chairs. The crocks she sold were rare, *Red Wing* Stoneware- Pottery pots and jugs in mint condition. The chairs were mid-century 1950s' diner chrome stools in great condition, and should have sold for no less than $40 each. It's certain that someone had received some wonderful deals.

Red Wing and Antique Stoneware Crock Pots

Church and School Rummage Sales

These sales are great because your spent dollars go toward a worthy cause. A lot of the time groups will mark items to sell quickly, so prices are low and affordable to their patrons.

At these types of sales, look for designer brand-high-quality clothing and designer handbags (especially in high-end neighborhoods), newer or vintage small appliances (e.g. vintage Farberware coffee percolators and makers, electric fry pans and rotisseries); mid-century home décor, vintage children books, and decorative collectibles.

Neighborhood sales are fun, but be aware of the traffic jams one can be up against. My advice is to find a close parking space as close as possible, then get ready to do some walking. Don't forget to bring a large handled canvas bag. As with other types of sale events-if you find something you want to purchase that is large in size-simply ask the owners if they would give you a piece of paper stating that you paid for that item with their signature on it along with their contact information on it. This contact information will also be used to arrange a time when picking up your purchase.

Auctions

In truth, I am an avid auction attendee and have been for years. I love going through the boxes and seeing so many unique reminders of the past. Oh, did I forget to mention, "I love the excitement of winning a particular treasure!"

Whether you attend a farm auction, business auction or personal property liquidation auction, be aware of the dreaded auction "fever". An *auction fever* is the excitement of the moment that may cause a person to bid more on an anticipated item-more then it's actually worth. Set a spending limit and stick with it to avoid the *fever*.

Picture of an Indoor Auction

Auctions that have an abundance of articles to sell- are those being held for the total liquidation of personal belongings. These types of auctions are indeed, a very tedious and unpleasant task for the surviving family members. Personal-property liquidation auctions are popular, because *everything* is for sale! Toiletries, paper products, vintage clothing, yard art, salvage...you name it... It's for sale.

Also popular are "living" liquidation auctions. This simply means, an auction is being conducted for people who are still- living, but they are in need of downsizing their personal possessions. With either type of liquidation auction, auctioneers all too often throw away potential treasures that could be transformed into cash.

Most auction regulars love a farm sale, with so many interesting and unique items to be found. I live in the Midwest so, it would be unlikely for me to find antiques dating from the 18th century or early 19th century, but it can happen. I find lots of 19th century primitives waiting to be, at farm sales.

Tip: Attend the sneak preview before an auction. Arrive an hour early to inspect objects being sold for any flaws. Avoid purchasing pottery, ceramics or porcelain if they are damaged; stains, rips, or holes found in any fabric related article; and discoloration to paperwork, LE (limited Edition numbered) prints, and books. Additionally, make sure all parts are complete to any game, puzzle or set. Ask if any electrical plug is present in order to test any electronics and appliances for making sure that they are good working condition.

When sifting through boxes at auctions, you may find one type of drinking glass in one box, and another glass of the same style, in another box. It's important to keep sets together, so politely inform one of the auctioneers—hoping he-or-she, will put the set back together again before the sale starts.

I remember attending an auction where I found two boxes full of Silver Age comic books dating from the 1960s. I found three that were very valuable-one of which was one the first "Green Lantern" *Marvel* comic books. The auctioneer had not taken the time to sort them out and I had discovered them. A truly great find—I sold the comic books for over $300 on eBay!

Tip: Before setting out to an auction, remember to bring boxes, packing paper, a quality magnifying glass (to check for flaws, hallmarks, back marks, signatures), and a fluorescent black light (Great for finding repaired areas in pottery and glassware pieces, and used for identifying glass and pottery authenticity.) A portable water misting fan is not a bad idea to endure the summer heat. I found a portable seat/cane comes in real handy, to get off my feet for a bit. For lunch, pack a lunch and a bottle of water. Otherwise, you may have to wait in long lines for lunch at the auction sight and miss out on possible merchandise deals.

Endure the elements-remember that umbrella-and stay to the end. Go to the auctions in the winter months that are scheduled to be held outside, and dress warm. I have gone to auctions in 97 degree heat, and outlasted 85 percent of the attendees, just to walk away with awesome deals.

Sign up to receive auction companies' announcements on future sales online, and to receive their upcoming sale flyers via mail. I have found some fantastic deals, just by seeing miscellaneous items in the background of preview photos which were posted online. Sometimes such items are not advertised correctly, meanly you have a greater chance of obtaining them for a low bid.

Tip: Buyer Beware! Be careful when bidding on auctioned items being shown via a monitor, TV, or computer screen. The buyer or bidder is unable to physically examine the item for sale. I once bid on some vintage clothing being shown on a monitor slide program for which I had paid over $600 on. Upon picking up these purchases—which had already been packaged —I opened the boxes and found them full of soiled and damaged clothing. I had failed to ask questions about their condition. "A valuable lesson learned."

How to bid at an Auction?

Upon attending a particular auction, you will need to get your own personal bidding card number to bid on items with.

Once the auction starts, the auctioneer will start the bidding at a high price-a price he thinks is a fair asking price-and will continue to lower the offer until there is a bid. The asking price will then be increased by regular increments, such as $2, $5, $10, $20, etc., depending on the amount of the original bid. For instance, high-end items such as oil on canvas artwork and limited editions, sterling silver dinnerware, appliances, cars and furniture; might increase in bidding increments of $100. Conversely, if an item receives a starting bid of $5, the auctioneer might increase the asking price per $2 increments. In any case, the winning bid will be last and final bid when no higher price is called out. If you were the last one to bid, then you are the winning bidder.

Mistakes *do* happen and often you might believe you are actively bidding on an item, just to have the auctioneer look at another bidder and announce, "Sold!" The auctioneer had missed your particular bidding technique, or hand gestures for bidding by mistake. In most cases, auctioneers will restart the bidding with these types of mistakes.

To avoid involvement in situations like this-yell out "Yes", or make sure the auctioneer can see you. I find that raising my auction card up, is the best way to be noticed. After the auctioneer finds you are interested, they will always continue to look your direction while the item is still up for bid. Once you node your head in a negative way, this acknowledges that you have decided to back out of the current bidding.

Most dealers and avid antique and collectible dealers who attend auctions-- may come for just one or two items. Once they have obtained these few items- they leave. These are the experts. They know what they want and have an idea of how much they will pay to get their item. So, stay to the end! This is where you will find your hidden treasures. Auctioneers will sell rows of boxes for $5 or even less, toward the end of the auction. You can find rare or first edition books, magazines, kitchenware, signed vintage towels, perfume bottles, and all sorts of goodies. Take what you want from the pile and sell what is left at your next tag or garage sale.

Always be, ALERT at auctions. Items can disappear or be stolen. I attended a school auction held at an old high school building, which was built in 1923. I had purchased some roll-down vintage maps from the classrooms (hot-to-sell), and when I went back to the previous classrooms to get the maps, they were gone. This happens all the time, especially in an auction where you have to travel from room to room quickly. **Never leave purchased items unattended!**

Intimidating and illegal behavior can, and does happen at auctions. Bidders may use scare tactics in their attempts to block out any competition. More blatant, are illegal practices, such as the "phantom bid. (Phantom bid, because the rival bidder-never existed). Here is how the phantom bid works: A bidder is dead set on winning a specific item so he or she might make a hand action or continually holding their card up through the entire bidding process, with the intent to show the crowd that they want that particular item, no matter the cost.

This is very risky to the bidder, as it opens the door to a dishonest auctioneer "bouncing" bids (taking nonexistent bids from the floor, the back of the auction hall, out of the air, etc.), which ultimately drives the price or amount up for that auctioned item, and the first bidder. Basically, the bouncing continues until the hand comes down or the bidder starts to show some hesitation. Then, suddenly, the 'under-bidder' stops bidding and the paddle-in-the-air buyer, wins the item. The first bidder has paid a higher unfair realized for the item.

While attending an auction, watch the crowd and learn how certain avid attendee's bid, such as winks of the eye, hand gestures, nodding of the head, or holding up a paddle. Learn what a fellow competitor's method of bidding might be. View the crowd at the sale to see what your competition will be. Watch for opposing bidders to start making gestures of exasperation, or some hesitation when bidding. This means they are reaching their limit. It is time for you to take over, so go for it! While watching-also LISTEN. It's very important to not chit-chat at an auction, because you could miss the item you have been waiting to bid on.

When I attend auctions, I stand towards the back of the crowd at an angle, so I can view my competition. I even attend auctions not necessarily to purchase, but to learn what the crowd is willing to pay for a particular item. It is a great learning arena.

Deciding What Auctions are Priority to Attend

Would you attend an auction well-advertised on the television or on the radio? Or, would you attend an auction that you discovered on a printed flyer posted on a bulletin board in a small town feed store or grocery store? Unless there is a certain item you desire-attend the less advertised auctions. There will be less competition, which means better value for your dollar. The absence of the competition is a plus for you. Small town auctions are even better. There are lots of treasures at these auctions, and the best deals.

Highly publicized auctions have their downside. At a well-advertised auction in Omaha, NE, over 400 people were in attendance for the once owned amusement park called *Peony Park*. Bidding started out high and because of such a large crowd, final bids were going to be high for any item.

Absentee Bidding

A person can leave an absentee bid if they are unable to attend the auction. You simply leave your highest bid with one of the auctioneers-if you won the item-the auction company will contact you after the auction is finished. Problem here is most auction attendees present, can beat your bid with just a few dollars.

Online bidding is the upside for those who can't attend an auction due to an illness or disability, he-or-she could bid online and win the bid of their desired item.

Here is a helpful online site I found online: http://www.auctionguide.com/tips/

Thrift or Secondhand Stores

Secondhand stores can be a treasure trove for people who like to buy for creating profits when reselling someone else's cast-offs; however, store owners are now savvy on how to mark their merchandise accordingly. Many hire knowledgeable experts who work with antiques and collectibles, to help determine values for donated merchandise. Better deals can be found at small town thrift stores rather than the larger city locations.

A great way to find a deal is to visit the store when carts come out of the backrooms. By asking a store clerk if it is okay to take a peek before the items are restocked, is a sure-fire way to getting some good deals before items reach the shelves.

Some stores bag accessories and smaller items with each other and sell them for a discounted price. Handkerchiefs, ladies scarves, doll accessories, and toiletries can yield an extra $500 to your bank account. I once found a designer Hermes scarf in a bag, which I paid $5 for. Another time, I purchased a bag full of vintage ladies handkerchiefs for only $4.99. Inside the bag I found several

Vintage Floral Handkerchiefs

Tammis Keefe Signed
Handkerchief

Lace Handkerchiefs on White

Tom Lamb Signature Handkerchief Print

Souvenir Handkerchiefs

 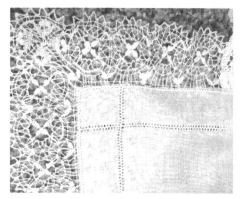

Lace Handkerchiefs

> **Tip**: When selling vintage white lace hankies-list them during the spring months for those summer weddings.

vintage, signed, novelty prints designed by Tammis Keefe-along with some fashion scarfs by "Vera."

Here is list of hankies that can sell for over $25:

- Hand signed hankies by *Tammis keefe, Tom Lamb* and *Carl Tait*
- Souvenir handkerchiefs and ladies scarfs that feature vacation destinations, maps of states, buildings, cities.
- Machine embroidered monogrammed handkerchiefs
- Nineteenth century Victorian lace handkerchief types (e.g., *Point de Gaze, Brussels* appliqued laces, and French- *Alencon*), can sell for $100 to $300 each if found in very good condition.

- Silk handkerchiefs/scarfs by designers, such as *Hermes, Gucci, Chanel, BVLGARI* and designer brands, can sell for over $100 each.

- Novelty children's themed prints of animals and nursery rhythms

Vintage Novelty Children's Print Handkerchief

- Valentine's Day and holiday handkerchiefs

Some of my thrift store bagged finds: I found an original 1959 BARBIE® doll with some vintage 1960s BARBIE® outfits; a toiletry bag yielded a vintage guilloche compact; and some '60s *Yardley City Slicker* cosmetics, which I sold on *eBay* for $130.

Flea Markets

Flea markets can be entertaining, but be careful especially in the mega-flea markets located throughout the south and east coast. Reproductions and knock-offs abound at big city flea market events.

A visit to a Florida flea market 15 years ago, taught me to not be so naïve and uninformed when dealing with their vendors. These huge flea markets are massive, with rows and rows of repeat merchandise meant to sell quickly to attending patrons. Walking along, I spotted with what I thought to be antique Flow Blue, earthenware soup tureen. I checked the hallmark on the bottom of the piece, and noticed it seemed quite large, which was unusual for an authentic English Flow Blue- porcelain piece. The vendors told me that the china tureen had come from their grandmother's china cabinet-of course. This must mean it could be an authentic piece, right? It had a sticker price of $38. This was too good of a price to pass up, since most Flow blue china pieces of that size would have sold for $100-or more. It turned out the dish was a newly-produced fake. It does pay to research, take note and pay attention.

Antique Flow Blue Plate/Saucer

Flow Blue Colored Soup Tureen

Antique Flow Blue Stamp/Mark

How to decide if an item-
which is said to be authentic-is a fake?

Simple, by noticing if the manufacturing and material of an item is of excellent quality.

The Internet is a great place to research the identity of fake items. In your search engine box, include the word 'fake' with your particular item's description. Within seconds thousands of web pages will appear on how to recognize fakes or reproductions. Look at the quality of the item. Does it appear to be cheaply made? Keep in mind the old saying, "If it seems too good to be true…it is."

The unique flea market events are those that are run by local small towns. Here is where you can find those one-of-a-kind antique or vintage items.

Tip: When you are attending flea markets events, bring a cart on wheels to hold your purchases; it will make the day a lot less tiresome.

Larger flea market venues similar to the one I previously mentioned in Florida; consist of inside and outside large buildings. The local vendors can usually be found under the outdoor tents and they love to deal. Name your price and walk away with a gold mine of treasure. I was lucky enough to find a large piece of amethyst crystal and some rose quartz, at one of these locations. Various types of semi-precious crystals (e.g., amethyst, rose quartz, aquamarine), mica sheets, agate and stones with embedded gold pyrite (fool's gold), can sell into the hundreds-of-dollars range. I would have paid dearly for the amethyst piece, had it had been purchased in a store found in Aspen, Colorado due to cabin-chic decorating in the mountain regions of the U.S.A. Rock and gem collecting is in demand!

Amethyst Crystal Rock

Rose Quartz Rock

Did You Know?
A large chunk of the Zagami-Martian meteorite, which fell to the earth in Nigeria, Africa in 1962-was auctioned off on eBay in 2006 for just under a half million dollars!

Find me any meteorite....PLEASE!

How to Become a "Picker"

One my favorite shows on the televised *History* Channel, is "American Pickers". Basically the series features two guys who travel the country in search of treasures and meet some interesting collectors of past memorabilia. With their pleasing personalities, a van and a full tank of gasoline, they are on a constant treasure hunt. To be a picker like these guys, you have to be willing to travel on dusty, gravel roads and unafraid to get a little dirt or grease, under your fingernails.

Here in Nebraska, there are a lot of rural areas with gravel and dirt roads. Many of these rural roads abandoned houses that were built in the late 1800s. My husband and I love an adventure. Pickers at heart-we've taken many weekend jaunts on these forgotten roads to find the remains of any old abandoned homes. We found quite a few of these ruins, over the years. We simply find out who owns the property, and if they would be interested in selling us any salvageable pieces from these-deserted structures. Remind the owners that you will enter at your own risk, as going through these old houses can be dangerous. The worst case scenario is they simply are not interested in your offer.

I have found some great architectural salvage pieces such as door knobs, old windows and screen doors; old springs to mattresses (Sought-after for creating upcycled art.), light fixtures, porcelain sinks and barn wood, which is used for creating weathered and worn projects. Even rusty-old auto parts found amongst the bushes and trees of a long forgotten farm, are valuable to upcycling artisans.

My Personal Antique Mattress Upcycling Yard-Art Photos

> **Tip**: Create a *wanted* ad section found in any small town local newspaper. Decide what it is, you would like to collect, then advertise that you will pay cash for those items.

Some years ago I decided to run a classified ad in several small town newspapers stating that I was interested in purchasing vintage clothes. We received good feedback from the ad and soon we began receiving phone calls. While visiting one of these prospects, a woman showed us some leftover garage sale articles of vintage clothing she had not sold. The woman we were working with also said she had some Christmas decorations she would be willing to sell if we were interested. We were invited into her home where she proceeded to take us downstairs into the basement. This is where I noticed a large industrial can full on tattered vintage blue jeans. I inquired about them and told they were just leftover rags. I asked this woman if we could have the rags for $5. She was happy to get rid of them.

In amongst the rags, I found some early 1950's *LEVI*, blue-denim cut-off shorts; and several pairs of 1960s' Blue Bell Wrangler jeans. Eventually, I sold them on eBay and made a profit of over $1000. Old and tattered jeans are the latest fashion rage today.

Hidden Treasures Found on E-commerce Auction Websites?

Auction Listing Mistakes Are Unfortunate-But Not For Everyone!

Every day thousands of misspelled or typos found in eBay listing titles end up unsold on eBay for one simple reason: buyers can't find them!

When it comes to hunting for treasures to resell for profit on eBay, or another ecommerce auction sites, watch for misspelled words in auction listing titles. This can be costly mistakes for the seller, but a great deal for a buyer looking to resell for profits.

Did You Know? A rare bottle of, *Samuel Allsopp's*-Arctic Ale Beer was sold on eBay in 2007, not once but twice. The first time around, the seller misspelled the name of the ale and only put up three pictures. It ended up selling for $304. However, the buyer knew exactly what he had—a very special beer that was brewed just for Sir Edward Belcher's 1852 expedition to the arctic. So, he decided to list the beer back on eBay again-with the proper description- and additional, detailed photos. This time the ale sold for $503,300!

Knowledge of markings to porcelain, pottery, silver, artist signatures and designer logos are of utmost importance when listing items for sale online. Unmarked pieces need to be researched before listing them. Therefore, I would stay clear of listing unmarked porcelain and pottery until the manufacturer has been identified. Once I know *WHAT* I am selling, then I proceed to list the item.

My Unknown-but Discovered, *Schuco* Toy Stuffed Animal Story!

Most recently I listed on eBay, an unidentified miniature, plush stuffed teddy bear I had found in a box at a recent auction. The label attached read, "East Germany". Other than the label and noting that it measured four-inches tall, I had no way of identifying its manufacturer. I did some research online to find out any information that might help me in identifying the bear, but found nothing on this particular jointed-miniature bear.

I was left with no choice but to list it with the auction title, "East Germany, Miniature Teddy Bear". I didn't receive any hits, or interested viewers, so I decided to go to the local antique mall where I found a teddy bear reference book. Eureka! I found the information I needed to know to list the bear correctly. It was in fact, a "Janus" Schuco miniature toy bear dating from the 1950s. I changed my listing to indicate my newly discovered information, and started receiving more views for my listing. It eventually sold for over $325.

Miniature 1960's Schuco "Janus" Two Faced Mohair Jointed Miniature (3.5") Bear-$315

Another surprise *Schuco* piece I came across was when I attended an auction last summer in Springfield, Nebraska, which was a farm auction. Towards the end of the auction, the crowd was thinning so the auctioneers started moving swiftly and selling boxes filled with items- by the row. (This is the best time to find your treasures for a miniscule cash investment.)

Earlier during the auction preview, I had spotted a cute miniature, red-furry monkey object that had resembled the vintage Schuco, mohair miniature, stuffed toy bear. I waiting patiently and during the

Miniature Schuco, Red Monkey Perfume Bottle (ca 1920-1930)

last 15 minutes of the auction, I was able to obtain this miniature monkey for a mere $10 for an entire box of goods. When I returned to my seat, I was surprised to find out the head lifted away from the body of the monkey. I discovered it was in fact a perfume holder vessel. When I returned home, I researched the three-inch jointed monkey figural bottle on the Internet and found it to be a rare German *Schuco* perfume bottle -a true collectible treasure. I listed it eBay and sold it for over $300 the following week.

Tip: When attending a local auction and viewing items that catch your attention as possibly being unique, or different found in boxes.....Take a chance, bid $5 and perhaps during that "mad dash" at the end of the auction, you will turn that original $5 investment into $100! Isn't it worth the chance? It's such a small investment for such a great cash return.

Since I have had a couple of hidden treasure stories surrounding *Schuco* toys; here is some information about the *Schuco Company*.

Schuco was the trade name for the German toy company, *Schreyer & Co.*, which was founded in Nuremburg, Germany in 1912, by Heinrich Muller. They started using the name "Schuco" in 1921, which was derived from the original name (the first three letters of the name- Schreyer, along with the abbreviated initials-Co). The first trademark featured a small tumbling man logo.

The company started making the now collectible, *Schuco* mechanical "Yes/No" Bear. It is believed to have made its debut at the "Leipzig Spring Toy Fair" held in Germany in 1921 after WWI.

Schuco teddy bears are unique in that they have a tinplate mechanical inner frame. They are made of various colored mohair and plush furs and come in different sizes. The *Schuco Company* is well-known for their manufactured mechanical and jointed teddy bears, and miniature teddy bear perfume bottles.

The "Yes/No" bear had a mechanism, which allowed a tail-operated lever to move the bear's head in an up and down - left to right, yes/no way. They were made in approximately six sizes, from 25cm to 60cm in height. The four smaller sizes contained squeakers, the two larger sized bears contained growlers. **Growlers** are little tubes inside the bear that make a raspy or moaning noise when you turn them over.

In the year 1924, *Schuco* introduced a series of miniature bears known as *Piccolo Bears*. They ranged in height from 9cm to 15cm with various colors of mohair.

In 1927 a cosmetic-*Compact* bear- was produced and designed to fit into a ladies bag, containing a mirror, compact, and powder puff. Additionally, a miniature perfume bottle, or a manicure set were manufactured.

The adorable "Yes/No" bear was made a comeback in the 1950s. The bears featured blonde, gold or brown colored mohair fur. Some contained growlers, Swiss musical mechanisms, and they came in seven different sizes. When identifying these bears, note they have distinctive down-turned paws, broad flat feet, and their muzzles were often shaved. The earlier, Tricky –"Yes/No" bears had short mohair and black boot button eyes. They wore a red bow and plastic medallion on their chest saying "Schuco TRICKY, Patent" on one side with the other side reading, "Made in the US zone of Germany." These cute bears were produced until the year 1970.

I can't emphasize enough how important it is that when you list any item for sale, that you don't misspell descriptive words in titles.

A notable online website to help with identifying the most commonly misspelled words used when listing items on eBay can be found at www.fatFingers.com

This website is dedicated to finding thousands of misspelled listings on eBay. The site was created 10 years ago, by Mike Sheard. This site is very useful and ultimately, can save you-the seller-lots of money.

Chapter III

A Beginner's Tutorial on "How" to sell Ephemera (collectibles) on eBay or other Internet Auction Sites

We have discussed the "Where" in my previous chapter. Let's move on and discuss "How" my interested treasure hunting rookies can flip their new found hidden gems, by simply listing them for sale on eBay, or other e-commerce auction websites.

What is eBay?

eBay is an online marketplace built to support trade on a local, national and international basis. eBay offers an excellent online platform where literally millions of items are traded each day through using auction-style listings, "Buy It Now", or instant Fixed price and eBay Store listings.

I personally use eBay because of its broad global marketplace access is superior. Your auction listings will be shown worldwide.

eBay has one of the largest ecommerce businesses with billions of dollars in goods sold on the site, and millions of active users. This makes eBay one of the largest e-commerce businesses in the world. Many of those hoping to profit from online marketplaces are over the age of 50 who are seeking either to change their career direction, or to supplement their pension or retirement income.

Did You Know?

- Pierre Omidyar who is the founder and Chairman of eBay, has a net worth of 9.1 billion dollars as of August, 2015.

- Items on eBay sell for thousands of dollars, and almost anything can be sold on this mega ecommerce site.

- In 2002, a golfing foursome date with the "Master Champion" of that same year-Tiger Woods, sold for $425,000!

Getting Started with Selling on the World Wide Web (Ecommerce) for Profit

First and foremost—start an online eBay and PayPal account. (PayPal is currently the most popular worldwide, online payment service.)

Potential buyers will need to contact you so you need an email address to link to your merchandise accounts.

I would obtain an updated laptop computer and an internet connection. Additionally, a good digital camera with a zoom lens used for taking quality photos. Ideally, you should have a room at home devoted to your e-commerce auction business. An area used for taking excellent, quality photos, and room for your shipping supplies.

Ultimately, you'll need the personal drive to achieve success for selling online. The rewards will come, when that extra cash starts appearing!

Here are some general guidelines for selling for profit on eBay:

- Buy off-season. Sell on-season.

- Timing is very important with regard to selling your wares.

For example, vintage Halloween die cuts and memorabilia will bring in a generous amount of profit in September versus selling them in the spring.

Vintage Christmas Décor will realize better prices if listing in October and November.

- Begin with listing no more than 20 items a week. Once you become accustomed to selling on eBay, you can increase the number. With the 20-items-per-week rule for beginners, you will have time to learn as you go. In no time, you will be able to bring in an additional $500 a week by selling the ephemera you found when researching and hunting for those hidden gems in the rough.

- Know your product (Is the item truly vintage, or could it possibly be a reproduction or fake.)

- The buyer is always right (even if he is not).

- Remember that UNIQUE and one-of-a-kind items are what sell, due to their scarcity.

When selling vintage clothing, jewelry and home furnishings online, keep in mind their timelines. These *timelines* are important to remember when you're adding keywords to your eBay titles and descriptions:

- Victorian Era, (ca 1837-1901)-The Victorian era is generally agreed to stretch through the reign of Queen Victoria (ca 1837-1901). It was a tremendously exciting period with the immergence of many artistic styles. It is also considered the beginning the 'Modern' Era

- Mission Era-c, 1895-1910 (Arts and Crafts movement)

- Art Nouveau Era, (ca 1890-1910)

- Edwardian Era, (ca 1901-1910) The Edwardian Era in the United Kingdom is the period covering the reign of King Edward VII.

- The Jazz or Flapper Era, (ca 1920s-1930s)

- Art Deco Era, (ca 1930s-1940s)

Did You Know? The term "art deco" arose in 1925 from the International Exposition of Modern Industrial and Decorative Arts held in France.

- Rockabilly & Post WWII Era, (ca 1940s-1950s)
- Space Age, Mid-Century Modern Hippie Era, (ca 1960s-1970s)
- Disco Mania Era, (ca 1970s-1980s)
- Punk, Pop and Hip Hop Era (ca 1980s)
- The revival of Goth, (Gothic), Grunge, Modern-Preppy Era (ca 1990s)

Online Listing Descriptions

Descriptions of your online auctions are extremely important. It is key, to use enticing language.

Your heading or title should draw interest to your website listings. Which title describes the item better- A "1950's Red Dress", or "Vintage '50s Lipstick-Red Wiggle, Cocktail Party Dress?" Make a description of the item you are listing on eBay sound attractive and enticing to view, by the usage of photos and wording in your eBay auction title and photo gallery.

Use powerful *key* descriptive words, such as magnificent, futuristic, amazing, enchanting, glamorous, rare, feminine, fabulous, and stunning in your auctions title page to draw attention. In your title mention the following: Eras, size or measurements, amount, age (new or vintage), and condition of the listed item/ items.

Spelling and grammar should be correct. It reflects your knowledge of the subject matter. Remember, mistakes in spelling can cost you money due to potential buyers unable to locate an item due to a misspelled (typo), or from identification mistakes.

Start your auctions at a reasonable price for you and your auction bidder. For example, if you would like to receive a profit on an auctioned item, but don't want to sell it at a low price; make sure you start it at a reasonable price to cover your eBay listing fees, and the price you originally paid for the auctioned item.

eBay listing fees currently are minimal. Most items I list cost me only .10 to .50 cents to list. You can add enhancements, but it will cost you more. By highlighting your seller auction titles and using bold letters on eBay's selling pages, it will substantially add up costs from your initial upfront listing fees.

Sell on eBay with a RESERVED Price

You can sell your wares on eBay with a set "Reserved" price (RPA)-meaning that you require the auction to reach a set amount (undisclosed amount), in order to start the bidding for that particular item. Another type of auction is the "Fixed Price" auction. This type of auction commands what price is expected for an item to be sold. "Buy-It-Now" buyers have the option of buying an item outright. Most eBay online stores use this option when selling their merchandise.

Use of eBay, and other Online Auction Related Acronyms

Acronyms and abbreviations will assist the seller for minimalizing auction listing titles and descriptions. These abbreviated letters, will allow the seller extra space for adding more essential information when listing their items... especially in the title.

Here is list of some common acronyms I have used when selling on eBay and other ecommerce sites:

AUTH (authentic)

MIP (mint in package)

NIP (new in package) Add the letter "B" first (brand new in package)

NIB (new in box)

NOS (new old stock)

NWOT and NWT (new without tags, new with tags attached),

MIB (mint in box)

OOAK (One of a kind)

NRFB (never removed from box)

HTF (hard to find)

AB (Aurora Borealis-jewelry stone term)

COA (certificate of authenticity)

CZ (cubic zirconia)

EXC (excellent)

HB (hard back)

LE (limited edition)

OOP (out-of-print)

PCGS (professional coin grading service)

PF (coin proof)

RET (retired)

VGC (very good condition)

VTG (Vintage)

For a vast list of other common used acronyms, visit the online web page:

http://www.bnibwt.com

Important Factors to Understand when Considering the Purchase of a Collectable Item for Resale

In your search for prospective "Cash Cows" to sell on eBay; you should consider following these basic principles in your pursuit of finding those vintage goods to sell online for achieving a favorable profit margin.

Supply and Demand - How many of the items were produced or manufactured? Supply and demand refers to the availability of an item, and the want or desire to own it. Whenever demands increase, or overtakes the supply of a collectible; it will drive the price up on that item. Simply put, the item becomes hard to find. The acronyms "DS" (dead stock) or "RET" (retired) can be used in referring to discontinued merchandise. Watch for the following: Limited editions, dead stock merchandise, retired items; and handwritten signatures found on--baseball cards, toys, pottery, flatware, dinnerware, books, prints and record albums.

Condition- Some guideline words used for describing the condition of a particular item you may be interested in selling are:

•	Mint: unused or untouched condition

- Very Fine (VF) or Excellent (EXC): Some usage, but kept in pristine condition

- Fine (F) or very good: The item has been used, but no notable damage.

- Good: The Item in question has some flaws and it is important to note them in your listings.

- Poor: The item has many flaws, but due to its rarity, is still very collectible. Be careful when listing items in *poor* condition. Remember to use the words "as is" when describing an item that is in- less than very good condition-in your listing; it will protect you from any issues the buyer might complain about.

Color- Pay attention to recent popular color trends that have appeal to the present day populous. Colors such as; pink, red, white, black, turquoise, teal, white, cobalt blue and purples are in demand currently.

Aesthetic Appeal-In other words, "That which is pleasing to the eye." For example, Rainbows, large floral prints found on vintage barkcloth fabric curtains; slim-line, mid-century furniture, Art Deco jewelry styles, Still-life artwork; and vintage pastel colored, bias-cut, satin nightgowns.

Individuality-Is the item found one of a kind?

Check your wares for the presence of embossed markings, hallmarks, acid etchings and engraved artisan or designer's name/initials.

Hallmarks found on antique porcelain, silver, pottery, designer-art glass, sculptures and pottery-if present-can help identify and improve value to your items listings.

Examples of Individuality:

- Author or writer signed books
- Signatures present on prints or oil/watercolor paintings
- Acid-stamped signatures on crystal, such as Waterford crystal. (Ireland's Waterford Crystal was one of my favorites since my Mom was born in Ireland.) Waterford crystal pieces will be marked "Waterford".

- Glassworks – Italian, Murano Glass, *Fenton Company*, Lalique- may have glass artisans signatures, or initials found on the bottom of their created vessels
- Raised relief signatures found on the bottom of *Roseville Pottery*
- Signed Metal mid-century sculptures (e.g. C. Jere)
- Embossed words on signage and antique bottles.
- Engraved artists information on sterling silver or gold pieces
- Manufacturer hallmarks or maker's mark, found on metal pieces of flatware and serving pieces (English, Danish, USA), pottery and porcelain wares (e.g. *Haviland & Company- Limoges*; *Meissen*, and English-Flow Blue)

Genre - Is the particular genre popular for collecting? Research what categories or types of paraphernalia are collectible in the present day, then pick those of interest to you. Remember to do research on those genres.

What particular genre is in high demand to own in the vintage toy arena? Some of the genres in the vintage toy category are:

- *Dinky Toys*- vintage die-cast metal miniature toy vehicles
- *J. Chein & Company's* mechanical toys made from stamped and lithographed tin. Produced from the 1930s through the 1950s.
- *Strawberry Shortcake* (1980s), *not* the reproductions made in the 21st century.
- #36-Vintage 1980's "Strawberry Shortcake" Tricycle
- Original 1970's *Star Wars* paraphernalia
- 1950's *Marx* brand toys
- Stuffed animals by *Steiff, Gund, Boyd's Bears* and *Rushton*

Size – The size of an item is a major factor when selling porcelain figures, pottery, blankets, bedspreads, fabric, mirrors and prints. Always keep in mind that even the tiniest sized items, can be far more valuable than the larger items.

Historic Significance to a Specific Group

Examples: Vintage Militia and *Boy Scouts of America* memorabilia from the 1940s are in demand to collect.

Vintage military artifacts, apparel and field gear-and *Boy Scouts of America (B.S.A)* related objects and accessories, such as vintage uniforms, equipment, patches, books, awards and pins--are selling for hundreds of dollars.

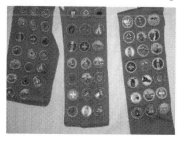  

| Vintage Boy Scouts "Order of the Arrow" Items | Vintage Boy Scouts Eagle Scout-Sterling Silver-Medal | Vintage 1950s/60s Boy Scout Merit Badges |

The Importance of Photos Used in your eBay/Online Listings

Photos are important. Make it a top priority to buy a good digital camera with a quality lens. Cheap cameras have cheap plastic lenses and the quality of the pictures is, of course, lousy!

The camera companies of *Canon* and *Nikon*-produce a fine line of digital cameras. Look for the ability to turn off your flash, change white balance, have optical zoom (at least 3x); a macro feature, and at least two megabytes. (The term megabyte relates to the method of measuring the size of digital photo files, as well as, the storage capacity of a memory card. Photos with more detail and image quality are larger files, and require more computer storage space.)

For more on understanding camera terminology, I found this helpful online site: http://www.rideau-info.com/photos/faq.html

The camera's "macro mode" setting is used for taking photos of smaller items such as coins and jewelry, and for taking photos used to show details to any particular item to be auctioned. Photos of existing signatures, porcelain/pottery markings, engraved names, as well as any defects, are important when listing your items for sale. Obtaining a tripod can help to avoid blurry pictures caused from unstable hands.

Use natural light to prevent glare on an item, when taking photos for your listing.

Early morning or late afternoon is generally considered the best time to photograph items. Direct noon-time sun can cause harsh shadows in the photo. Experiment with different areas located inside the home, to find the best lighting. I find indirect early sunlight, or an overcast day is best. Have at least two lights, one for either side of the item, to eliminate shadows.

Usage of image editing software similar to 'Photoshop' (used to edit or fix-up your photos), will aid with fixing poor lighting situations, color balances and cropping. This is particularly important if you're trying to achieve optimum color and detail to your item. I use this regularly for most of my photos. I want to attract attention to those potential buyers!

Carefully crop photos to single out necessary details in your auction listings. Always show photos detailing damage to an item you will list for sale, such as cracks, chips, flea bites, discoloration to paint, book pages, soil or holes in fabric; scratches to furniture, or canvas art fading. If the buyer is well-advised of any flaws described in your listing before-hand, you shouldn't have to worry about any flaws they might complain about after purchasing, receiving and upon examining it. This avoids a headache for you and your buyer.

Camera flashes are often necessary for photographers to use to illuminate their subjects, but remember using this method of lighting, can be tricky.

You can have trouble with your camera flash for a variety of reasons. Flash photography doesn't work well on reflective surfaces, such as metal, plastic, glossy paper surfaces and glass (e.g., picture frames, glass bottles, jewelry with diamonds, or zirconia pieces). Camera flashes don't work on objects at a distance, as they are out of the range of the flash unit and the flash may not be powerful enough to counteract the strong light that comes during sunset hours.

When a flash camera or attachment is used when taking photos indoors, and when some light is streaming through a window, a camera flash can be a useful counterbalance to the light. Direct sunlight tends to create glaring contrasts, especially when only coming from one side. The camera flash *can* provide full light on the front side of the subject to eliminate dark shadows.

The following accessories will greatly enhance your images by softening, diffusing and altering the color temperature of the light created from a flash from the camera:

A <u>diffuser,</u> which is a special opaque filter, fitted over the top a flash unit. It will reduce flash intensity and soften the flash by blocking some of the light it created.

A <u>reflector</u>, which is a matte, reflective surface onto where a flash unit is aimed, instead of aiming the unit at the subject. This will alter the intensity of the flash used.

An <u>umbrella</u> attached to the flash unit, or a studio light, is used to direct light around the room and subject, and also to used diffuse the subject.

A <u>Softbox</u> can be placed behind the flash unit. This piece will catch and direct light toward the subject; some types also diffuse light.

Here are a couple of homemade methods used to make diffusers and reflectors when taking your eBay photos:

- Use a white styrofoam cup placed over the flash, when taking your photo.

- By placing a white business card about one inch in front of the flash and held at a 45 degree angle to the flash; it will create a nice balance of light needed to enhance your photo.

- Cut part of the plastic handle on a half-gallon milk jug. For correct placement and quick instructions, see the short video link currently found online at: <u>https://www.youtube.com/watch?v=-DPQsXmuAtk</u>

- Take photos at night with a flash. This creates a non-glare environment, especially for merchandise such as clothing. When taking photos of vintage clothing, I use a full size mannequin and several torso forms for taking photos of jackets, blouses, shirts etc. Some of the most successful vintage clothing online sites use real models to photograph their outfits.

- For enhancing backdrops behind the clothing forms or mannequins, I use neutral shades, such as grays, beige, black or white wall color. I sometimes use large or flat bed sheets tacked against a wall, for a backdrop. Velvet fabric is nice for taking photos of some finer pieces, but be sure to take off any traces of lint or dust. Lint on darker fabric shades show up in your photos and is distracting from the object you want to enhance.

- The placement of small boxes placed under fabric will aid in propping up items on flat surface tables. Beeswax is used to hold pieces steady for the set-up for photos in catalogs used for selling fine jewelry and collectible porcelain. It works great because it is a clear neutral color, and it doesn't usually show up in the photo. Replace it often though, as it easily picks up dirt and fuzz on fabric pieces.

Tip: Create attractive listing backgrounds found on the internet, for your auction listings.

Free online listing backgrounds used for auction listings can be found online at: http://www.grsites.com/textures

This website features over 6000 backgrounds and are available at no cost.

Use of Cloud Domes and Portable Photo Tent Light Cube Soft Boxes

When photographing jewelry, collectible coins or other metallic items, you can become quickly disappointed in the poor quality of your pictures versus what is seen by the naked eye. When viewing jewelry or coins being sold on televised shopping networks, such as QVC; notice the shimmering glow from the displayed merchandise. The shiny luster of the subject makes me want to rush to the telephone and order the advertised merchandise. These glorious pieces are definitely pleasing to the eye.

Let's face it, all women like shiny- sparkling- anything!

Equipment, such as the portable tent light cube soft box can be purchased in order to enhance photographs of jewelry, collectible coins or other metallic items.

A *Photo Tent Light Cube Soft Box* is an ingenious product that will alleviate glare, harsh shadows, and burnout on item details.

Another great feature to include with a camera purchase is a translucent white plastic dome called the "Cloud Dome." The Cloud Dome will make original colors photograph accurately and allows for crisp, clear, close-up photos. The dome also gives you the best images for those gemstones, bringing out the luster in those lovely facets!

Here is a site to help you understand how the *Cloud Dome* works:

www.clouddome.com

Other helpful points when taking photos for your eBay listings include:

- Clean up the area around the subject, or use a backdrop.
- Always avoid clutter in the photo-no one wants to see "Fluffy" the cat, hanging around in the background when spreading out that delicate vintage clothing apparel on a floor for a photo.
- Shoot photos outdoors on a cloudy day.
- If comparing size is an issue, show something such as a ruler or coin to indicate the dimensions of an item.

Use of Auction Management Services

Automate your auction listings with an auction management service, which will provide some superb online auction listing amenities. They feature auction templates where you type in your titles and text, insert your images (image hosting), list your price, specify listing terms and conditions, length of the auction, and schedule your auctions to launch at any day or time specified.

The management service includes the incredibly popular scrolling gallery, allowing your viewers to see additional items you are currently listing for sale by cross-references. Once potential buyers have viewed your gallery photos, they might be interested in purchasing more than one of your auction listings.

Other amenities to these services are tracking inventory and sales, sending automated emails to your clientele, and automatically post feedback once payment has been received by the buyer.

These auction management online sites are easy to set-up, and the cost is low (approximately $10 a month) to use. It's a wonderful service and will help your auction listings look professional.

Here is a list of some of the most noted ecommerce management services:

- *Auctiva*
- *Inkfrog*
- *AuctionSplash*
- *Vendio*
- *Pagemage*
- *Prostores*
- *Sellersourcebook*

Most of these companies will offer a free "30 Day Trial" period so, make sure and research each online program to match your particular needs.

Building Positive Feedback

The customer is ALWAYS RIGHT, even if they are not. There are always going to be faultfinders when selling online. To keep complaints low from buyers, have an accurate description, and remember to **ship your merchandise out on time**. When mailing out packages, always add a "Proof of Delivery" receipt and purchase postal insurance. I can't stress this enough.

It is eBay's goal is to create a secure transaction when a buyer wins an online auction. They have strict rules that need to be followed when selling on their site. Be careful about selling potentially infringing items. This is an area to be especially careful of before selling an item. If you list a potentially infringing item and use another sellers existing copyrights, trademark or registration; it will result in penalties to you-the seller. Ultimately you can be banned selling on eBay.

An unfortunate personal experience

I once used the phrase, "Shabby Chic" on my eBay listing, to describe a vintage

76

chenille bedspread in my auction's title which, resulted in the listing being removed from eBay. I later found out that someone had trademarked that name to a store in California. Because of this trademark, the words-shabby and chic-can't be used together, but each word can be used separately. Similarly, one of eBay's policies states that the word, 'like' not be used in an eBay auction listing title. This is called "Keyword Spamming". The word *like* denotes comparisons to the real thing-not-the actual brand. Example: "Louis Vuitton *Like*- Handbag"....definitely a no-no.

An online link for more information on eBay's rules and regulations for buying and selling can be found at: http://pages.eBay.com/services/tsindex.html

Shipping

USPS (United States Postal Service), UPS (United Parcel Service) and Fed Ex Ground are the most widely used shipping companies. The eBay and PayPal Companies have an automated shipping system integrated with UPS and USPS on their site. These companies can mail shipping supplies to any address— home or business—so you don't have to leave your house. Be sure to add the delivery tracking number or confirmation to all your packages.

The time it takes to get your packages to the post office and the cost of gasoline -will verify your reasoning for wanting to add the necessary postage right from your own home.

For more details, visit: http://www.usps.gov and http://ups.com

When weighing packages, there is no need to purchase an expensive postage meter. Instead, get a scale that is functional, cost effective, ounce-specific, and easy to find in any neighborhood. *Target, Wal-Mart*, or other discount retail department stores have low-end food and diet scales (less than $15). For heavier packages you can just use a regular digital bathroom scale then add a pound to the weight that is displayed.

Aside from stamps and mailing materials, keep bubble wrap and styrofoam peanuts on hand. These items can be picked up, free of charge, at pharmacies, furniture or home décor stores. You can find boxes placed in dumpsters behind retail store buildings for shipping larger items.

eBay Tutorial Information

Here are some tips to help you become a topnotch money maker by learning how to sell your merchandise on eBay:

- Attend local eBay seminars in your area.
- Join in on any eBay online workshop.
- Use the various eBay online tutorials available to view for free.

eBay teaching guides can be found in their website links.

Additionally, here are some helpful books on how to excel in the e-commerce, eBay selling arenas:

- *How to Buy, Sell, and Profit on eBay: Kick-Start Your Home-Based Business in Just Thirty Days* by Adam Ginsberg

- *The Six-Figure Second Income: How to Start and Grow a Successful Online Business Without Quitting Your Day Job* by David Lindahl and Jonathan Rozek

- *eBay 101: Selling on eBay For Part-time or Full-time Income* by Steve Weber

- *Part Time Selling: 90 Days to Online Success by Selling on eBay & Amazon* by Jason Guarino and Susan Myers

With a little patience and a lot of research you will be on your way to being the next eBay "Power Seller", or one of their top-rated Sellers.

Using eBay's Search Engine to Determine Current Merchandise Prices

This is my favorite way to discover ephemera that are the current market trends. What are people looking to purchase or garner? Additionally, it assists in identifying antiques or collectibles, and what they *sold* for.

Here are some pointers to help you to get starting using eBay's search engine:

Find the "Advanced" search link on eBay's online site. This link is located in the far upper right side of the home page and to the right of the royal blue "Search" box. Once you click onto this link, enter keywords in the box that reads, "Enter keywords or item number". Here is an example of a title search: vintage red heart brooch, antique picture frame, *John Deere* tractors etc. (You don't have to use capital letters in your searches.) Next, scroll down on this page to the heading that reads "sold items" and check the box located there.

This area will tell you WHAT these particular items "sold" for in the past few weeks (past sold items). If you don't check this box, you can also check the "Completed listing" box. Completed listings, will show you sold, and unsold recently completed auctions. Remember, your goal here is to find out what a buyer *will actually pay* for merchandise, not its appraised value.

Scroll further down to the "sort by" area. Highlight the option that reads, "Price-highest first" and click the blue "search box" area.

A full list of sold items will appear with prices starting from "Highest price to lowest price". This is where I learn how high a price someone will pay for a particular item. This method of searching helps in figuring out if your item is worthy enough to list. If you discover an identical piece to the one you are researching, and it didn't even fetch $10…Will there be a profit made?

This page has other categories to assist you with narrowing down your searches. When I use this page, I add descriptive key words to narrow down searches further. (e.g., brands, colors, gender, patterns and timelines.) Example: vintage pink high heel shoes. When I apply these words in the search box and follow the above method, I get *all* the vintage pink, high heel shoes that have sold in the last couple of weeks, starting from the highest to low price range. Walla! I have now, figured out *what* pink shoes brought in the highest dollar amount.

Find a particular niche product and research it; it may take time and effort on your part, but it will be rewarding in the long run. By becoming an expert in selling a certain niche or genre, it will ultimately help to earn that extra cash.

Google's search engine is perfect place to research prices and find out what's the newest, super- hot, collectible trend.

When searching for items to list and sell on eBay, search for items that will cost you under $20 to purchase as an initial investment, to start the ball rolling. As you learn more and become experienced, you can increase these amounts.

Other Online E-commerce Sites for Selling Second-Hand Treasures

The classified advertisement website called Craigslist, is a great site to sell merchandise (especially appliances and furniture) and it is FREE to list items-no fees, whereas, eBay and PayPal have fees based on the percentages of the item sold (final fair value fee) in addition to their listing fees. Craigslist allows several photos and has a large description area in which to list information about your merchandise for sale. Craigslist will require contact information for potential buyers. I personally just use the email address preference until I know I have a serious buyer. Once I know the person is legitimate, I will release my phone contact number.

Unfortunately, there are a lot of scammers who enjoy taking advantage of online sellers. Be aware of broken English, confusing text, puzzling instructions and misspelled words from potential buyers. Please don't waste your time with them. Once contact is made via email, these scammers will try to confuse you with puzzling instructions and word content. This is your raised black flag to back out while you still can!

Etsy Website

Etsy is a popular online site where you can start your own store. A buyer creates a blog or Facebook that will draw buyers to their listings on Etsy and eBay websites. Usage of blogs, YouTube, Twitter and Facebook are all great marketing tools to help draw prospective buyers to your listings on these online ecommerce sites.

Here is a list of online reference books I would recommend, to help you get started on your quest to making a profit by selling used or new merchandise on the internet:

- *Sell It Online: How to Make Money Selling on eBay, Amazon, Fiverr & Etsy* by Nick Vulich

- *Million Dollar eBay Business from Home - A Step By Step Guide* by Neil Waterhouse

Selling Books Online

Here is a list of some of the most notable online websites for selling all sorts of books and music CD's:

- **Amazon.com, Inc**

  Would you want to get rid of a few unwanted books that are just lying around on shelves or bookcases, and at the same time make a lucrative amount of income? Amazon.com is one of the world's largest online retailers and multi-leveled ecommerce sites; additionally, it is a noteworthy website for selling used or new books.

  On Amazon, a buyer can find new or used beauty supplies, clothing, jewelry, gourmet food, sporting goods, pet supplies, CDs, DVDs; computers, furniture, toys, garden supplies, and everything in between.

  Since Amazon is the number one book marketplace in the world, I would strongly suggest investigating this worldwide marketplace as a place to sell your collectible books. They sell hundreds of millions of books every year.

  You can choose the option of selling as a professional or individual.

  Here is a helpful link to help you to get started selling on Amazon.com: http://services.amazon.com/content/sell-on-amazon.htm?id=hm1&

- **Alibris Retailer Company (Alibris.com)**

  Alibris.com is an online marketplace where books can sell quickly. A small fee is collected when signing up as a book seller on the site, but it's worth the money spent. Inventory is sold on Books-A-Million, Half.com, and Barnes and Noble-currently at no extra charge.

  Here you can sell books, movies, and CD's. You will need a PayPal bank account, or a U.S.A. address to receive payments. There is a yearly fee to sell on Alibris, which will be due upon signing up as a book seller; however, it is well worth your time as books sell fast on this site. With the click of a button, you can upload your inventory to be sold. It's just like selling on four websites at one time and with Alibris UK, and other worldwide affiliates, you'll be able to ship your books to buyers international.

- **Half.com-an eBay Company**

  http://www.half.ebay.com/

  Half.com is an eBay company which focuses on the sale of games, CD's -but mainly books. Half.com does require sellers to have an eBay and/ or PayPal account to make and receive payment. The fastest way to get rid of a book is through any company associated with eBay. When customers are seeking a particular book, not only does the result of eBay come on the screen, so does half.com.

- **ABeBooks.com**

  For more information on ABeBooks website, go to the following link:

  http://www.abebooks.com/books/Sell/professional-sellers.shtml

---

Tip: When attending auctions, books usually aren't sold until the last hour. This is unfortunate for the homeowners, but beneficial for the buyers that attend the auction and have waited patiently for this moment. Crowds typically thin to ten bidders or less, towards the end of an auction. For only ten dollars or less, a buyer can walk away with huge boxes of books. Finding rare

first editions, and signed copies for literally a dollar a book, is not unheard of. Bring a metal two-wheeler, or extra help if you plan on purchasing boxes of books at an auction.

Selling books online can be an easy hobby and a great way of earning extra income. Just look for the 'sell' button on any book ecommerce website, and get to work.

This will conclude the chapter on *How* to sell your purchases to create a profitable cash flow. The following chapters will discuss *what* some of those hidden bargained treasures are-depending on current demand factors. These chapters will cover a multitude of vintage sought-after consumer goods. Consumer goods are products that are purchased by the average person. These goods have changed in nature throughout the history of the decades. They were manufactured and placed on the store shelves per current demands, but these past, manufactured wares have now brought back a revival of interests to own them once again.

Items, such as clothing, food, home furnishings, automobiles, and jewelry are all examples of consumer goods.

So let's get started on discovering those *less obvious* treasures that can found in the home, farm, office, yard, shed or garage.

Chapter IV

What Hidden Treasures Might Lurk in the Kitchen?

The nostalgic kitchen collecting category can span to a wide range of objects, from pots and pans to canisters, and cookie jars to salt-and-pepper shakers. Even though these items came from the past, if they are still functional and appealing to the eye, they may be presently in demand.

Particular kitchen utensils, such as eggbeaters with red or green-handles from the 1930s through the 1940s may only sell for $5, but the more unusual types, such as the "E-A-S-Y" eggbeater-which sold for $2,100 at a Kansas auction in 1994; is what you're looking for. (This is an egg beater I would like to find!) Those old-fashioned gadgets may be unusual in nature, but are clever in function and have an interesting appeal.

The first kitchen appliances developed and sold during the Art Deco Era were designed to be attractive as well as useful. Some of the designs were actually attractive and the engineering that went in to some of them were brilliant.

I had an old '50s *GE* stove, which I kept in our garage and was more dependable than our newer, 2002 *GE* model! Those old appliances are now HOT to find, buy and resell (refurbished or not). Quality is everything and vintage appliances are known to be tried and true. The 1930s -1940s years, brought about stove brands like *Roper, Tappan, Chambers, Dixie, Magic Chef,* Gaffers & Sattler and *O'Keefe & Merritt.* Oh, I forgot to mention those vintage (ca 1960s-1980s) toy, Kenner Easy-Bake Ovens, which I so much cherished as a young girl, sell for around $80 online.

1939 Frigidaire Refrigerator

Vintage 1980's Toy, Easy-Bake Oven

Refrigerators replaced turn-of-the-century wood and metal clad ice-boxes in the 1920s. If you are lucky enough to come across those primitive ice boxes (e.g., *Coolerator, Windsor, Grand Challenge* and *Baldwin*)-BIG MONEY!

Vintage refrigerator names that are sought-after are *Frigidaire, Philco, Admiral, General Electric* types with ball (globe) tops, *Hotpoint*-they sell for hundreds of dollars if their aesthetic appearance is desired, and in very good working condition.

Antique Wood Ice Box

Kitchen Textiles

Watch for mid-century Tammis Keefe tea towel prints; and fine Irish linen tea towels. Vintage '30s and '40s aprons and apron sewing patterns; and the whimsical, bright colored and themed '50s print tablecloths by *Wilendur* (i.e. *Weil & Durrse Company*) and *California Prints.* These durable, beautiful table coverings featured themes. Designs with large floral and fruit images; Christmas Holiday images, Atomic Age prints (bold geometric patterns); quirky cartoon depictions, and kitchenware utensils-on a white background. During the mid-century timeline, these tablecloths were widely used at neighborhood barbecues, cocktail parties and social events. Most of the printed tablecloths were made from sailcloth fabric. Vintage tablecloths depicting "Black Americana" (mammy prints), mid-century "Leacock" prints and "Vera" designs are also in demand.

Below is a guide to *Vera Neumann's* logos, and how to date her designs:
- Early 1950s – small signature with no copyright or ladybug marks.
- Mid to late 1950s – small signature with copyright symbol and ladybug.
- Early 1960s – larger signature with copyright symbol and ladybug.
- Mid 1960s -1980s – the signature became larger. Still has the copyright symbol, but no ladybug symbol.
- 1993 to present – small signature with copyright mark.

For more information on *Vera Neumann* and her merchandise you can check out the book: *Vera: The Art and Life of an Icon, 2010* by Susan Seid.

Vintage 1950's
Wilendur
Company Label

1950's Wilendur "Lobster-Clam"
Print Tablecloth-selling price
over $200

Vintage Pinecone Themed
Tablecloth

Tip: The textile designer/artist, *Vera Neumann* (1907-1993) should not to be confused with the other "Vera" designer names of *Vera Bradley* and *Vera Wang*. Vera's earlier signature/logo textiles, which include her fabulous line of designer ladies scarfs- are valuable, especially those with original labels still intact, kept in pristine condition, or never used.

Vintage Vera Neumann
Kitchen Tea Towel-Lady Bug
symbol (ca 1950s-1960s)

Circa 1960s-1980s
"Vera" Signature on a
Silk Neck Scarf

Cleaning kitchen linens and tablecloths

Before purchasing a vintage tablecloth, always check to see if there is any soil present it may be considered worthless to sell for a substantial profit. I have spent hours attempting to remove stains on tablecloths. Some unfortunately, ended up being discarded. Minor staining may be remedied. In fact, if there are but a few spots of yellowing or light soil. I would still buy the tablecloth and try to remove the stains.

Cleaning vintage tablecloths and home linens:

- Use oxygen products (e.g., OxiClean), by first rinsing the cloth thoroughly, then continue to launder with the oxygen product. Since most chemical detergents can damage some vintage cloth types, oxygen products should not be used with any cloths containing metallic threads or dyes. Check your cloth carefully before soaking.

- Take approximately a 1/4 cup of *OxiClean*, and dissolve it in two of cups of *hot* water. Add the mixture to very warm water. Soak your cloths overnight, but be sure to check them immediately in the morning as soaking for too long can be risky (the shorter the soak time-the better). Be patient-it may take a few tries to see satisfactory results . The small yellow stains will most likely be bleached out once hung out to dry. If not, try again! I would recommend doing this process in a porcelain sink.

- Stain sticks are enzyme-based cleaners available at grocery and discount stores. They are most effective on food, grease, oil, protein, and dirt-based stains and can be used on any fabric and color. Stain sticks can remain on fabric for up to one week. The *Carbona* product line is one of best at removing specific stains, especially rust.

- Mother Nature can be the best bleacher on fabrics. Hanging tablecloths from a clothesline, or laying them outside on a sheet in the grass for two to three hours after washing, will do a beautiful job of lightening yellow stains. Make sure that if you hang your tablecloth on the clothesline, you are not stretching the ends or using several non-metal wood pins.

Tip: Always open up a tablecloth and hold it up to a light source (in front of a large window or lit ceiling overhead light) to inspect for any noted discolorations (stains and yellowing spots), which will affect its value substantially.

How to remove rust:

- Be careful not to damage the cloth
- Carefully use the rust remover product called "Whink." Some stronger detergents will eat away at vintage fabric and create even more damage by disintegrating the textile and cause holes.
- Make a paste of lemon juice and table salt and apply the mixture to a rust stain with a soft, clean white cloth. Gently work the paste into the material-then set it outside on a clothesline under the sunshine for two to three hours -repeat if necessary.

Removal of Yellowed areas

Small yellow spots on white can be removed by simply dabbing a Q-tip with *Clorox* liquid and applying it to the stain. When you attempt this, make sure you have a white rag cloth underneath when placed on any hard surface. Remember to rinse the cloth in warm water after dabbing.

For those tablecloths that can't be saved. Crafters who upcycle may buy them as "cutters" to make "Cottage Chic" items, such as stuffed toys, pillows, quilts, chair and footstool covers, appliance covers, pot holders, pillow covers and much more.

Tip: Tablecloths made prior to 1935 will have dyes that may not be colorfast and may fade or clean unevenly. Watch for any signs of the colors running out of the cloth-the water will be tinged with red, green or orange. Remove the tablecloth immediately-then rinse in cold water. Always check your tablecloth while you are soaking or cleaning it, to check for fading colors or possible damage of the fabric.

Removing Mildew

Mix water with white vinegar in equal parts into a spray bottle and then spray the mildew stains. Set the tablecloth outside to dry and repeat if necessary.

Here are some favored reference books to help in researching vintage tablecloths and linens types:

- *Elegant Table Linens from Weil & Durrse Including Wilendur* by Michelle Hayes
- *Colorful Tablecloths 1930s-1960s Threads of the Past* by Yvonne Barineau & Erin Henderson
- *Collectors' Guide to Vintage Tablecloths* by Pamela Glasell
- *Terrific Tablecloths* by Loretta Smith Fehling

Decorative Kitchenware and Useful Consumer Goods in the Kitchen

Vintage Holt -Howard's Cozy Kitten line of kitchenware

Who was *Holt Howard*? During the 1950s and 1960s—Holt-Howard was the king of whimsical ceramics. Some of their wares included: salt and pepper shakers, string holders, ashtrays, bud vases, cottage cheese crocks butter dishes, sugars and creamers; condiment jars, spice sets, match holders, cookie jars, meow mugs, soap shakers and the "Keeper of the Grease" crock.
They created many fine household lines which became best sellers. *Pixiewares* by far, was one of their leading lines.

Here is some information about *Pixieware*, and other Holt Howard lines:

- *Pixieware* (ca 1958-1962), started with a striped mustard, ketchup and "jam 'n jelly" ceramic jar. Each came with lids or toppers in the form of funny, elfin heads. The line expanded to include coffee containers, "Spoofy Spoons," sugar and cream crocks, and jars for cherries (cocktail and regular), olives (cocktail and regular), onions (same), relish, honey, mayonnaise, chili sauce, salad dressings, liquor decanters; cruet sets, hors d'oeuvre dishes, salt and pepper shakers, tea pots, planters, and even towel holders.

1958 Holt Howard
"Pixieware" Jam & Jelly
Condiment Jar

- *Red Rooster* (ca 1960-70s)—Rooster images, or wares were the latest rage in the kitchen in the 1950s through the 1960s, so Bob Howard designed the *Red Rooster*, "Coq Rouge" dinnerware. Pieces included were pitchers, figural salt and pepper shakers, vases and ashtrays.
- *Merry Mouse* (ca 1950-60s)- cocktail kibitzers (Toothpick holders used for placement of olives and cherries on the edge of cocktail beverage drinking vessels.), coasters and crocks.
- Christmas Collectibles (ca 1950s-1970s)- The *Winking Santa* and *Merry Whiskers* beverage sets, which included pitcher and mugs and usually changed designs each year and the *Starry-Eyed Santa*-party ware

Vintage Holt Howard "Winking Santa" Figure

- The *Cozy Cats* line was introduced 1959.

1950's Holt Howard Cozy Cat
Jam 'n Jelly—$475

- "Moo Cow" salt and pepper shakers
- "Dandy-Lion" Bobbing banks, and other whimsical coin banks

Identifying *Holt Howard* Items

Most Holt Howard creations were marked with an ink stamp and a date; the smaller pieces usually just had a foiled label sticker since they were too small for a stamp. The sticker would read "Holt Howard" and the year in which it was made, or "HH" and the year stamped in black ink. The "HH" mark was used until 1974. Additionally, a black and silver label or foil sticker on items marked "Japan", can be found for items produced aboard; and later (c, 2000) pieces were marked GHA (*Grand Howard Associates*). The *Pixieware* pieces marked GHA, were produced for one year with guidance from 1960's Holt Howard designer, Curt Blanchard. The GHA labeled pieces command a higher price for collecting, since only a limited amount of pieces were made.

Holt Howard (HH) foiled
sticker label

Cookbooks:

Late 19th century and the following cookbooks can sell over one hundred dollars:

Mastering the Art of
French Cooking Cookbook
by Julia Child

- *Mastering the Art of French Cooking 1961* by Julia-Child--if signed-all the better!
- *Betty Crocker* and *"Joy of Cooking"* First edition cookbooks
- The Art Culinaire Cookbook Collection
- *Larousse Gastronomique Culinary* cookbook-1938 edition
- Black Americana--*related* cookbooks
- The Good Cook Time Life Cookbook Series (a set of 28 cookbooks)

Vintage '40s-'50s
Chalkware French Clown
String Holder

Vintage kitchen chalkware string holders sell into the hundreds range as well. Vintage lightweight chalkware "string holders" are very collectible. They came in an array of different caricatures depicting cartoon personalities, Black Americana Mammies, animals, famous movie and storybook characters, such as Roy Rogers, "Popeye the Sailor" and "Little Red Riding Hood".

Vintage metal *COSCO* rolling carts, swivel bar stools and chair-stepping stools are in demand, selling in the hundreds.

Vintage Pink Cosco Utility Cart—$210

Vintage Cosco Step Stool— $110

Boscul -Peanut Butter Glasses

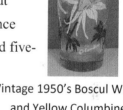

In the 1950's the *Wm. S. Scull Company*, Inc. distributed their products of tea, coffee, assorted nut products and peanut butter in vivid, floral-decorated glass tumblers to enhance interest in their *Boscul* product. These glasses measured five-inches tall and held 11-ounces of liquid with the newer sets being a bit smaller in size and boring the name of the flower in small script usually at, or near the base of the glass. These glasses can sell in the hundreds range.

Vintage 1950's Boscul White and Yellow Columbine (Peanut Butter) Drinking Glass-$30

Fire-King *Anchor Hocking* Restaurant ware, white coffee Mugs with "C" shaped handles (moreover "D" handles were also made and can be valuable) that have particular advertising logos added to them (e.g., *Burger King, Dairy Queen*), and those with iconic cartoon images, such as *Charlie Brown & Snoopy* of *Peanuts* fame-sell in the hundreds. Additionally,

Vintage Fire-King, Burger King Restaurant Ware Mug-$75

the *Fire-King,* Jade-ite (i.e. Jadite) "Jane Ray" opaque green glass and turquoise blue dinnerware sets can be quite collectible. *Fire-King* "Kimberly" patterned mugs can also fetch over $100 each. The early 1940s Fire-King mugs will be marked "Fire-King" in block raised lettering on their bottoms. In the mid-1940s and into the 1950s, the words--oven, glass and ware were added.

Vintage Fire -King Blue
Turquoise Mugs

Fire King Logo on
Bottom of Mug

For a more detailed look at dating *Fire-King* pieces, I found the following online website quite helpful: http://www.fire-king-mug.com/faqs-for-fire-king-collectors/

Coffee Pots/Percolators: *Cory* Rubber-less Glass Vacuum Coffee Pots; *Chemex* Pyrex Coffee Makers; Mid-century Sunbeam, Deco *GE* Pot Belly, *Revere Ware* Copper Clad stove-top 8-cup, *Pyrex's* Flameware Range-top and *Farberware* Percolators all sell over $100 if found in excellent working condition. The series and volume of coffee cups produced are factors as well.

Vintage Revere Ware copper
bottom Drip-O-Lator

Revere Ware Cookware

Revere ware Signature

Pyrex "Flameware" Stove Top
Percolator-Coffee Pot

Wagner ware-Roasters, Dutch ovens with handles; fry pans, Bundt pans and ovenware are always desired and profitable to sell in very good to mint condition.

Vintage *Wear ever*, *Presto* Cookers, chicken fryer's and pressure cookers sell for over $150 if they are in very good condition and come with original instructional booklet. Those huge dinosaur (Old), cast aluminum, pressure cooker/ canners, can sell over $300!

Tip: To add value to any vintage or newer appliance you plan on selling; make sure to look for their instructional booklets and original boxes.

Pressure Cooker/Frying
Bucket

Antique Cast Aluminum
Cooker/Canner

Griswold Cast Iron #9, 12 and 20 fry skillets with lids sell for over $300. Not to mention the Holy Grail of *Griswold* cast iron pieces, the "Turks Head"

95

muffin pan #13 is currently selling for over $1,000.

Antique Griswold Cast Iron Skillet/fry pan-#13

Magnalite-cast aluminum cookware is in demand with roasters selling for over $150-with the *Magnalite* tea kettle sells for over $100 alone.

Mid-century *Dansk*, Jens Quistgaard's line of *Kobenstyle*- enameled steel cookware; and *Raymond Loewy's*, "Le Creuset" enameled cast iron ovenware can bring in over $300 each.

Mid-century, Dansk Kobenstyle blue,
Enameled Covered Steel frying pan

Mid-century modern, *Cathrineholm* Enamel Kitchenware

In the kitchen there are several collectible mid-century wares, I would like to discuss one of the most popular in the enamelware group-Cathrineholm.

Contrary to popular belief, *Cathrineholm* is not the name of a person or a designer (I admit I thought it was.). It is the name of a factory where these lovely enamel treasures were manufactured. The factory was located on the outskirts of the city of Halden, Norway.

Originally an ironworks factory that produced wrought iron, but due to economic circumstances the company ventured into making kitchenware with mid-century Danish modern designs and motifs in the 1950s and '60s. By the end of 1960s, the company closed, but in recent years, the company's designs and products found a renewed interest among vintage collectors and mid-century modern design connoisseurs. It was their 'Lotus' design that turned out to be *Cathrineholm's* signature design. It is now coveted by collectors around the world. The enamelware became icons of the Scandinavian design movement was based on functionalism and democratic design.

Some types of kitchenware the factory produced were: Various mixing/serving bowl sizes, fondue sets, coffee pots, tea kettles, various casserole dishes, cookware, ice buckets and more. Moreover, some of these pieces are collectible.

#60A- 1960's Cathrineholm "Lotus" Pattern Coffee Pot from Norway-$137

Cathrineholm , Blue on White 'Lotus' Enamel Bowl- 5.5"-$125

Cookie Jars: Several brands of vintage cookie jars, are hot collectibles from the mid-century to the 1990s. Specific favorite cookie jars made by Star Limited Editions (especially the Wizard of Oz Series), *Walt Disney Company, Shawnee,* American Bisque, *McKee Glass Company* of Pennsylvania; *McCoy, Haeger, Metlox, Red Wing* Stoneware, and the highly sought after- *Glenn Appleman* designed automobile cookie jars from the '70s and '80s, which can fetch over $1,000 each.

Some other notable cookie jars selling for over $200 are the 1980's Strawberry Shortcake character jar by *American Greetings* and *Fitz and Floyd brand* novelty and the Christmas themed cookie jars.

Vintage Fitz and Floyd Cookie Jar

Vintage Disney Themed Cookie Jars Lot

Vintage Disney Themed "Cinderella' Cookie Jar

Did You Know? 1960's Pop Icon, Andy Warhol loved cookie jars. In fact, in 1988, hundreds of interested bidders filled *Sotheby's galleries* in New York to bid on over 175 cookie jars he once owned. The bidders came from Florida , Paris. France and Halifax, Nova Scotia-to browse and bid on the pop artist's collection, which included pigs, mice, goats, sheep (animal types). "Humpty Dumpty" and a plump-panda. The total amount of money paid for the entire lot of cookie jars was $247,830.

Tin Metal Advertising Pot Scrapers: In the early 1900s the tin pot scraper was a favored giveaway ad. Ads for: ice cream, flour, bacon, kitchen cleansers and other consumer goods, were pictured on the tin scrapers. The straight edge of the scraper was used for the frying pan with the smaller edge was used for the rolling pin, and a large curved edge was used scraping the roasting pan. These metal ads are hard to find as once used,—the ads usually wore off. These early pot scrapers can fetch over $300 if the ad is still in very good condition.

Vintage Early 20th Century "Sharples Tubular Cream Separator" Advertisement- Metal Pot Scraper

Frisbie's **tin pie pans** from the early 1900s, sell for over $100. In 1871, William Russell Frisbie managed a branch of the *Olds Baking Company* located in Bridgeport, Connecticut. Soon after, he bought it outright and named it the *Frisbie Pie Company.* W. R died in 1903, with the company being under the directions of his son, Joseph, Joseph's wife, and a long –time manager; the pie company grew to making over 80,000 pies a day by 1956. These are the tins that held the pies the company made.

Vintage Frisbie
Metal Pie Tin

Vintage Frisbie Pie
Delivery Truck Photo

Vintage small appliances lightly or never used in their original boxes, such as any 1980's *Black & Decker Spacemaker*-products under cabinet small appliances (e.g., can openers, toaster ovens, coffee makers); *Farberware* (e.g., electric griddles, open hearth electric Broiler/rotisserie's); and vintage slow cookers (e.g., *Rival, Westbend, Farberware*), can sell in the hundreds. Those huge floor '40s *Westinghouse* roasters/slow cookers sell for over $200.

Farber ware Open Hearth
Electric Broiler & Rotisserie
Indoor Grill-Model 454A

1970's *Rival* 4-Qt Slow Cooker-
Crock Pot with Removable
Stoneware

Vintage General Electric Broiler Oven

Black & Decker Spacemaker,
Under-the-Counter Can Opener-
NIB

**Vintage 1940s-1950s, tin metal canister sets with matching bread boxes sell
for over $150.**

Pyrex Fever!!

Hot to collect are those cheerful vintage *Pyrex* mixing, nesting and Cinderella-
handled bowls; pie plates, lidded casserole dishes, nesting bowls, refrigerator
dishes, chafing and warming dishes; Chip and Dip sets; and kitchenware in
favored patterns. Here is a list of some of most desired patterns: "*Amish
Butterprint*", "*Gooseberry*" (pink color), Atomic Era 'Eyes', "*Starburst*",
"*Snowflake*" (blue color), "*Friendship*", "*Polka Dot*", and "*Blue Hex
Signs*". Other factors to garnering these kitchenware serving receptacles is
their color** with pink and turquoise, leading the way in popularity.

Pyrex "Dots" Nesting
Mixing Bowl Set-
Size-#401, 402 and
403-$225

1950s Pyrex Pastel Custard Cups-
Made in England -Very rare-$495

Vintage Pyrex Corning Vi-
sionware Cookware-Amber
Glass-$350

Recently, I found a Pyrex

Vintage Pyrex Nesting Mixing Bowls

1960's Atomic Age- JAJ (made in England) Pyrex, Red "Gooseberry" Pattern Serving Dish with Lid (Cinderella Model 443) and Warming Stand- $462

covered dish sold for over $4,200 (2015), in the HTF pattern called "Lucky in Love"!

Vintage mid-century pressure cookers:

Presto, Wear-Ever, All American and *Mirro*
- brand canning, pressure cookers and chicken fryers complete and in excellent working condition are sought-after.

Vintage "*CUTCO*", Homemaker knife sets and cutlery, and Counter-"*LUX*" Minute Minders/Timers are HOT!

Breweriana
What? Selling Old Beer Cans are Profitable? You Bet!

Beer Can Garnering or Breweriana

Beer has been around for thousands of years, but sealed, liquor bottling in America began in the 1870s. Before this time, barrels and kegs held the ale or brew. The advent of pasteurization in 1876 made it safe to bottle fermented products.

Since bottling of beer was costly, the metal "Beer Can" was introduced in January, 1935.

Beer Cans Collecting Intro

People have been collecting vintage beer cans ever since the first can was commercially produced for overall consumption in 1935. Because of this, there is a beer can grading system ranging from numbers 1 thru 5, with the number 1-

being in excellent condition and 5 being poor. The majority of collectors will only look for the cans with low numbers (1-3). Beer cans sold online can sell for thousands of dollars.

Here are some examples of rewarding beer can finds, I found sold online in the last year:

- A vintage Bock Budweiser Beer-sold for $2,500.
- Omaha, Ne, Storz- All-Grain, Flat-Top cans can sold for over $1,235.
- An Iroquois Cone-top Can, sold for over $1,000.

Sorry. But the 1970's "Billy Beer" is not listed as valuable, due to millions of cases of beer being sold.

Yes! These various types of beer cans were all found by treasure hunting in what others consider to be **Trash**!!

"Mark…Get set….Let's Go Beer Can, Dump Hunting!"

In order to become a vintage/antique bottle and can collector, a collector literally, looks for old dumping sites. Old dumps are the best place to find these highly collectible pieces and this means getting dirty -- not donning your favorite clothes. Large open dump pits were once used to toss beer cans and other rubbish away, most of these pits are found in the Pacific Northwest where the particular type of soil is favorable for digging. In the New England States, you can find old beer cans under layers of decomposed leaves near old buildings or homes.

Both of these digging styles require a good metal detector, rake, trimmers to get through bushes and trees; a good shovel, and bug spray to ward off any pesky insects (chiggers, mosquitos, gnats and black flies).

Personally, I have even endured going dumping for old bottles myself. As the story goes, my family roots started in picturesque New England with my parents residing in the Mt. Monadnock region of New Hampshire. On one particular journey to visit with my parents; my dad told me and my husband, that he was aware of one of notorious "Machine Gun Kelly's" old hide-out camps just across the river near Surrey, N.H. Seeking out this hide-out sounded intriguing we decided to investigate and headed to New Hampshire's, White Mountain region.

Once we arrived in the general area, Dad pointed to approximately where he had seen this presumed hide-out location during his teenage years. Long story short, we had to cross a small river, (despite the lack of a bridge) crossing the stream via an old fallen tree, and search for what appeared to be an old road going into the dense woods. The road was now hard to detect because of an abundance of foliage and greenery. Walking a short distance, we found an old stone foundation and the remaining ruins of what once was some type of stone home structure. Sadly, due to vandalism, broken bottles and dishes had been scattered everywhere, some dating from the early-20th century.

We didn't discover much at the camp remains, but decided to walk toward the embankment of the river where we found the original dump site. Eureka!! We started digging and found a few old bottles still intact. Unfortunately, while digging, my husband happened to come across a beehive. All I heard was my husband yelling "I just found the bees!" He had been digging in the dirt slopes by the stream when he thrust his shovel right into an obscured hive. With my husband being allergic to bee stings, this was not the time to find a bee hive. Thankfully, we found a local medical clinic, within the hour. The point of this little story is when you go dumping, make sure you are careful. Always bring a medical kit and bug spray/lotion along with the necessary equipment you need for digging.

When beer cans were first produced, they stated, "When empty, throw away." So that's exactly what beer drinkers did. Think about where you would find a can from the earlier days. Places such as fields found near old buildings and abandoned homes. In earlier constructed homes, look in attics, basements and garages. Look in car junk yards in the back of those rusted old forgotten cars, in hill caverns, in old outhouse pits (look for the abandoned, brick privy foundations) near a home that was built before they had bathrooms. My cousin in New Hampshire, remembered finding a beer can dump on his parent's acreage in an expired fire pit. He believed when the contractors originally built the house dwelling, they had used this location to take their breaks.

Another fantastic area to find old bottles is a partially dried up lake bed. There is an amusement park located in Salem, New Hampshire called *Canobie Lake*, a park that has been in existence since 1902 and is still going strong today. Back in the 1980s, a drought hit New England causing the lake to dry up along its banks. That same year we were on vacation visiting family members near Salem. While there, my brother and I decided to visit this amusement park. The park was situated by a lake-which was at a record low level. Strolling along side of the lake, we could literally see hundreds of vintage beverage bottles-including some early *Coca Cola* brand bottles. Wow, what a discovery! My brother climbed over an 8-foot-high chain-link fence to acquire some of those bottles, which he still has today.

For information on searching for beer cans, go online to:
http://www.beercancollectibles.net/BeerCanDumping.html

Dating and Classifying Beer Cans
So now we understand HOW to find these treasures. Let's discuss *what* you should be looking for. Here is a dateline of beer can types and some of their characteristics:

- Flat Tops- (ca 1935 – 1960)
    These first cans, were opened by means of a "church Key" which had flat lids. The church key was a device invented to open the can. It was placed onto the side of the can of beer being sold for consumption, and used to punch holes in the can's flat lid, in order to pour out its

contents.

The early flat top cans (approximate circa, 1938-1945), had opening instructional (OI), directions on how to open the can with the church keys. The instructions changed a bit through that decade and even into the early 1950s. Beer can collecting online sites show photos of these earlier cans and have loads of information on this collecting category. Another way to determine the flat-top can's age differences, is by the production of the single and multi- panel instructions on how to open the can with a "church Key", which date the can between the 1940s-1950s.

- Cone-Tops- (ca 1935-1960) Cone-top beer cans were typically used during '30s and '40s. Their production ended because they could not be filled as fast as, the flat-top cans.

There are four types of cone-top cans:

1. The J-spout, which was produced by *Crown Cork & Seal* from 1937-1942. This type had an elongated spout on its top.

2. Low-profiled cone-top cans: This type of can was produced from 1935 until 1942 by *Continental Can Company*. Its spout is shorter than the high-profile or J-spout. There were a few exceptions as a few west coast breweries used them in the late 1940s.

3. High-profile cone-top cans, which featured a prominent *high* spout.

4. *Crowntainers:* Manufactured by *Crown Cork & Seal Company*, were unique in that they had a continuous can form instead of a separate cone -top. Between 1940 and 1955, over 70 different breweries in the United States used the *Crowntainer,* which developed over 250 designs incorporating the metallic background.

Additionally, cone-tops originally had flat bottoms, from 1935-1936, which were replaced in 1936, with concave bottoms. *American Can*

Company made some flat bottom cone-tops in the 1950s that they sold to a few Eastern United States Breweries (*Easlinger, Schmidt's* and *Gunther*).

The first cone-tops were made by *Continental Can Company* in 1935- (Hmm, *Continental Can Company* had a factory located in Omaha, Nebraska (Time for me to do some research since I reside in that city.). The cans featured inverted rib flat bottoms (FBIR). This meant that they had flat bottoms and inverted ribs on the top. In 1936 they were replaced with concave bottoms and had raised ribs.

Vintage Beer Cans-Note Flat Tops

Vintage Cone-Top Beer Cans

- Pull-Tabs, which were produced 1962 to the present. These were called "Zip Tabs" in the beginning and it took nearly a decade to become be standardized. Invented in 1962 in Pittsburgh Pa, the "zip- tab" allowed the can to be opened with an attached tab to the lid, instead of with the original idea of the separate

Vintage Beer Cans

Vintage Beer Can-Regal Pale Beer

"Church Key." The pull-tabs originally had the tabs that were thrown away, but anti-littering efforts in the 1970s and 1980s, warranted their replacement with the "Stay-Tabs." For a brief time a "Push Tab" or "Press Button Tab" was used in the late 1970s. This consisted of two small round openings that were pushed in, one after the other.

Determining a Beer Can's Age at a Simple Glance

Early cans had date stamps applied on the bottom of the can. Copyright dates were applied to the year that the label design was actually copyrighted. This doesn't necessarily note its exact age, but the copyright date will help when identifying the can is not any older then this date. *Schlitz Company* cans were an exception as they changed their copyright dates every couple of years.

Tax Statements (1935-1950)-If the can has a statement, such as International Revenue Tax Paid (IRTP), it means the beer can was produced between 1935-1950- in various forms.

If the presence of the statement "Withdrawn Free of IRTP for Exportation" is found on a can, they were designated for U.S military installations between the years 1942 to 1945.

Here is a list of other "beer can" identifying methods:

1. Non-IRTP statement - This will date the can between the timeline of 1950 through 1970.

2. The presence of brewery dates. When was the particular brewing company in business? When did it close its doors? There are a few exceptions to this rule.

3. *American Can Company Cans (CANCO):* The *American Can Company* put a very tiny date code on their cans dating from 1935-1953. Watch for the word *Trade* and *Keglined* along with a code appearing along the bottom edge of the can. First on this code, will be a two digit number, this designates the city the can was made at followed by the letter "A", which it is believed, refers to the *American Can Company*. Before this,

there will be a symbol of sorts such as a "/" which denotes the calendar year in which the printed can was made.

The term 'Keglined' related to the usage of steel in the production of beer cans. To separate the steel from the beer, a lining had to be added to each can to prevent spoilage. The Keglined *American Can Company* trademark is often present on earlier produced beer cans. This term ceased to exist on cans into the 1960s.

4. Is a UPC code present on the can? If so, it was produced from 1978 or later.

5. Is the can made of aluminum? If it is, it dates the can to pre-1960s, although, beer can companies did produce aluminum cans from 1960-1964 with the "EZ" lid or "Soft-top" on their lids. The lids were made of aluminum. Earlier 1900s' flat top cans were made of steel and weighed in at four ounces.

6. *Crimped* steel cans were used from 1970s - 1980s. *Crimped*-meaning the body of the can was indented slightly to fit into the lid and then into the bottom section. A total of three pieces used to produce the can.

An online site I found extremely helpful in dating beer cans is:
http://www.breweriana.com/beer-can-appraisal/how-to-date-cans.html

Beer Can Cleaning Tips
Just because you found a corroded old beer can, doesn't mean it's worthless. Cleaning, removing corrosion and rust from beer cans is not hard to do.
The first beer cans made, were of a heavier gage of metal and had thick coatings of paint.

The early base coat colors of *Crowntainers*, was one of five colors: silver, cream/yellow, white, dull gray and a drab olive shade. Because it is of utmost importance to save as much of the original labeling on a beer can as possible, here are some safe beer can cleaning tips.

1. Never use soapy water or hot boiling water to clean a can. You can use hot tap water, just not boiling water. Rinse your cans in the warm tap water.

2. Make a bath of one gallon of hot water, and add approximately three tablespoons of citric acid powder to it. (Don't add water to powder first as this can cause a bad chemical reaction.) Wear long rubber gloves with ribbed finger tips when adding this powder, wear old clothes or an old apron to protect your good clothing. If you use oxalic acid, it is wise to use a real ventilator, not gauze masks, to cover your face and eye goggles. When using oxalic acid, use one-half cup acid to one gallon of water.

3. Soak cans from two to three hours for light rust, and up to two days for

> **Tip**: If using oxalic acid, please don't apply this acid near or under the sunlight, it will result in a yellowish residue left on the cans.

heavy rust. Check every couple of hours.

4. If you need to scrub, use an old toothbrush and run under warm water while scrubbing—a gentle sponge rub is preferred.

5. After they have reached an acceptable appearance, put them into a mixture of one of gallon lukewarm water with one-fourth cup of baking soda. Let the beer can fill with this water to neutralize the acidic mixture inside the can as well as the outside of the can.

6. Dispose of this solution, and do one last final rinse on the cans, under faucet. This last rinse will prevent the can from having a white powdery residue left on them.

7. Dry on a rack placed over sink or wash tub.

You won't believe how cleaning those old rusty cans, makes such a huge difference.

For information on cleaning old rusty cans, visit the online page:
http://www.rustycans.com/DUMPING/cleaning.html

A few breweries used paper labels on their cans instead of painting right on the metal. The Ebling cone-tops from 1930s, the *Crowntainers* for *Gluek's Stite* beer from 1950s, the first *Michelob* Cab, and the first *Schlitz-* Malt Liquor cans from the 1960s-are rare to find. Be on guard for fakes being sold as these vintage, earlier produced beer cans.

Research the history of food packaging in your region. In Omaha, you could discover old cans, containers, or tins from the "Big 4" breweries of *Storz, Krug, Metz* and *Willow Springs Distilling* Companies/Breweries; *Kellogg's Company* and *Kitty Clover Company* (potato Chips). Employees from these factories would bring home promotion products as memorabilia. (I should know, my husband has been employed at *Kelloggs Co.* for over 42 years, and we have four large boxes of *Kellogg's* memorabilia in the attic.)

My neighbor had a large garage sale for their relative, which I attended. I was talking with the people who were conducting the sale, and they told me their relatives-whom had lived in the house-were linked to *Storz Brewing Company* here in Omaha. I found some lucrative vintage Storz beer related items from this sale, along with some fantastic vintage goodies to sell.

I have only given the reader a heads-up on the profits that can be made by selling beer cans, but the subject of collecting antique liquor and beer bottles; is another area of collecting. High-dollar profits are waiting to be discovered in the Breweriana category.

Collecting Vintage Tin-litho-Tobacco, Coffee Tins and Other Consumable Canned Goods

In the 19th century, the first processed can/container food products featured applied paper label product advertisements, and information— which were printed or stenciled onto those labels. In 1875, machines were introduced that could trim and stamp sheets of tin-then between 1869 and 1895-manufacturers developed a process that allowed them to use lithography to transfer images directly onto the tin boxes.

Did You Know?
Tins, in fact, are not totally made of tin, but were originally from tinplated sheets of iron which was later replaced by steel.

Coffee was added in tin containers as long ago as the early 1800s. They come in many shapes and sizes, such as cylindrical, rectangular, and trapezoid shaped. Size ranges were anywhere from one-ounce sample tins to large containers carrying over 50 pounds of coffee.

Lids are very important to the value of your tin if they are present, but, be watchful for fake lids (not original to tin). Keep in mind earlier tins had lids that could be pulled off and had hinges. Later tins were made with pry lids, slip lids, and lids that could be screwed on and off. Let's not forget those cans with keys to remove lids called "keywinds".

Invest in a collector's book to help determine brands and dating vintage consumer tins, and attend any local tin can auctions and shows-you can find a list of area shows online. A popular event is "Indianapolis Antique Advertising" show. This show is held at the Indiana State Fairgrounds, held three times a year. If you find what is believed to be an old tin in a box inside a barn, garage, attic or basement of a home, does it have any tarnish or wear to the can or label? If yes, it is most likely authentic. Always keeping in mind where, and who you are purchasing the tin from, to avoid fakes.

Condition of the tin
A very rare, old tin, in mint or near mint condition-can fetch big money. The more elaborate *lithos* (lithographed) found on one pound size tall coffee tins, can

range in selling prices from $150 to more than $1,000. Early labels were made with paper or stenciled on, usually in black as the main color and used with green, red, blue or yellow. By 1914, the process called chromolithography allowed for the mass production of wonderful multi-colored tins with stunning graphics-considered today as works of art.

Vintage tins have some exquisite graphics to them, which makes them desirable to the collecting realm.

Branding-Tins with advertising sold from local products from years ago, may be valuable in the area where they were manufactured, but have little value outside that region. Tins from national brands no longer available to purchase (dead stock), are highly collectible.

Omaha, Nebraska is a great place to find *Butternut* and *H. P. Lau Company* tins. Benjamin Gallagher went into partnership with his friend, Omaha capitalist William A. Paxton in 1879. By the turn of the century, the wholesaler name of *Paxton and Gallagher* was renowned throughout the West for it's line of staple and fancy groceries. In its four-story building in Omaha--Paxton and Gallagher manufactured baking powder and extracts, ground spices, packaged teas from their own Japanese warehouses, and blended and roasted coffees from around the world.

There are so many other valuable collectible tin containers, such as peanut butter, kitchen spices and other consumer products.

Recent Photo of Old Paxton Coffee Building located Downtown Omaha, Ne.

Vintage Golden West, Closset & Devers, 2 lb Coffee Can With Cowgirl
Advertising-$62

Doing research is by far the key to success in finding treasure.
Study your reference books so that you can become familiar with different brand names as well as online ecommerce sites, to study what people are actually willing to pay for a particular vintage or antique item. With research I found the *Uneeda Biscuit Company* was the precursor to *Nabisco*, one of the biggest cookie and cracker manufacturers in the world. The company had changed hands, meaning- the manufacturer no longer existed, thus we have the factor of rarity for the *Uneeda* Biscuit tins.

A late 1800's *Blue Bird* coffee can which came from the *Stone Ordean Wells Mills* in Duluth, Minnesota can sold for over $600 online currently, versus an ordinary easy-to-find 1960's *Maxwell House* coffee can that sold for $20. Rarity rules!

Tobacco Tins
Early tobacco tins with lithograph colors applied, can sell in the thousands of dollars range.
The tin *must* be in very good to excellent condition, and *not* be of a common brand, such as those by Sir Walter Raleigh, Prince Albert, Velvet and Union Leader etc. The tin litho design shouldn't be scraped and graphics should still be crisp and legible (no fading). Additionally, free of rust and dents and any other noted defects, to be considered valuable. If the tin found, is of an unknown brand- it is definitely collectible. Certain designs, and those with multi-colors, similar to the "Gold Dust" and "Taxi" tins are in high demand to the tobacco collector.

A recently sold—1910, John B. Stetson tobacco tin made in Binghamton, N.Y. by M.W. Goodall, brought in over $6,000 on eBay auction!

Miscellaneous Vintage tobacco cans

Vintage Early 20th Century
Sweet Burley Tobacco Tin

Antique Tiger Chewing Tobacco
Tin...Vintage Primitive Folk Cigarette
Advertising Historical Country Store-
Pipe Storage Container-$220

Historical Bering Cigar
Building Advertisement, Tampa, Florida

> **Tip**: A very rare old tin, in mint or near mint condition can fetch thousands of dollars, while the same tin in poor condition may only be worth a few dollars.

How to Grade a tin

Here is a numbered grading system that many collectors have adopted: Grades running from 1 - 1 (10 - mint, 9.5 - near mint, 9 - outstanding, 8.5 – excellent etc. with number 1 being poor condition.).

Generally, I would not advise in buying any tin less than an "8" grade, if you plan on reselling it. A grade "8" is basically a tin in excellent condition and is free of any dents, fading or rust. Always keep in mind, the paint (lithographs), should be intact, and the surface scratch free. These factors will undoubtedly bring down their resale values.

Never scrub an old tin or use anything abrasive to clean it; no bleach as it will destroy the tin. If a tin is dirty, simply clean it by soaking in warm, soapy water.

> **Tip**: When attending estate sales, make a bee-line to the basement and the garage in any house. Home owners would keep used tins around to store nuts, bolts, screws and nails in.

Last but not least, I will close this chapter with a quirky collectible found in the kitchen freezer: A 1960's *Swanson*-TV Dinner Box with aluminum tray-currently is selling fr over $150 on eBay.

Vintage Swanson TV Dinner with
Original Aluminum Tray

Chapter V

Dining Room Dough!

Union Outfitting Co. Catalog

Surely, there are valuable treasures in the dining room. We all know this to be a factual statement. This is the room considered off-limits when I was growing up, except on special dinner occasions. I remember the fancy china cabinets, Sideboards and buffets, which held all the favorite china, table linens, silver flatware and serving utensils.

Currently the values of china, dining room sets and crystal have taken a downward direction-this chapter will discuss some easy-to-find treasures still to be found in these elegant rooms of a home.

So, let's start with the setting the dining room table.

China and Porcelain Dinnerware

Lovely china sets have drastically tumbled in their values. Paper plates and cheaper dinnerware are currently the norm for serving dinner. Hopefully, this trend will change in the near future and class will return to the dinner table.

Two of my favorites-Ireland's famous *Belleck* porcelain and England's Flow Blue earthenware-have decreased substantially in values during the last 15 years. I know this is a major disappointment, as you're grandparents special set of china so delicately wrapped and saved for generations to enjoy, has basically lost 75 percent of its monetary values during these last years. Of course, they are *priceless* to family members who cherish them for sentimental reasons.

Currently, still quite valuable are various china/porcelain patterns by the following manufacturers: *Minton, Noritake, Wedgwood, Haviland Limoges; Spode, Meissen, Dresden, Royal Doulton* and *Lenox*. A majority of the higher valued pieces are gold encrusted, or hard to find retired patterns, such as "Jewel" from Lenox.

Vintage Gold Gilt Accented Plate

Rare (ca 1953-1971) Spode "Irene" Pattern, Scalloped-Rim Dinner Place Setting-$340

Vintage Royal Copenhagen "Blue Fluted" Full Lace China Set

Royal Copenhagen's "Flora Danica", "Blue Flower" and "Blue Fluted" dinnerware patterns can sell in the thousands.

The *Royal Copenhagen* collector Christmas plates dating from 1937-1945, are quite collectible due to low production quantities during WWII years. The first Royal Copenhagen Christmas plate came out in the year 1908. The plate's title is "Madonna with Child" and it can sell for over $3,000.

Unfortunately, if you have a *Royal Copenhagen* Christmas plates dating from the 1960s on—they're values have dropped dramatically. *Bing and Grondahl* Mother's Day, and Christmas plates, have followed the same unfortunate downward trend plates prices.

Remember, it may take some research to identify the manufacturer and the pattern of china sets, but it may be worth the effort. If the name of the pattern is on the dish, you are in luck. If not, there are several ways to help to identify a pattern. An excellent resource for china pattern identification that I use avidly is *Replacements Ltd.* Their database is free to access and has images of thousands of manufacturer's patterns. I found a reference book titled: *English China Patterns & Pieces* by Mary Frank Gaston-very helpful in helping to discover china identifications.

Watch for vintage *Aynsley* English China– Floral tea cup and saucer sets signed A J. Bailey; gold encrusted sets, and those with rose motifs.

Vintage 1950's Aynsley JA Bailey Teacup and Saucer China Set-Handpainted Rose Motif With Gold Accents-$350

Aynsley Stamp

> **Tip**: If a dish is unmarked, the first thing you must determine is whether it is made of porcelain or earthenware. Hold the dish up to a 100-watt light bulb. If any light shines through the dish making it appear translucent, it is made of porcelain. The light won't shine through earthenware pieces.

These extraordinary hand painted tea cup sets can sell for over $300 if in excellent condition.

Dinner Flatware and Accessory Serving Utensils

Sterling serving pieces and flatware are selling in the thousands of dollars especially the repoussé (i.e. raised relief), floral patterns by *S. Kirk and Son*, *Scrofield* and *Stieff*;

Repoussé Sterling Silver Pattern

Vintage Stieff Sterling Silver "Stieff" Pattern flatware

Stieff Hallmark

Vintage Sterling Silver Wallace "Rose Point" Pattern Flatware-Never Used

Renowned sterling silver flatware sets by Tiffany & Co.; mid-century sets by silver artisan "Georg Jensen"; and Gorham's "Grand Baroque" pattern.

Jens Quistgaard Teak Handled Fjord By Dansk
Flatware—$100

Furthermore, complete sets of mid-century, stainless flatware that feature teak wood handles by Dansk Fjord, and are designed by Jens Quistgaard, can sell for over a thousand dollars.

An Interesting Stieff Discovery Story: Most recently, I listed a set of Stieff sterling silver flatware on eBay in the ever-so-desired "Rose" pattern. I also had some similar patterned, repoussé *S. Kirk* fork and Scrofield pieces, but I wasn't going to add them to this listing-thinking they didn't belong together. With some research, I discovered *Stieff Company* eventually had bought out these other companies. As a result, the *S. Kirk* and Scrofield marked pieces were discontinued after the year 1980, and their names were combined. *Stieff Silver Company* was known for their repoussé floral carved designed sterling silver pieces. These raised patterns are very collectible, due in part to having intricate ornate patterns. Finding out this information, I was able to add all pieces

Vintage Filet Lace, White Tablecloth

to the Stieff lot of flatware, and sell them together for a better profit margin.

1950's Italian "Point de Venise"
Floral, Handmade Needle Lace
Tablecloth

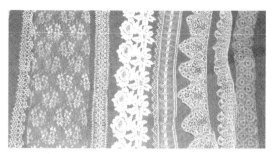

Vintage Lace Trim Examples

Vintage 1900-1909 Hand Embroidered, Circular
Tablecloth with Reticella Lace -$125

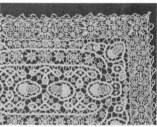

Vintage Italian Reticella
Needle Lace Place Mats Set-
$129

Vintage 1940's Italian
Alencon Lace and Linen
Napkins Place Mats Set-
Asking Price-$125

Antique lace tablecloths made in the following lace techniques: *Alencon, Bobbin* **lace,** *Point de Venise, Tambour, Appenzell* **and** *Reticella* **are selling in the hundreds.**

The art of lace making was developed in Europe during the 16th Century. Italy and Belgium were the chief centers of early lace making. During the 1800's, British inventors developed the "Bobbin Net Machine." This machine became the basis for many of the machines used today in making lace. Designs that are most popular are, floral or figural such as "Cherubs." Other designs feature columns and scrolls. It is important to note how to recognize antique lace versus newer machine made lace.

There are two main types of lace: *Bobbin* and *Needlepoint*. In making needle-point lace, the lace maker draws the design on parchment and sews it on a linen backing. Then, she uses a needle and thread to fill in the pattern with embroidery stitches. *Bobbin* lace-the design is drawn on parchment attached to a pillow. In this case, the lace-maker uses several bobbins of thread. The thread is worked around small pins that are stuck into the pillow along the lines of the design. *Cro-chet* lace is yet another type, and *Tambour* lace is made by embroidering designs on netting.

Here is a brief definition of these types of laces:

- *Venetian* - These are among the oldest types of needlepoint lace. The floral design being called, "Point de Venise"
- *Reticella* - Also Reticello (or in French, *point coupé* or *point couppe*) is a needle lace dating from the 15th century and remaining popular into the first quarter of the 17th century.
- *Reticella* was originally a form of cutwork in which threads were pulled from linen fabric fto make a *grid* on which the pattern was stitched, primarily us-ing buttonhole stitch. Later, *reticella* used a grid made of thread rather than a fabric ground. Both methods resulted in a characteristic geometric design of squares and circles with various arched or scalloped borders.
- *Alencon* - A needlepoint lace made in Alencon, France.
- *Appenzell* -Some of the finest white-on-white hand embroidery has come from a small town at the foot of the Swiss Alps, since the late 1700's.

Hollywood Regency Era Furnishings

As Zsa Zsa Gabor might say, "Speaking of Hollywood Regency, Darling, a touch of elegance is back"! (By the way-Zsa Zsa is age 98 as this book is being written. "You rule, Zsa Zsa!")This elegant '30s style, is one of those areas re-volving around a particular current culture trend with home decorating. It has been named the "Hollywood Regency Era" because of lavish style of architecture and decoration, especially popular in during the mid-century in the Los Angeles area. It combines the elements of the "French Regency" (early 19th century) and the limelight of Hollywood -the revival of classical regency style through a modern lens. Hollywood Regency decor adds a layer of pattern, decoration, opulence and glamour to the minimalism found in mid-century modernism decor.

Vintage Elegant Hollywood Regency Furnishings in Home

From the 1930s until the 1960s, the Hollywood Regency style was a favorite of celebrities ranging from actresses like Joan Crawford and Zsa Zsa Gabor-- to the former First Lady of the White House, Nancy Reagan. Hollywood Regency design, however, is not a relic of the past anymore. It has been revived. Today, the over-the-top style is not just for the rich and famous. Fancy fringe lampshades, large crystal chandeliers, highly lacquered furnishings, bold and showy fabrics (yellow, orange turquoise, red), silk lampshades and thick sculpted, and ornate gold gilt wood mirrors are all examples the Hollywood Regency style.

Rooms done in the Hollywood Regency style are designed to present a dramatic showcase for entertaining, while also providing guests with a feeling of lounging comfort. Low sofas, swivel stools and movable chairs are arranged for ease of conversation. A relaxed setting is highlighted with touches of luxury by the use of lush fabrics like silk, velvet (drapes, bedspreads) and faux fur that adorn hand-picked accessories, such as drapes, pillows, lampshades and rugs. Animal prints and Chinoiserie (meaning, "in the Chinese taste") patterned wallpaper with bamboo, parrots or pagodas are often used to indicate a sense of exotic opulence.

In the era when Hollywood Regency evolved, people really wanted to impress each other with their luxurious home decor. The Hollywood Regency style takes furniture from the Georgian and Regency periods, and then mixes them in modern interiors. Hollywood Regency is Neo-classical lines mixed with Hollywood glamour. If there's one color scheme that anchors this style, it is *strong color*. Black and white epitomizes the sharp contrast that characterizes Hollywood Regency interiors (and shows up well in films), but jolts of bright, luscious color lend the energy the look demands. Think of bright and cheerful turquoise again combined with zebra stripes.

Hollywood films that come to mind with using this decor would be, "Breakfast at Tiffany's," James Bond's 1960's- movies (e.g. "Gold Finger"), Doris Day and Rock Hudson Movies, such as "Pillow Talk" and "Thrill Of It All."

Vintage items thought of as Hollywood Regency styles are: *Bouillotte* metal tole desk lamps; *Henredon Company* furniture accented in faux bamboo wood branch styles; elegant tufted Velvet sofas; Ornate carved wood Chairs; and Ornate French or Italian gilt wood and metal wall mirrors-all selling for over $500. Additionally the following home furnishings: Italian (Florentine and Venetian, Italian-style), tole and gold gilt painted pieces, such as those seen on nesting, or stacking end tables, trays, Bombe chests, jewelry boxes; side and pedestal tables and consoles; and French, Louis XV- XVI-style table and chair sets.

Vintage Brass Boudoir
Vanity Stool

Vintage Gold Gilt
Mirror

Vintage Florentine Gold Gilt Painted Bombe
Chest of Drawers

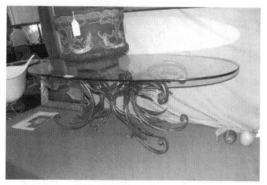

Vintage Glass Coffee Table with Gold Gilt
Frame

Vintage Florence Gold Gift
Stackable Nesting TV Trays

Vintage Faux Bamboo Nesting
Tables

Hollywood Regency lightening fixtures or lamp examples:

- Antique bronze or gilt French ornate electric light sconces
- Art Deco slip shade light fixtures and Medieval/Gothic light wall sconces
- Italian floral metal Tole and crystal chandeliers-(*Tole* or *Toleware*, as it was called, was shaped and painted tin or metalware used for decorative objects and accessories, such as Italian-made floral chandeliers)

Vintage Italian Toleware Chandelier

Italian Toleware Table Lamp

#85-Vintage 1960's Reticulated Blanc de Chine, (Chinese White Porcelain) 25" Table Lamp-$200

- *Blanc de Chine*, reticulated table lamps sell in the hundreds

Reticulated: Having a pattern of interlacing lines—especially pierced

work, forming a net, or web

- Mid-century, Venetian, Murano Art Glass tall, table lamps with large shades

Vintage Glassware and Crystal

Cambridge Glass (Rose Point pattern), *Sandwich, Vaseline* glass, *Opalescent* and *Slag* glass; Satin glass and Tiffany glass, have maintained their high-dollar values. The glass collecting arena is vast, so it's important that you research vintage glass reference books at the library or online. I have only mentioned various types considered worthy of garnering for monetary profit when selling online.

Profitable early Depression glass patterns are: *Mayfair* by *Anchor Hocking Company*, MacBeth-Evans, "American Sweetheart" and *Jeannette Glass Company's* "Cherry Blossom".

Macbeth-Evans, "American Sweetheart" Pattern, Depression Glass Set-Monex Color.

Vintage (1935-1938) Pink, Hocking Glass "Miss America" –Diamond Pattern

Carnival glass (Not to be confused with 1960's-1980's, *Indiana Glass.*) is highly desired in the earlier 20th century. Iridized carnival glass patterns by *Dugan, Fenton, Imperial, Millersburg, and Northwood Art Glass Company* pieces can fetch a pretty penny if in excellent condition.

⚷—⚐ **Tip**: Carnival Glass "Peacock" patterns, figurines and sculptures are in demand!

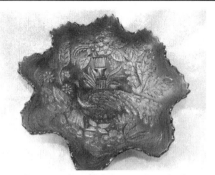

Vintage Blue Iridescent Carnival
Glass Bowl in "Peacock" Pattern

Tiffany Studios Glass

Tiffany glass was a free-blown type of glass. A whole range of unique glass-ware pieces were created by trying out and perfecting new techniques in the furnace. The glass used was of the best quality; its colors were achieved by the addition of metallic oxides in the molten glass to create the chosen colors of subtle greens, blues and gold etc. Louis C. Tiffany created his renowned hall-mark iridescent "Favrile" (hand-crafted) glass. With *Favrile* glass, the color was ingrained in the glass itself. This beautiful iridescence can be seen in the many different wares of Tiffany's glass.

Charles Tiffany was the founder of *Tiffany & Co.* (Originally called- Tiffany & Young), in 1837 in New York City. His son, Louis Comfort Tiffany (commonly known as LCT), founded *Tiffany Studios* in 1885, and the store remained open until 1930. Louis C. Tiffany was famous for making stamp boxes and metal components, but he was also famous for his wonderful iridescent glassware, leaded, stained glass lamps and chandeliers and jewelry creations. Louis's work exemplified the Art Nouveau style of design, but he was also a fan of the *Arts and Crafts* movement and endorsed their goal of making art more readily avail-able for purchase.

Watch for Tiffany's vast majority of lustered wares used to in creating vases with a few dishes and bowls, additionally, his famous early *Tiffany* lamps.

Vintage 20th Century L. C. Signed Tiffany, Favrile-Vase (10-1/4" H) selling range $1,000-2,000

Vintage (1900-1909) 5.5" Tiffany Gold "Favrile" Tumbler With Blue Iridescent Hue—$799

Tiffany Gold "Favrile" Tumbler Stamp

Fakes and Reproductions Abound

To identify antique *Tiffany* glass can be difficult. Some original pieces were not signed but instead, had applied paper labels. With signature markings, it is hard to detect if they could have been added by another source. Be careful, imitated signatures are everywhere. They could be sold as Tiffany signed pieces, but in essence, they are not stating it to be authentic-they are just saying it is signed. Anyone can say an art glass item is a signed *Tiffany* piece-this doesn't mean it is authentic? Paper labels are currently being reproduced so the following tips can help in deciding if the piece is truly an *authentic* piece.

Always note these signature markings on Tiffany glass pieces:

- Signature engraving or stamps can be found by the pontil-"LCT", Louis C. Tiffany", *Tiffany Studios* N.Y. (bronze wares) and "Louis C. Tiffany Favrile". Tiffany used the word Favrile as a general trademark for his glass—and later for his pottery and metalwork. Tiffany used this word on his created glass pieces, to suggest its handmade quality.

- Often each piece also had noted dating numbers.

- Signatures, nine times out of ten, were etched on the underside base, courter-clockwise. When you turn a glass piece over and look at the base, yo will see the signature under the center pontil mark-going from left to ri

There are some exceptions to every rule, but this is what you will find on the majority of pieces that were created by Tiffany.

- Hold the top of the lampshade and lightly knock on the glass. According to Tiffany experts, a firm glass shade that *doesn't* rattle usually indicates the lamp is a forgery.

- Inspect the glass. *Tiffany* lamps are known for deep, vibrant colors and a variety of textures. Glass containing specks of color, also known as "confetti" glass, is commonly seen in originals.

- If the shade contains any gold glass, it should have a translucent amber sheen to it. If any gold glass has a greenish tint or a very pale, translucent gold color, it is not an original. Additionally, any other color of glass with a silvery sheen to it is not authentic Tiffany glass.

Here are a few resource books for identifying antique glass:

- *Warman's Depression Glass Identification and Value Guide* By Ellen T. Schroy

- *Collector's Encyclopedia Depression Glass (Glass Encyclopedia)* By Gene Florence

- *Depression Glass and Beyond: A guide To Pattern Identification* By Doris Yeske

Crystal

French lead crystal has seen resale prices plunge due in part to mass-productions.

Exceptions- Rare antique cut crystal sorts, crystal created by Ireland's *House of Waterford*; Edinburgh, Scotland's "Thistle" pattern crystal; *Baccarat*, and genuine *Jules Lalique* Crystal.

Waterford Crystal Decanter

Waterford Crystal Stemware MIB

Lalique and *Baccarat* Crystal

Lalique created crystal vases, inkwells, decorative boxes, and bookends, then in 1921 a larger factory was established at Wingen-sur-Moder in Alsace-Lorraine. By the 1930's, *Lalique* was world renowned as the most important designer of his time.

During the 1920s and 1930s, *Lalique* designed several elaborate vases and bowls reminiscent of American Indian art. He also developed a line in the Art Deco style decorated with stylized birds, floral designs, and geometrics. In addition to his vases, clocks, automobile mascots (hood ornaments), stemware, bottle creations, and many other useful objects were produced.

While not well-known, *Lalique* also experimented with bronze and other materials as well.

If you're lucky enough to find an original 1920's Lalique automobile masco, than guess what? You'll possibly have enough cash for a **new** automobile!

How to Identify *Lalique* Crystal:

- *Lalique* glass is lead based, either mold blown or pressed
- It features wonderful motifs from the Art Nouveau period (1890-1914), with dancing nymphs, fish, dragonflies, and foliage.
- Characteristically the early glass (pre-1930) is clear with a partially frosted finish. Later, Lalique pieces a satin crystal glass was used.
- Some items were made later, in as many as ten colors, (red, amber, and green among them) and were occasionally accented with enameling. These colored pieces--especially those in black, are highly prized by advanced collectors.
- The earliest *Lalique* pieces were signed "R. Lalique France" in script writing, and quite small-less than 1/8" tall- and included a model number. The succeeding applied *Lalique* signatures were either done via engraving on the base of the mold "R. Lalique", or the name of "Lalique" in capital letters

that were acid-etched onto the piece by using a template. Lalique signatures can be molded, engraved or wheel-cut.

The R. Lalique signature was used until 1945, upon the death of Renè Lalique. At that time, *Renè Lalique's*, son Marc took over the company. Production of many pieces produced prior to 1945, ceased following R. Lalique's death; although, some are still in production with a different marking. After 1945, the signature can be found in many different variations. The marks dating from 1946 and after are usually signed "Lalique France". If you find a piece marked, "Lalique h. France" it is the work of Renè's granddaughter, Marie-Claude.

1930's Lalique Opalescent St. Francis, French Art (Birds), Glass Vase (7" H x 6-3/4" W x 2-1/4" W at Base)-Signed R. Lalique France-Online Listing Price-$2,900

Lalique Crystal, Elephant Sculpture/Figurine

Lalique Etched signature mark (R. lalique France)

Lalique Frosted Crystal Cat Figurine

Lalique hallmarks and signatures…Buyer Beware!

Currently, there is a very big problem with modern Czech glass bearing *Lalique* signatures.

Watch out for fakes, and buy pieces from reputable sources.

Don't buy the signature, buy the piece. Always examine the piece in question from a reliable *Lalique* glass dealer, for its authenticity.

Baccarat Crystal

In 1765, France's *Bishop of Metz*, Louis de Montmorency-Laval, first encouraged artisans in the little village of Baccarat to use its collected talents to establish a mecca for the world's most luxurious crystal for the royal houses per France's, King Louis XV's, authorization. He couldn't have known that the brand would remain one of the world's premier fine crystal glass companies for royalty, over 250 years later.

The French firm's trademark lead-crystal glassmaking techniques have won medals for quality, design and workmanship and are respected around the globe. Over time, the company expanded its product offerings to include jewelry, paperweights, chandeliers, decanters, bottles, vases, serving dishes, figurines and more.

Baccarat Crystal Stemware

How to identify *Baccarat* Crystal?

Baccarat Crystal Etched Decanter

Turn a Baccarat crystal piece over and check it with for the Baccarat etched logo featuring a carafe, a decanter and a drink glass in a circle. The words- Baccarat and France will appear around the circle. According to Anne Geffken Pullin's book, "*Glass Signatures Trademarks and Trade Names*," *Baccarat* registered this unique mark in 1860. Today's Baccarat logo features the name "Baccarat."

In discussing glass acid- etching, I would like to define its meaning to my reader. Acid etching is a technique for engraving blown or cast glass or a metal by the use of an acidic substance; especially the use of hydrofluoric acid to etch a pattern onto a glass or metal surface.

Here is an online reference site I found to help my readers identify some known artist etchings and embossing identification types:
http://www.20thcenturyglass.com/glass_encyclopedia/glass_signatures/glass_signatures.htm

Search for the acid-etched mark, a paper label, pattern, designer and style to determine an approximate date Baccarat created the item as many earlier pieces were void of acid etched marks.

Replacements, Ltd. Companies online website features an identification guide for confirming dates for crystal, silver, flatware, serving pieces, dinnerware, porcelain, fine china and so much more. They can confirm your estimated date by comparing your item with *Baccarat* line drawings. Additionally, there are many other free antique appraisal online sites available to contact.

Getting free antique appraisals online is easier than you may think. The appraisal allows you to identify and evaluate your antiques without spending money on a professional appraisal. Several free appraisal services can be found online, and with an accurate description and proper photos of your piece, you may be able to obtain a fairly accurate appraisal.

Here are a few free online sites for appraisals on antiques:
www.countryliving.com/antiques/appraisals

If you have a piece of crystal that you believe is *Baccarat* and you want to be reassured of its identification or value- go and the closest *Baccarat* dealer in your area. It could be a boutique, or high-end department store that is selling today's new line of Baccarat collections. I found *Neiman Marcus* and some *Bloomindale* Department Stores are authorized distributors of *Baccarat* Crystal in the U.S.A.

Bring a couple of photos of the crystal piece in question, so the store merchant can contact their *Baccarat* sales representative via email, or faxing of the photo to that representative on your behalf, as a facet of the store's customer service policies.

Swedish, Crystal Glass from *Orrefors* and *Kosta Boda*

The early 20th century *Orrefors* and *Kosta Boda* art glass pieces are quite valuable-selling in the thousand-dollar range.

The *Kosta Gasbruk* was founded in 1741 and is one of the world's oldest, still operating glassworks, but in 1990 the Swedish Glass companies of *Orrefor* and *Kosta Boda* merged to form "Orrefors Kosta Boda AB", and in year, 2005 the glassworks were then sold to *New Wave AB*, a company that focuses on lifestyle and design. *Orrefors Glassworks* came to an end in 2012.

From the 1920s, cut glass produced by Orrefors is characterized by being thinner than the later designed 20th century pieces. This helps to distinguish early glasses from later ones. The cut glass was engraved by the usage of fixed copper wheels by skilled workmen.

Watch for pieces created by glass artisans: *Simon Gate, Vicke Lindstrand, Swen Palmquist, Nils Landberg, Carl Fagerlund and Knut Bergqvist.*

Vintage 1960's "Sunflowers" Candle Holders by Kosta Boda-Design by Ann & Goran Warff-Rare 7-1/4" H , 4-3/8" H and 3-1/2" H-$86

Orrefors Crystal Cat Figure

Swarovski Crystal-_Walt Disney_ themed Swarovski crystal pieces are highly desired. Additionally, amongst other favorite Swarovski crystal creations is the "Annual Edition of Christmas Ornaments". Swarovski issued the first "Star" ornament in 1991. It is highly collectible and can fetch around $1,500. Other "Star" ornaments were created in 1993, 1995 and in 1997. Along with earlier ornaments Swarovski made in the latter part of the 1980s, they created the crystal "Snowflake" ornament, which debuted in 1992 with each ornament featuring an absolutely beautiful, sparkling snowflake shape. The year of each ornament is inscribed on a metal tag attached to the top of each ornament. The 1992 ornament has a red hang ribbon; years following 1992, mostly featured a navy blue ribbon. This ornament can sell for over $400 especially if listed prior to Christmas. If you find any complete sets, they can sell in the thousands range. You may find these ornaments hidden among boxed Christmas decorations at auctions and estate/garage sales.

Swarovski Crystal "Snowflake" Ornament

Swarovski Crystal "Star" Ornament

Disney Themed "Mickey and Minnie
Mouse" Swarovski Crystal Set

Walt Disney themed Swarovski crystal pieces are highly desired. A limited edition Cinderella Castle by *Arribas Brothers*, features a sculptured, hand-enameled metal castle with over 28,000 Swarovski crystals set by hand, and has a selling price of $37,500. This 20-inch high by 11-inch wide piece, is truly a collectible masterpiece fit for any princess. It comes in a custom metal case with a "Certificate of Authenticity".

Steuben Glass-Engraver Thomas G. Hawkes and English glassmaker Frederick Carder founded *Steuben Glass Works* in 1903. Carder Steuben Glass was made by the *Steuben Glass Works* in Corning, New York (which is in Steuben County), while the company was under Frederick Carder's (the chief designer) direction from 1903-1932. It was during his time as Steuben's chief designer, Carder had been extraordinarily creative by producing more than 5,000 shapes, some 60 unique colors, and designs. Some of the glasses made by Carder and Steuben were *Alabaster, Aurene, Cintra, Cypian, Diatreta, Intarsia* and *Jade*.

In 1932 the *Steuben Glass Works* concentrated on clear crystal and of a pure limpid color. Their most famous objects produced and created by Frederick, were in the *Gold Aurene* line, which was introduced in 1904; and the *Blue Aurene* line introduced in 1905. Because the pieces were handmade, they were definitely a work of art and are very valuable. These particular *Steuben* glass lines are highly collectible and sell into the thousands of dollars.

The given name-*Aurene*- is classified as a surface technique with iridescent pieces that shimmer with their metallic glazes creating a luminous and lustrous visual appearance to the piece. *Steuben's Aurene Glass*, can be found with original paper labels, some were acid stamped with the word "Steuben" and a fleur-de-lis pattern; and some pieces were left unsigned, which makes it more difficult recognize.

Steuben Glass Owl

Steuben Glass Gold
Aurene Glass Candle
Holders

Vintage Wall Art on Canvas Paintings and Prints

The field of art collecting is quite vast and most of us know artwork can be extremely valuable. It takes a tremendous amount of knowledge and research-ing to be an art dealer. Therefore, I will only bring up a few types of vintage art you might come across easier then a piece of art painted by Leonardo da Vinci (1452–1519).

Art Deco Maxfield Parrish Art Prints

Maxfield Parrish (July 25, 1870 – March 30, 1966) was an American artist, painter and illustrator. Maxfield was most active in the first half of the 20th century. He is known for his distinctive saturated hues and idealized neo-classical imagery. He was the highest-paid commercial artist and muralist in the U.S. by the 1920s. He is best known for his depictions of fantasy landscapes populated by attractive young women. Original, oil on canvas paintings by Maxfield Parrish can sell for over a million dollars. His most famous piece of artwork was called "Daybreak," 1923— with those prints selling for around $400 with ornate Deco frame included and in excellent condition.

Maxfield Parrish, "The Lantern Bearers" Print (c,1908)

The field of collecting artwork is massive. Here is a short list of some sought-after works of art types:

- Contemporary Modernism Abstracts from the mid-century
- Thomas Kinkade, signed oil paintings
- Terry Redlin, signed paintings and LE edition prints
- Primitive Folk Art oil paintings
- Antique Realism and Surrealism Genres
- Vintage drawings and etchings finished in various applications by pencil, pen/ ink, charcoal, and pastel shades and drawn by specific artists.

Still Life "Roses" Oil on Canvas Painting

- Original Currier and Ives lithographs and prints from the 19th century
- Vintage Japanese Woodblock Art

Be careful when purchasing prints-valuable modern print reproductions prints abound. How do you decide whether a print is truly an original or vintage?

Because of modern technology, amazing printing capabilities are relatively easy to create an exact duplicate of any original old print. However, it is possible to learn the knowledge needed to recognize what the differences are. One way to identify a reproduction is by the usage of a magnifying glass, which will reveal the regular pattern of dots found on a modern photographic reproduction. Most of the reproductions will have a shiny surface that looks similar to vinyl. Look for signs that an old print would exhibit, such as wear and tear, spilled printer's ink, a smudge, slightly misapplied watercolor, a plate mark, or a watermark.

Where did you find the artwork? If the painting was discovered at a local farm auction, look at its frame. Is the frame vintage? Chances are if it was found in an aged frame; it is a vintage print. Know the print or arts basics such as its origin, history, and documentation or more simply, where has the art been and who's owned it? Verbal information can come from friends, collectors and others who are familiar with the art or artist in question. Always ask questions about art you're interested in when attending estate sales and auctions.

One question of importance to ask the art dealer or seller "Is the art an original, or reproduced by mechanical means?" This question is especially important with limited edition prints. Many limited edition "works of art" are little more than digital or photo-reproduced copies of originals that are printed not by the artists who sign them, but by digital printers or commercial publishing companies.

The more you focus on, and are savvy about a particular genre, artist or medium that captures your interest, the better off you'll be.

Oil on Canvas Art, will need to be researched to find its worth. Research artist websites, gallery websites and exhibition catalogues (either online or printed material); online artist database resources, exhibition reviews, art reference books and databases including dictionaries of artists, art indexes, art or artist encyclopedias.

Chapter VI

Valuable Vintage Household Textiles

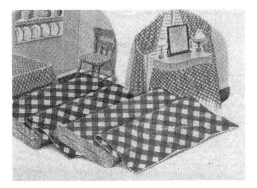

Sears Spring Catalog, 1946

Vintage textile types can indeed be-quite valuable! Let's talk about a few of those types that can be purchased with only a small amount of cash and resold for profit.

Early 20th Century Feedsack Cloth

Feedsack Fabric, also known as "chicken linen" or "textile bags"

In the '20s and '30s "textile bags" were used for packaging products, such as grain, seed, flour, and feed. The fabric was then used for making clothing and quilts. The fancier, themed, novelty, bordered feedsack prints were admired by housewives of yesterday and the quilters of today.

In America's earlier years, farm and food products were shipped in barrels, then from 1840 to 1890, cotton sacks gradually replaced barrels as food containers. Many of the logos on the flour sacks were circular, which was a legacy from the time when these logos had to fit on the top of a barrel. Women quickly discovered that these bags or sacks could be used as fabric for quilts and other needs. During 1914 to 1928, cotton had been king until its price dropped due to the introduction of synthetic fabrics like rayon, which became popular for creating dresses and undergarments. With the drop in the price of cotton, even more companies began using cotton sacks as packaging. Earlier, these bags were made with plain, unbleached cotton with product brands printed on them. The branded bags are very collectible and can be found at farm auctions.

The manufacturers saw the popularity of these sacks and decided to market them. Colors were added to the feed sacks first then around the year 1925, colorful prints for making dresses, aprons, shirts and children's clothing began to appear in local mercantile stores.

By the late 1930s, there was an intense competition in the textile industry, to produce the most attractive and desirable prints. Artists were hired to design these prints. This turned out to be a great marketing plan, as women picked out flour, sugar, beans, rice, cornmeal and even the feed and fertilizer for the family farm based on fabrics they wanted to acquire. Some sacks displayed lovely border prints. Scenic prints also were very popular. Manufacturers even made pre-printed patterns for dolls, stuffed animals, appliqués and quilt blocks. Printed feedsack cloth bags were used for sewing post World War II because of its popularity, but by the 1960's, the cotton fabric was replaced with plastic, or heavy paper bags because it was more economical to produce.

Today, vintage feedsack cloth is very sought-after for making quilts. At the top of the popularity list are feedsack cloth made with themes, such as Disney, movie, and nursery rhyme characters from the mid-century.

Vintage Feedsack Novelty, Children's Print Fabric

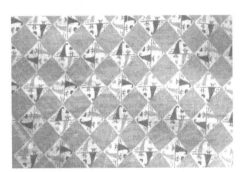 

Vintage Feedsack Fabric Example

Sun Bonnet Sue Quilt Pattern

Tip: Genuine bags can easily be distinguished by long machine chain-stitches, or large holes in the fabric where stitching has been removed (usually made from removing early branding labels).

Vintage Handmade Quilts

Although, some vintage handcrafted quilts have lost prior values, here are some of the most favorite to garner.

 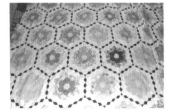

Feedsack Fabric Bag "Indian Head Stone Ground White Corn Meal"

Vintage Feedsack Fabric "Pinwheel" Quilt

Victorian Era ((1837-1901), Crazy Quilts

During the late 1800s Victorian Era, hand appliquéd "Crazy" quilts had their heyday. Crazy quilts were usually made using velvet, silk and brocade fabric that were cut and pieced in random shapes. Ladies of the house would create these decorative quilts using silk thread and then create attractive and intricate, decorative stitches for piecing together each seam. They used elaborate stitches,

Vintage Crazy Quilt

such as the feather, herringbone, fly and chain stitches. An array of hand embroidered motifs (animals and floral themes) with odd- shaped fabric pieces (e.g. triangular, diamond-shaped, miscellaneous strips), were used to put together these decorative quilts.

Vintage Hawaiian-Themed quilts

These beautfiful handcrafted quilts used traditional Hawaiian botanical and flag designs with boldly colored, large-scale, "Papercut" appliques typically applied on a solid white background, using two or three colors at most.

Folk Art quilts from the late 1800s and early 1900s- Folk Art quilts were appliqued or pieced together with antique textiles. These quilts will feature unusual cultural piecing configurations and/or with unusual varieties of colors and fabrics. Fabric can be cotton or wool. A folk art quilt might be embellished with embroidered drawings or paintings depicting the life of the particular quilter.

If kept in pristine condition, these quilts can sell in the thousands.

Vintage Barkcloth Fabric

Barkcloth fabric was avidly used during the 1940s until the 1960s. The heavy cotton fabric was used for making draperies, or covering a pillows and upholstery fabric, used in the covering of sofas and chairs.

Named *Barkcloth*, because of its nubby feel-much similar to tree bark (a rough textured surface). *Barkcloth* is usually made of densely woven cotton fibers. It is also known as "Pebble Cloth." Historically, the fabric has been used in home furnishings for making curtains, draperies; used to upholster chairs and as slipcovers. These fabulous prints can sell for over $500, depending on condition, amount and rarity. Pay attention to bold colorful tropical graphics, floral patterns (roses lead the way), novelty, and Atomic Age, mid-century patterns. Some of the most notable mid-century patterns are the abstract "Boomerang" patterns.

I once sold a 3-ft x 2-ft piece of *Barkcloth* for $325. Why so much for such a small piece? Because it was a whimsical- novelty print depicting circus animals. Totally adorable!

Here is an online link to viewing some of these unique patterns:

Http://www.barkclothhawaii.com

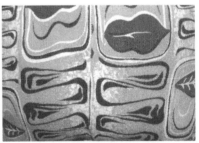

Barkcloth "Red Lips" Pillow

Barkcloth-Bold Floral Print

Barkcloth Novelty Western Themed Pillow

In The Bedroom (Bedspreads, Blankets and Bed Sheets)
Vintage Chenille Bedspreads

One of my favorite vintage bedspreads is made from "Chenille".
Chenille yarn is quite thick, soft, and fuzzy pile mostly made from cotton.
Manufacturers of chenille begin by creating a tightly wound core for the yarn
then short lengths of fabric, which are referred to in the industry as piles, are
wrapped about the core.

This special yarn is characterized by a pile protruding on all sides, resembling a
hairy caterpillar. The yarn is produced by first weaving a fabric with a cotton or
linen warp and a silk, wool, rayon, or cotton filling.

Chenille bedspreads, as we came to know them in the twentieth century, were
originally developed by a young lady from Dalton, Georgia named Catherine
Evans. In 1917, Addie Evans, Catherine's sister-in-law, opened the first chenille
bedspread manufacturing company, *Evans Manufacturing*. The industry grew
rapidly during the roaring '20s. From the 1940s -1960s chenille bedspread
making saw its peak manufacturing period.

Companies like, *Cabin Craft* in Dalton sprang up which had developed
machinery to make chenille bedspreads even faster while still maintaining the
original vintage look. While there are dozens of family run chenille tufting
businesses in around Dalton, Georgia-larger manufacturing companies in other
parts of the country also got in on the action-*Morgan Jones*, *Bates*, *Cabin
Crafts*, and *Hofmann*. Hofmann, 'Daisy' bedspread patterns are in demand
currently. Tags or labels on the vintage *Hofmann* bedspreads will read "*W.
Hofmann Textiles Inc*. Englewood NJ".

As always, fashions change constantly. Chenille bedspread making lasted for about 60 years, in the old way. Peacock Alley, which once was the location of the *Crown Cotton Mill-* the major supplier of chenille cloth, is no longer active. There were different types of chenille bedspreads manufactured. The needle-tuft spread featured loops that were raised way up like they are in standard chenille, but the *loops were not cut.* Needle-tuft loops were very often used in creating the floral patterns favored be collectors. Just as with needle-tuft spreads, the loops of hobnail chenille are not cut, but the loops are much more compact. Hobnail most closely resembles chenille's candle-wicking predecessor.

Popcorn-style chenille bedspreads consists of rows of little chenille tufts that resembled popcorn on the spread. The *Bates Manufacturing Company* was the primary manufacturer of hobnail chenille, which they used for the Martha and George Washington, patterned bedspreads.

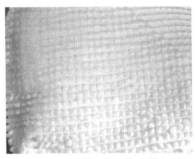

"Popcorn" Type Chenille Bedspread

Other products made in the 1940s and 1950s from chenille other than the bedspreads were bathroom rugs and toilet tank covers; cuddly bathrobes and ladies bed jackets.

Notable chenille bedspread motifs are those featuring depictions of peacocks, roses and rosebuds, daisies, hearts, cowboys and wedding rings.

Vintage "Peacock" Pattern Chenille Bedspread 92" x 96" sold for over $200

Vintage Hofmann Chenille Bedspread-Daisy Pattern Example

Vintage Child's, Western-Cowboy Motif Chenille Bedspread

Vintage "Hearts" and Flowers Motif Chenille Bedspread

Even if you own a damaged chenille spread, quilt or *Barkcloth* drapery section, it can be sold as *cutters*. Upcycling vintage chenille to make household items, such as pillows, upholstered items, garments, toys and crafts is very common in the crafting arena currently.

Cleaning Chenille Bedspreads

When dealing with material that is made of woven yarn, you would know how delicate they are. A simple run or a loose thread and the spread can be substantially damaged. If there is a small hole-hand stitch it before washing the piece, otherwise it will definitely enlarge the damaged hole.

When washing vintage chenille bedspreads always pick hand wash over machine wash. Check it over to see if there is any damage before trying to remove stains and grime.

Begin by soaking the spreads before washing them. This helps loosen up, or remove any stains and age discolorations. To soak the spread-fill a big tub with hot water and add a double dose of OxiClean, or other such deep cleaner (Biz is great, too). Stir the OxiClean into the water to dissolve it as much as possible. (Dissolving the OxiClean is especially important with colored spreads, because it can leave damaged bleached white spots into the ground cloth if you are not careful.) Add a couple of cups of vinegar (to prevent color bleeding) to the hot water, and stir the mixture up before you put the spread in-then spread and swirl it around gently. When cleaning chenille bedspreads you need patience. Check it now and then, until it appears to. If not, continue to soak and add some baking soda, or more vinegar to the water, and give it a bit more soaking time.

Empty the used bath water out, and rinse with new warm water-then remove from the bath tub and put it in the washer. Spin on low cycle until most of the water on the spread is gone. Reset your washing machine on the gentle wash cycle in warm water with a cold rinse. It's a good idea to add liquid fabric softener to the final rinse cycle to care for a soft bedspread. Machine dry on the fluff setting is recommended, or line dry (Be careful not to hang for too long, it may stretch the spread out of shape.) until it is almost dry, then finish drying the piece in the dryer. *Don't* dry the bedspread if you still see stains that were not removed because once it has is placed into the dryer-it can the stain into the fabric.

For any small blood stains that didn't come out in my soak, I use almost straight Clorox on a Q-tip (only if it's on the white threads of the spread). For colored spreads-put peroxide on a Q-tip for stain removal. Repeat until its gone or almost gone-follow with a water rinse. Laying the spread on a large white sheet

---

Tip: The Dollar Store carries a great spot remover called "LA's Totally Awesome All-Purpose Cleaner" for $1 and it works great on spots when cleaning chenille bedspreads.

---

on the lawn, in the sun will help brighten up the spread.

The *Matelassé* Bedspreads

Matelassé (Mat-lasei) is a French technique used in quilting. The *Matelassé* bedspreads are made out of a superior quality, 100 percent cotton material. These spreads have a luxurious appearance. The all-cotton fabric has amazing designs raised to create a soft texture that makes you want to touch it. The texture is so detailed that many people describe it as being sculpted. Intricate patterns are created by literally thousands and thousands of stitches that give the material the appearance of being padded or quilted, but this illusion is created by the many stitches sewn in a tight and close machine stitch. These stitches are made by a quilting machine or loom.

Many times, you will find a *Matelassé* that has been designed to be reversible. *Matelassé* designs, such as the "William and Mary" spread, were inspired by an antique coverlet discovered in a collection of textiles from Colonial Williamsburg and was instantly in demand as creating a reproduction. This pattern has stylized fauna and flora motifs that were popular choices during the reign of joint sovereigns of England, King William II and Queen Mary II, which is commonly known as the "Baroque Period." Other patterns are the "Rose Medallion" which has a rose raised texture, the basket weave pattern and newer contemporary patterns. These beautiful spreads sell for over $150 in excellent condition.

Vintage 1950's Bates Blue and White, Matelassé-Americana
Bedspread (112"L x 96" W)-$90

Beacon Indian Camp Blankets

First of all, camp blankets were never sold to Native Americans. They were originally manufactured from 1920 to 1940 to accommodate the East coast summer camp industry (Adirondack Retreats). Folks purchased them for the beach, their cars and cabins, basically, vintage outdoor leisure. They were sold at the local dry good stores, *J. C. Penney's* and *Sears Department Stores* by the *Beacon Manufacturing Company* in New Bedford, Ma, and *Esmond Mills* of

Esmond, R.I.

Early mid-century, Beacon Indian Camp blankets were made with cotton (or cotton-wool blend) and are easy to clean. In later years, blankets were made with synthetic blends.

Bathrobes and coats were also produced with the Beacon Indian patterns and fabric. Their colorful 'Ombre' pattern was the name given to colors that blend into one another. The patternized, Ombre cotton blankets are highly admired. Beacon's Manufacturing was the master of the Ombre patterns.

Primary colors are very collectible, especially those with lavender and violet shades. Original patterns, copied American Indian hand woven blanket designs. At their peak, *Beacon* produced as many as 1,500 unique styles of blankets. These collectible blankets are in the selling range of $500-$700.

For more information on *Beacon* Blankets, visit the online webpage: http:// www.deseretnews.com/article/600108622/ Collectors-snuggle-up-to-Beacon-cotton-blankets.html?pg=all

1910 Camp Trade Indian (70" x 80") Joined Robes/Shawl Blanket, Listing Price-$284

Vintage *Pendleton* Wool Apparel

Vintage *Pendleton* wool found with Native Indian designs-In 1909, The *Pendleton Mill* opened in Oregon where they first produced Indian blankets. The mill then started making bathrobes and coats. By 1924, they started making the famous *Pendleton* men's wool shirt and in 1929 they were producing a full line. By 1949, *Pendleton* started developing a line of sportswear separates for women. Most notable was their '49er jacket (in demand). The '49er is a hip length, long-sleeved casual jacket with wide collar, patch pockets, and large shell buttons down the front. The 49er is still being made by Pendleton today due to its popularity.

Additionally desired is *Pendleton's* "Big Lebowski" style sweater. This sweater was worn by "The Dude" in the 1998 classic movie, "The Big Lebowski" The actor who played this role was Hollywood's Jeff Bridges. The "Big Lebowski" sweater was actually a comfy and stylish vintage Pendleton 'Cowichan' style sweater they named "The Westerly" cardigan in 1974. It was this movie that started the craze to actually own one. Cowichan style sweaters sell for over $300.

Vintage *Pendleton* Westerly, Cowichan "Big Lebowski" Sweater

Pendleton Wool Indian Trade Blanket "Suwanee Stripe" Pattern

Vintage Hemp Textiles in fabric bolts—unused, can sell for hundreds of dollars for several yards.

Vintage Bed Sheets
House of D. Porthault:
The most admired classical and fanciful bed linens in the world come from the D. Porthault of Paris, France. *D. Porthault's* line of luxury bed linens, terry towels, and tablecloths feature lovely designs (some embroidered) in garden and floral prints and are known for their quality, craftsmanship and detail. Some of Madeleine and Daniel Porthault's clients have included: Charles de Gaulle, Sir Winston Churchill, the President-J.F.K and his First Lady-Jacqueline, Coco Chanel, Audrey Hepburn, Grace Kelly, the Duchess of Windsor, and many other figures in government, fashion, cinema and society.

Whimsical, novelty printed children's bed sheets- from the 1960s-1980s-are sought-after. Novelty bedspread sets can sell from into the $300 range.

There is nothing like those nostalgic TV cartoon characters from our past. These memorable cartoon characters from the 1960s and 1970s were printed on bed sheets during that timeline and their popularity has been rekindled. Here is partial of character prints to hunt for: *Huckleberry Hound, Flintstones, Yogi Bear, Quick-Draw McGraw, Pound Puppies*; *Pac-Man, The Jetsons, Smurfs, Rainbow Brite, Superman, Charlie Brown's* and the *Peanuts* gang and *Scooby-Do*.

Other notable collectible character prints are: The TV Series characters "*Star Trek", Care Bears and Gremlins*. Additionally, *Walt Disney's cartoon characters, Spiderman, WWF Wrestler, Hulk Hogan; Transformers, "Kliban" Cat, Garfield, Peter* Max (of 1960's Beatle's artwork fame); and *E.T. the Extraterrestrial*

1980's Child's Sesame Street Sheet Print

Vintage "Pacman" Sleeping Bag

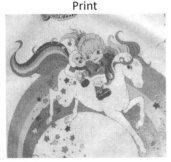

Vintage 1980's Rainbow Brite Sheet Print

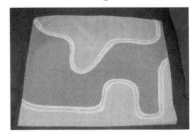

Mod 1960's Bed Sheets/Linens

Other desirable vintage bed sheets, are the floral prints from *Ralph Lauren* and *Laura Ashley* from the 1990s-today.

Fab patterns from the 1960s are also popular in wild Op-Art, psychedelic "Flower Power" themes; and any vintage sheets with lace, and those with machine embroidered monograms applied to them. Depending on the condition of the sheets and if they are still in their original packages unopened, they can fetch up to $350.

Vintage 1960's Inspired, Psychedelic "Peter Max" Shroom Bed Sheet Set by *Cannon*-Valued at $175

Any vintage large sheet that has damage to it, can be cut up to make a number of upcycled curtains, pillow covers, totes and bags, table napkin, or for any handcrafted project.

This will conclude the chapter on finding valuable vintage textiles, but I have only mentioned a few. The vintage clothing industry incorporates the usage of many different types of fabric. This subject would be yet another book in itself.

Chapter VII

Garage, Shed and Yard- Cash Cow's

Valuable vintage collectibles can be found not only in the house, but in the garage or shed as well!

Ladies, this is where you can find some wonderful hidden treasures, but you may have to get a little dirty and meet a few spiders, when moving boxes around to find those hidden moneymakers.

Let's mention a few of those treasures.

Ducks Decoys-Late 19th Century and Early 1900s, Folk Art Wood Carved Duck Decoys.

Used to lure their prey, a duck carver would craft the desired shape of the decoy's body using a hatchet and then they would fine-tune it with a long drawknife. He would create the head separately from a smaller block of wood using an axe, rather than a hatchet; then, the carver would whittle the head down with a sharp jackknife and attach it to the body using nails or long spikes.

Lastly, the finished carved decoy would be sanded, primed, and painted in natural colors to lure the particular fowl effectively. By the time of the Civil War, this technique had matured almost to an art form. The 19th century, crafted ducks are extremely sought-after today selling in the tens of thousands of dollars range. Ranges differ for particular carvers as well as the type of position the duck is carved in.

I think next time I visit the Northeast area of the U.S.A, I will watch for garage sales on any low-maintenance dirt road that leads to a lake!

Antique Wood Duck Decoys

Household Canning/Fruit Jars

Jars from 1840 through 1850, with cork and wax seals and odd closures are valuable. The clear, aqua jars are not as valuable because they were commonly produced. Other colors created were olive green, yellow, teals and cobalt blue (not "Milk Of Magnesia" blue), milk glass, black and purple. These colors are the most valuable as they are harder to find with the cobalt blue jar's being the most desirable. Vintage 19th century canning jars can sell into the thousand dollar range.

Pontil marks and indented rings found in the bottom of the jar denotes it was hand finished by a glass-blower. These marks will usually be found on jars made before 1858, with only a few made after that time. Variations of *Ball* canning jars can also be very valuable. If a canning jar is found with the Ball logo "Ball Perfection" embossed on it, (not to be confused with Perfect Mason) their values can range between $100- $4000. Always try to find matching lids and any closure mechanism to a canning jar, as values can drop substantially without these components.

Vintage "Improved Gem" Pint Canning Jars, with glass lids; Made in Canada

Vintage "Atlas Strong Shoulder", Aqua Glass Canning Jar with Zinc Lid

Vintage Olive Green Glass Canning Jar

Wrought iron patio furniture from the 1950s-'60s, Mid-century Era

Wrought iron is lighter than cast iron and more pliable, making it easier to wrap into a variety of fanciful designs. Many mid-century chairs and tables of that era, feature metal acorns, intricate fern leaves, grape vines, and have legs and arms that wrap into scrolls and cylindrical designs. There are even chairs and chaise lounges that rose up on the back to create little roofs to shade one's head. Some of these notable patio sets were Russell Woodard's "Sculptura" pieces, *John B. Salterini* luxury chairs and tables; and *Maurizio Tempestini* for *Salterini*-"Clamshell" chair pieces. These vintage sets are in high demand.

Vintage 1940's Carre
Sunburst Spring Iron
Garden Chair

Antique Ornate Italian Cast
Iron Bench

#Vintage Mid-Century Salterini Hoop
Tete a Tete Patio Table and Chairs

Vintage Wrought
Iron Lounge Chair

A summarized list of vintage items found outside the house that can be valuable:

- Vintage 1960's, vinyl fringed, floral patio umbrellas are currently desired, selling for over $250. (Though, remember packing these babies to ship might not be so fun.)
- Rusty, garden architecture such as

Vintage '60s Patio Floral Umbrella

antique metal wire gates, pails, milk cans

Old 1940's Rusty Childs Push Pedal Car

Antique Milk Can

- Wrought iron TIKI Patio torches
- Large vintage standing and desk-top, early 1900s electric fans by GE, D. L Bates, Westinghouse Company; the revolutionary, 1946 Vortex tornado "Vornado" (Model "A" 12D1) fan and Emerson brand fans can bring in the hundreds-to-thousands range. Architectural selvage-antique kitchen chrome exhaust fans-can sell in the hundreds, as well.

Vintage Westinghouse Vornado
Tornado Fan

Vintage Brass Metal Fan

- Large cast iron kettles used for horticulture containers are sought-after especially for yard décor during the summer months, and during the fall for those spooky Halloween, yard decorations.
- Antique bed metal mattress springs and antique farm equipment-Used in

upcycled "junk art."

- Primitive farm, wood and metal pie safes!
- Antique washing machine tub basins

Antique Wash Tub Set

Primitive Clothes Washer

- Antique gray *Graniteware* (unique vessels), and *Enamelware* camp-fire cookware-Look for objects with swirled cobalt blue, brown or green shades on a white background cookware in very good-plus condition fetch in the hundred-dollar range.
- Antique glass car battery jars-Repurposed for fish tanks-sell for $70
- Antique metal medical cabinets and stools-sell in the hundreds
- Vintage Industrial metal and wood filing cabinets (all sorts, especially those with drawers used for index card cataloging or tool storage), sell in the hundreds range.

Antique Blue-Swirl enamelware Coffee Pot and Bowl

Antique Oak Filing Cabinets

Vintage Industrial- Heavy Metal Card Drawers

What does "Steampunk" mean?

It is a subgenre of science fiction and fantasy literature, but has developed in recent years to become a craft and lifestyle movement that commonly features some aspect of the usage of steam-powered, machinery. Although, its literary origins are sometimes associated with cyberpunk, steampunk is often inspired by industrialized Western civilization during the 19th century.

Vintage Luggage and Steamer Trunks-Lightly used vintage hard-shell, *Samsonite-Shwayder Bros,* suitcase sets can sell for over $250 with original keys. Popular exterior shades are Rose, Hot Pink, red, marbled green and blue; and faux leather, brown. Vintage hat box and cosmetic train suitcases, sell for around $100 with their original keys present.

Vintage Red Samsonite Train Case

Vintage Red Samsonite
Luggage Set

Vintage Large Bermuda Green Marbled
Suitcase-$250

Vintage 1940's-1950's, Samsonite Colorado
Brown Carrying Case

Vintage Alligator or Crocodile hide covered luggage pieces, or briefcases sell for over $200. Hard-shell, Aero Pak and tweed-covered suitcases from the 1940s, sell for over $100.

The Italian brand "Bottega Veneta Luxury House" is best known for its luxury line of leather-goods. Their vintage leather briefcases—if found in excellent condition can fetch over $600.

Vintage 1940's Aero Pak Stripe Hard-Shell Suit Case

Victorian Flat-top, industrial and military- trunks sell for over $300. (Any souvenir stickers applied to them? Leave them alone. Buyers love the nostalgia!

Antique miscellaneous small animal traps produced by *Newhouse*- can sell over $500.

The first *Newhouse* traps were **all** hand forged in the 19th century, and are the most sought-after of the antique animal traps.

Blow Mold Yard Art

Plastic blow mold lawn ornaments have been available in the United States in the 1950s to the present day. These ornaments rocketed into popularity with the original "Pink Flamingo" blow mold. Companies, such as *Union, Poloron* and *Empire Plastic Corporation* made blow-mold yard ornaments along with popular toys. Many American companies created blow-mold hollow plastic light-up yard art ornaments from the 1950s through the 1990s. Blow mold yard decorations are still available, but only a few blow mold companies are still operating in the U.S. today, thus their popularity to collect.

There are blow mold figural character ornaments for all seasons: Christmas, Halloween, Easter, or just as fun yard art (e.g. the infamous "Pink Flamingo"). Some of the most collected are: nativity scenes, Santa Claus, Snowmen, Holiday Caroler's, Candlestick's, Jack-O-lanterns; Ghosts, Turkeys, Easter Bunny, Walt Disney characters and hard-to-find molds. Blow molds can sell in the hundreds of dollars. The rarity of a character, along with its condition, warrants its current value.

Vintage Holiday Nativity Blow Mold Set

Vintage '50s Noma Light-up Santa Claus Blow Mold

Vintage 70s Halloween Black Cat and Jack 'O Lantern, Yard Art-Blow Mold

Cast iron door stops by *Hubley Company*-especially various dog types- sell in the hundreds

Antique Padlocks and Keys-American padlock companies, as-well-as padlocks from particular companies, seem to attract a lot of collecting interest. Padlock key companies, such as *Wells Fargo, Winchester, Yale & Towne Mfg. Co., Eagle Lock Co.* and *Miller Lock Co* are sought-after. Furthermore, railroad padlocks and those made of brass and iron. If the original keys for the locks are found-all the better!

Rusty antique metal paddle cars, bicycles, and even just the bicycle frames themselves (specific Schwinn and international brands, such as the French and Italian brands), can fetch into the hundreds of thousands-of-dollars range. Don't forget those old tricycles and "Taylor Tot" brand vintage baby walkers from the early 20th century used for unique yard art-CASH!!

Recently, I came upon an original 1980's "Strawberry Shortcake" tricycle at an estate sale for which I paid $25 for. I hope to flip for $100 cash. Hoping!

Vintage 1968 Schwinn Sting Ray "Orange Krate" 5-speed Bicycle

Vintage 1934 Schwinn Aerocycle Bicycle

Vintage Speed-Bicycle Frame

Vintage 1980's Strawberry Shortcake Tricycle

Primitive Early 20th "Taylor Tot" Baby Stroller

Antique Fishing Gear-Hard-to-find, lures (e.g. Heddon), early Bamboo wood rods; and reels by Hardy, Bogden, Talbot and Jack Charlton to name a few.

Vintage Fishing Gear: Wood Lures, Reels

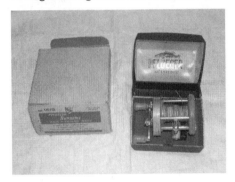

Vintage Mid-century "Snap-On" Tool Cabinets, chests and tools, sell in the hundreds.

Vintage Stanley Tool Planers (#1 and #2 models are among the most valuable), and vintage chisel sets can sell for over $500 in very good condition.

Vintage Stanley and Miscellaneous Hand Planes

Vintage License Plates….especially early 20th century, motorcycle plates can be quite valuable. Can you believe they can sell for over $2,000!

Primitive and vintage Axes/Hatchets are in demand.

Most of us know an ancient hatchet, or various Broad ax head artifacts are valuable; I want to bring reference to the 19th and early 20th century Steel Double Bit, and Single Bit head-wood handle axes, or hatchets with embossing found on them. Watch for: *Keen Kutter, O.A Norlund's Hudson Bay line*; *W. C Kelly* (*Black Raven, Flint Edge* and *Perfect*) to name a few of the most collected types.

Vintage 1950s-1970s Coleman manufactured, picnic and camping equipment is HOT!—Metal ice chests/coolers, kerosene lanterns, house tents, single, two and three burner stoves and camping heaters. They must be in very good to excellent condition to fetch the highest amount of cash. Early 1900s portable mantle lamps/lanterns, and camp- cooking stoves are in HIGH demand -selling in the hundreds.

Vintage 1950s Coleman Coolers

1950's Coleman Heater Ad

Vintage 2-Burner, Coleman Stove

Vintage Igloo Galvinized Steel, Water Cooler

Mad for Plaid!

Vintage 1950s, Plaid/Tartan Litho covered- grills, coolers, thermoses, jugs, and wicker picnic baskets are hot! Company names to watch for: *Hamilton Skotch*, *Poloran* and *Redmon*. Finding these items in lightly used condition; could fetch an easy $100.

Vintage 1950's Skotch Hamilton Picnic Set (Grill, Cooler and Beverage Cooler)

Vintage Skotch Hamilton, Plaid Standing Grill

Priceless Sewing Patterns

Vintage sewing patterns can be found in trunks or boxes found in the attic, garage or basement of a home. Currently, they are highly desired by seamstresses to recreate the fashions of yesterday.

Sewing patterns came in different sizes; printed on tissue paper, cut and folded-then inserted into envelopes complete with instruction sheets used when creating a particular sewing project.

Here are some of today's most collectible vintage patterns and their timelines:

- Any pre-1920's pattern
- 1920's- Flapper clothing and accessories (hats, handbags); and children's clothing
- 1930's-Day dresses, Bias-cut nightgowns, evening gowns, children's clothing and aprons (with original embroidery or

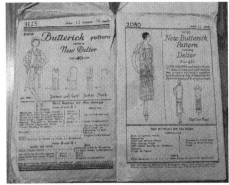

1920's Sewing Patterns

applique transfers included).

- 1940's -Ladies designer clothing by Vogue; nightgowns and sleepwear; evening gowns, Men's clothing, girls' dresses and stuffed toys (dolls).
- 1950's -Women's and men clothing, household items, designer Vogue patterns, wedding gowns, doll clothes, toys and crafts

Vintage '40s and '50s
Sewing Patterns

BARBIE Doll Clothing
Patterns

- 1960's- Mid- century Vogue, women's designer clothing; Clothing for-BARBIE®, Betsy McCall, Chatty Cathy and Shirley Temple dolls.
- 1970's –Vogue designer clothing and accessories, doll clothes and crafts
- 1980's -Halloween costumes, craft patterns, doll and toy patterns.
- 1990's- Halloween costumes, craft and doll patterns, children's clothing

Vintage '70s Vogue, Diane Von Furstenberg–
American Designer Original Pattern (Wrap
Dress) -$145

Vintage Batman
Halloween Costume
Pattern

Disney, Peter Pan, Captain Hook
Costume Pattern

Vintage Vogue Hats Pattern

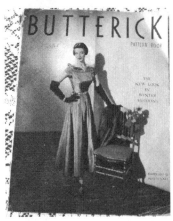

Vintage Butterick Winter
1947-1948 Pattern Book

Sewing Pattern Tutorial

Ebenezer Butterick, invented the commercially produced and graded, home sewing pattern in 1863. He started with children's patterns, and in 1866 he added women's clothing patterns. Vintage 1930s-1950s Butterick patterns for ladies fashions are among those patterns desired to acquire.

In the late 1910's, a pattern called the "Deltor" was introduced- which came with its own instructional sheet as well as, with the paper cut-out pieces.

In 1870, James McCall established the *McCall Pattern Company* in New York City. It was not until 1919 that the company started printing information directly onto the pattern pieces. In the 1920's, selected patterns had full-color illustrations on their envelopes. Finally, in 1932, the company started printing full-color illustrations on all pattern envelopes.

McCall's was the only pattern company that usually printed the date of issue on their envelopes, which nowadays, makes it easy to identify their age. The age of undated patterns can also be determined, by comparing them to clothing of a particular era. Vintage McCall sewing patterns from the 1930s-1950s, can also fetch higher dollar amounts.

Vintage 1940s-1950's, McCall's Pattern Lot

A helpful online sewing pattern-dating guide can be found at:
http://www.sovintagepatterns.com/

This site is filled with information and photos illustrating their patterns over the decades.

Additionally, the online, general vintage sewing pattern dating guide at: www.cemetarian.com is very helpful. Patterns are organized by decades, and the site is bursting with photos of patterns, pattern catalogs and fashion magazines giving the viewer a good sense of era styles.
Yet, another way I have found to date patterns is simply noting the price printed on the envelope. A 10 cents price means the pattern was created pre-1940s.

Vogue patterns started in 1899. In 1909, *Conde Nast Publication Company* bought *Vogue*, which resulted in the "*Vogue Pattern Company*" in 1914. In 1916, Vogue patterns hit the department stores. Their Couturier line entered the market in 1932 and their Paris Originals in 1949. It is the Vogue Women's Couturier and Paris Original clothing patterns can sell for over $200 if found with uncut pieces. Early '50s and '60s, Vogue pattern catalogs, sell for over $500. By reselling vintage Vogue patterns, there is definitely money to be made. So, as Madonna would say, "Strike a pose, there's nothing to it....Vogue, vogue!"

Simplicity patterns entered the market in 1927. *Simplicity* was one of the fastest growing pattern companies as they were sold around worldwide. *Simplicity's* goal was to produce an easy-to-use, lower-priced pattern. Their pattern pieces were void of any printing until after 1946.

Dubarry patterns were made by *Simplicity* from 1931-1940. They were made for *F. W. Woolworth Company* of five-and-dime store fame.

The *Hollywood Pattern Company* was started by *Conde Nast* in 1932 and highly collectible today. Their envelopes featured photos of iconic Hollywood stars printed on some of their pattern envelopes. The *Hollywood Pattern Company's* production ended at the end of World War II.

The *New York Pattern Company* started in 1932, and continued until the early 1950s. They were unique, because the pattern envelopes had drawn characters, rather than photos and the paper used weren't glossy.

Tip: The most valuable collectible patterns are UNCUT, with the appropriate pieces, and envelope being in excellent condition. When selling online, remember to make sure all pieces and instructions are in the pattern envelope before listing them.

Advance patterns started in 1933, which was sold exclusively for the *J. C. Penney Company*, until 1966 when it was sold to Puritan Fashions.

If you discover a favorite pattern is missing pieces or instructions, head on over to www.pattern rescue.com, which is a non-profit website that can help someone find random missing pattern pieces for vintage patterns.

A recommended pattern collecting reference book is: *A Beginner's Guide to Pattern Collecting* by Jennifer Warris.

We have only reviewed a few of the many hidden treasures found outside the house, found in garages, sheds, or someone's barn. Antique tools, automobile and different vehicle parts, *John Deere anything*, iron anvils and so much more-are moneymakers. When I conduct an estate sale, it is my savvy, female second-hand buyers who head for the outbuildings before even looking at the jewelry and contents inside the home.

This will conclude the chapter on finding hidden treasures found in the backyard, in an outbuilding, shed, or garage.

Chapter VIII

Nostalgic Memorabilia

(Ephemera and Paraphernalia) from Our Past

Most of us enjoy reminiscing about our past, whether it pertains to a place, event or some famous celebrity or team we once idolized. Our own personal nostalgic, memories are what creates the desire to own or collect articles that would rekindle those fond memories. These items may seem less important to many individuals, but valuable to some. Even if they are only made of paper or cardboard, they are considered valuable nostalgic paraphernalia to particular collectors.

This chapter will additionally, discuss a few of those cherished areas of ephemera collecting such as 20th century movie, event and concert posters/ broadsides, and tickets- originally meant to be discarded after use but have since become collectibles. Past memorabilia, such as vintage Halloween paper products and die-cuts, vintage napkins with fun graphics; personal photos, old restaurant menus, Christmas wrapping paper, greeting cards from the 1950s; event flyers, RPPC (real postcards), Pin-up girl cards and posters; '60s psychedelic posters, records and much more--can bring in the hundreds!

So, let's take a walk down memory lane.

Vintage Personal Photos

Finding specific vintage photos are the latest collecting rage.

Vintage photos can be worth a substantial amount of money for individuals who are searching for local public past events, buildings/dwellings or individuals. For instance, I lived in Massachusetts during the '50s and '60s in my childhood years. Thus, any photo or postcard pertaining to events/places that I once visited during those years, are important for me to own. If I was to come across any historical postcard of Hampton Beach, N. H., or someone's own personal photo representing a day at that particular beach-I would pay a substantial amount to acquire it.

Here are some types of personal snapshot paraphernalia, "Tintype" photos and "real-photo" postcards (RPPC's) that would appeal to collectors:

- Defunct amusement park haunts
- Past local town/city hangouts such as swimming holes, beaches, buildings and parks.
- Favorite regional football/baseball teams-along with sporting events held in the early 1900s.
- Photos of people dressed in a certain manner or in a specific fashion era (e.g., Victorian, Flapper and Depression Eras).
- Militia memorabilia (e.g., Civil and Revolutionary Wars, WWI and WWII- battles & troops), and militia items from international troops.

- Early Native American and Black Americana historical depictions
- Past people dressed up in Halloween costumes-HOT!

Tintype Photos

A tintype photo was one of the first photographic process methods introduced in 1856, and very popular until about 1867. They were used up to the 1940s. The general public used this type of photography to have their portraits taken. Size range for these types of photos are usually 2 ½" x 3 ½". Tintype photos were also known as a "Ferrotype" or "melainotype" photos. The tintype photograph was produced on a piece of lacquered iron, then blackened by painting, lacquering or enameling, and coated with a collodion photographic emulsion. The tintype process was promoted in the mid-19th century as a type of first version to the later- instant photograph.

You can identify a tintype photo especially because a magnet will hold to the photo, but keep in mind that this method of identification isn't totally foolproof as another type of photo called *ambrotypes*, have a metal backing behind a glass plate. A tintype photo is typically cut out quite roughly and is thinner than the ambrotype photos. Earlier tintypes were put under glass, but later were placed in a cardboard sleeve.

Vintage Tintype Photo-Black Americana

Nostalgic Postcards

It is of utmost important in being able to date a particular postcard you may have found. The earlier post cards can bring in hundreds of dollars. Starting in the late 1800s, postcards appearance has changed on their backsides, the card stock used to create them; and the presence of a border around displayed front photos or graphics.

The late 1800s marked the beginning of the postcards era. In their heyday, postcards played an important role in social media just as text messaging does today. Essentially, they provided a way to send an inexpensive greeting, particularly at holidays. They maintained their popularity until around the year 1918. Before the postcards entrance into society, there were "Trade Cards".

Trade Cards-Pre 1900s

With Chromolithography becoming the most popular printing method after the Civil War, trade Cards were cheap to produce and the public loved their colorful designs.

The trade cards became popular with the enterprising merchants as advertisements for their businesses. During the 1870s, many companies sold these card stocks to merchants.

A merchant would then add his own stamp on the back, or on a space in the front of the card. The printed trade cards depicted pictures on their front side in an array of assorted, popular 1800's culture and society subject matter, which would likely include people in everyday scenes.

Vintage Trade Card

The backs of these cards were left free for the purchasing merchants, particular ad. These cards were distributed from the 1870s and ended approximately by the turn of the century.

Certain Victorian Era -trade cards can sell for over a thousand dollars.

Birth of the "Real-Photo" Postcards (RPPC's)

The first documented photo postcard was mailed in 1899, but wasn't fully used until *Eastman Kodak* began to sell Velox photo paper with a pre-printed postcard back in 1902. That following year, Kodak released its # 3A Folding Pocket camera, which used film specifically designed for postcard-size prints. Amateur photographers were now able to have their own images printed directly onto postcard paper and send them through the mail.

Early 20th Century, Real-Photo Baseball Team Postcards

RPPC'S may or may not have a white border, or a divided back, or other features of postcards, depending on the paper the photographer used.

Dating Postcards into the 20th Century

In 1901, postcards, as we know them, entered the postal system in America. Prior to that time (late 1800s), postcards were often called mail cards and souvenir cards, which usually carried advertising or printed messages. It was the *World Columbian Expo* held in Chicago, Ill, on May 1st of 1893, that attendees were able to buy postcards, or souvenir cards with Illustrations made on government-issued postal and privately printed souvenir cards. Up to the year 1901, messages were not permitted on the address sides of these cards.

WWI Soldier, Real Postcard

After some time, the U.S Postal Service adopted the message "This side is for the address only". In May of 1898, an Act of U.S. Congress on May 19, 1898 granted private printers permission to print and sell cards that bore the inscription "Private Mailing Card." Today these cards are referred to as "PMCs".

The first actual postcard timeline dates between 1901- 1907-These cards had undivided backs with new U.S. postal regulations added on December 24, 1901, with the words "Post Card" printed at the top of the address side of privately printed cards. Cards previously, had to have a "Private Mailing Card" statement added. So if your card is marked "Private Mailing Card," it dates the postcard from 1893 - 1901.

Backs of early 20th Century postcards

It was this postcard timeline that black and white "real photo" postcards were photographed by citizens, and printed on paper with postcard backs.
Other dating tips:

- American postcards that measure 3.5" by 5.5" inches were likely produced before the 1960's. After this date, the 4" x 6" size was implemented.
- Does the postcard show a white border on the front? If it does, then it can be dated from 1915-1930.

Early Postcard Depicting People in Costume.

To save on ink, publishers left a clear border around the view so these postcards are referred to as "White Border" cards.

- The postcards with undivided backs date before 1907. Divided backs on a postcard were allowed in the U.S after the year 1907. (One half of back was used for the personal message and the other half, for the address information.)

Here is a quick tutorial on dating postcards by viewing their printing process:

- Postcards that were produced using high-quality chromolithography with six or more ink shades, is a tell-tale sign meaning they were probably made before 1917.
- If the post card has a flat-textured surface and is printed with a limited range of low-contrast inks, it was probably made before 1930.

Tip: A unique way of discovering if a real-photo postcard is a copied photo or an authentic photo is to hold it under a magnifying glass; it will show a smooth transition from one tone to another.

- Does it have linen-textured surface and is printed with sharply contrasting bright inks-the postcard is likely dated from the period 1930-1960.
- Postcards with a shiny surface and printed in color using a halftone process (little dots of magenta, cyan, yellow and black) were probably made no earlier than 1939. Before that date, printed post cards used black and white ink.
- If the postcard in question has a cost amount code of .01 cent, or U.S.A. Postal Service stamp in the required amount increment, which was located in the upper right hand corner in a rectangular shaped stamp box on the card-it was made before 1952.

Furthermore, two major postcard publishers, Curt Teich and the *Detroit Publishing Company*, used numbering schemes, which are helpful in dating a postcard.

The *Detroit Publishing Company* began numbering its cards with, number one.

Numbers one through 1000 were published between the years 1899 -1901. Some of these same cards were later reproduced in the 5000 series. Detroit postcards are easy to manage by the number.

Postcards on the top of the list for collecting are the RPPC's and those representing the pagan celebration event called-Halloween.

Halloween Postcards and Memorabilia-CASH!

With the popularity of postcard greetings in the late 1800s, people sent these cheap greetings for any reason particularly around celebrated holidays and events. They maintained their popularity until around 1918.

Early 20th century Halloween postcards typically featured cute, plump, jack o' lanterns with children; black cats and beautiful witches. Yes, you heard right— beautiful witches—not ugly ones. Interestingly, the witches printed on these cards were not the wicked type, but were often depicted as pretty ladies bringing forth love.

Because of these beautiful witch depictions—they are highly desired by postcard collectors and are quite valuable. Other Halloween greeting postcards can be desirable depending on condition and the artists and publishing companies who printed them.

Between the years of 1911 - 1915, John O. Winsch of New York was one of the most notable Halloween postcard publishers. Mr. Winsch used heavy, rich inks and embossing on his cards, then sent them to Germany to be printed. Most were packaged in sets of four, but some appeared in sets of six. Making them even more special, some of these postcards had booklets attached, and still others were offered with diecuts.

The most collected Winsch, artist-signed Halloween postcards were designed by American artist Samuel L. Schmucker, who painted beautiful women in lush, bright colors, signing some of his artwork with the monogram "SLS."

Additionally, Mr. Jason Frexias, produced holiday cards for Winsch with round -faced toddlers with starfish hands.

Other admired artist designed, Halloween postcards were the following:

- Ellen H. Clapsaddle, one of the most creative American postcard artists of the era, produced some of the most collectible Halloween cards today for the *Raphael Tuck and Sons, International Art Publishing Company, and Wolf Publishing Company--a subsidiary of Inter-Art* that Clapsaddle launched herself. Her style is distinct, particularly her illustrations of children.

Ellen H. Clapsaddle
Halloween Postcard

John O. Winsch Halloween Postcard

- H.B. Griggs is another highly collectible holiday postcard artist (with over 350 designs created), using the signature H.B.G. He or She—as gender is not known--published almost exclusively for *Leubrie and Elkus of New York.*

Vintage Halloween Postcard

- Grace Gebbie Wiederseim Drayton—famous designer of the "Campbell's Soup Kids"—designed cards for *Raphael Tucker and Sons*--with that same character appearance.
- Clare Victor Dwiggins, a comic-strip artist (cartoonist), also created designed cards that were left unsigned. His designed art, postcards would feature a beautiful, fantasy-style "witching queen" figure.

Today, some of the highly collectable postcards can sell for up to $700. Watch for the heavier embossed cards in excellent condition with no creasing to the cards. It pays to go through all those discovered old greeting card scrapbooks found in boxes, trunks, basements or attics.

Vintage Halloween Decorations

Diecuts

When I think of a diecut, I think about those long ago, special cardboard Halloween classroom wall decorations-especially those depicting scary images.

A diecut, (c, 1920s-1960s) refers to any flat, paper, cut-out decoration. In most cases, the shape will follow the outline of the graphic image. The term, diecut or die-cut, comes from the process by which they are made. After the image is printed onto a larger sheet of card stock or stiff cardboard, the image is then cut out by what printers refer to as a "die." A die basically resembles a giant two-piece cookie cutter. Many of the early diecuts were also embossed, which is a term that refers to stamping a raised image into the piece for the purpose of providing depth and emphasis to the printed image.

In reminiscing about my own past, I remember helping my parents put up several Halloween diecuts on the wall. We had some diecuts with images of Jack-o-lanterns (JOL's), skeletons, owls, ugly old witches, black cats, and scary-moon depictions. Who would have known those simple diecut decorations could fetch up to $700-based on condition, scarcity and age.

Vintage Beistle Halloween Diecuts

Vintage Luhrs Halloween Diecuts

Vintage 1920's Halloween Décor-
Heavy Embossed German Black Cat
Die-Cut-$165

The earliest diecut Halloween decorations were made of a stiff cardboard or heavy card stock; some had jointed legs and arms made of honeycomb crepe paper. The diecut table centerpiece party decorations by Hallmark and American Greetings Corp, used diecuts with honeycomb crepe paper for a dimensional effect.

Honeycomb Witch Decoration

Some notable diecut companies were Beistle and Dennison. These companies manufactured paper diecuts in the U.S.A. during the 1920s-

1940s. The *Beistle Company* has been a family owned company for over 100 years, it's the largest and oldest manufacturer of decorations in U.S.A., and has continually produced diecut decorations over the years. Beistle's art was certainly the more sophisticated of the two companies.

While often their products can be identified by manufacturers' trade names, each company has their own unique and distinctive artwork.

Did You Know? Many diecuts from this period are sometimes marked "Copyright H. E. Luhrs". This has created one of the most common misconceptions that "Luhrs" was a separate company, when in fact H.E. Luhrs was a graphic artist who took a job with Beistle and later marrying into the Beistle family; eventually he became the company's CEO. Because of this, all products marked "Luhrs" were made by Beistle.

Another Halloween diecut company was the *Gibson Company*. During the 1920s and 1930s, the *Gibson Company* produced some wonderful Halloween diecuts, games and centerpieces as well as other specialty party goods.

Some of the most collectible diecuts were made in Germany during the period between both world wars and also for a short time in the late '40s. They were made of a heavily embossed cardboard featuring artistry and quality that was superior. Embossing on these cardboard pieces were so heavily detailed, they are nearly sculptured into the cardboard. Their character depictions and graphic styling are exquisite. These hard-to-find decorations can sell in the upper hundreds range.

> **Tip**: Recognize the age of a diecut by the thickness of the embossed cardboard, will help determine how old the piece is. The thicker it is, the older the decoration is.

While we are on the subject of Halloween, here are some other valuable Halloween decorations that are prized among collectors.

Vintage Halloween Paper Mache (papier mache) Lanterns

Popular during the 1940s, these very collectible pieces were inexpensive and fun items to use for decorating and festive lighting. They were also used as candy containers and nut cups.

Many of these lanterns featured paper inserts for their facial features. Most of them depicted Halloween characters of pumpkins or Jack-O-Lanterns (JOL's), but some came in the shape of black cats, devils and other spooky themes. These lanterns can sell today for up to $600. Additionally, vintage Paper Mache' was often used to make toy figures and for children in the early 1900s. Popular items were German-made holiday candy containers (e.g., Christmas, Easter

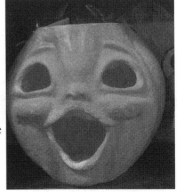

Vintage 1940's Halloween Paper Mache "Jack 'O Lantern (Paper Eyes Missing)

themes), and "Bobblehead Nodders", which are highly desired to collect. These pieces were made using clay molds, which they could reuse over and over for mass production-a process much the same as todays. In the early years, the pieces had bases with natural colors with brightly colored details. Paper mache makers paid attention to bringing a durable and polished finish for their piece. However, in each era, the paints and finishes were different.

Holiday Plastic Candy Containers

Yet, another missed money-spinner is the whimsical, plastic candy containers that were manufactured between the 1940s and '60s, than sold during celebrated holidays. Very collectible! They were made of hard plastic celluloid in a variety of spooky forms such as witches and black cats. Some of the brand names to take note of are *Irwin, Knickerbocker, E. Rosen, Rosbro* and *Union Products*. These were not the only companies making polystyrene and celluloid plastic novelty items for Halloween, but they are the most notable. Vintage plastic Halloween candy containers are currently selling for up to $700.

Vintage Rosbro Plastic Halloween Witch Candy Containers

Vintage Halloween games (board and Paper) and tin litho noisemakers
from the early 1900s are also included in this
collectible group. Tin Lithograph (Litho)
noisemakers were fun and inexpensive toys and
came in many varieties featuring the typical black
and orange Halloween colors. Halloween
noisemakers depicted similar themes and symbols:
witches, black cats, ghosts, clowns, pumpkins, owls
and devils.

Vintage Halloween Tin
Litho Noise Maker—$47

Vintage Halloween Paper Products

Vintage Monster Magazines

Vintage Monster magazines from the 1950s and 1960s are sure money-makers
in the magazine category.

Famous Monsters of Filmland Magazines-The World's First Monster Magazine– These magazines can sell for over $900 each-in excellent condition.

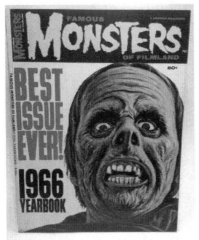

Famous Monsters of Filmland
1966 Yearbook Horror Magazine

In the late 1950's, "Famous Monsters of Filmland" magazine's founders, Forrest Ackerman and James Warren acted on their love for science fiction and old horror flicks by publishing scary magazines that featured classic horror movie monsters, such as *Frankenstein, Dracula, The Wolfman, The Phantom of the Opera* and others. The magazine proved to be a success and was the foundation for Warren's publishing empire, which later comprised other classic titles such as *Creepy, Eerie,* and *Vampirella.* Another collectible/valuable monster magazine from the past they are was "Mad Monsters".

Miscellaneous Nostalgic Paper Products (Ephemera)
Other items in this category that are hidden gems waiting to be discovered are the following:
• Bygone movie films and entertainment venue paper products, such as theatre programs, ticket stubs, posters, signed autographs of famous

silver-screen entertainers and brochures.

- Past, now defunct, restaurant menus, napkins, placemats, photos and postcards. Additionally, with the mention of defunct restaurants; should you happen to come upon any mid-century furnishings from that particular establishment such as fountain bar stools, booths, vintage cookware, dishes with restaurant logo placed on them, and barware—CASH! Especially found in very good condition.

Vintage Mid-century Bar Napkins

- Vintage Greeting Cards-Please don't toss away old greeting postcards or cards, until you have researched their possible values.

Not all vintage greeting cards are collectible.

Here is a list of some of the most desired by collectors: Early 20th century-3-D Valentine's Day greeting cards; heavy card stock-Diecut greeting cards; POP-UP cards, 1960s Hallmark cards representing favorite animated characters (e.g., Peanuts and Snoopy of Charlie Brown fame and Betsy Clark) '50s Christmas cards with glittered scenes, unused boxes of vintage greeting cards and gift wrapping paper from the '50s and '60s.

Vintage 1950s Greeting Cards

Vintage '40s and '50s Christmas Greeting Cards

Vintage Charles Schulz, Charlie Brown and Peanuts Memorabilia

- Vintage 1970's Sanrio's "Hello Kitty" (any Sanrio "Hello Kitty" merchandise) is very hot currently for collecting.
- Vintage 1970's Hallmark "Betsy Clark" Character-Paper products (e.g., stationary and postettes) are collectible.

Vintage Hallmark "Betsy Clark" Paper Products

- Vintage Stickers-Scratch and Sniff stickers (SNS) were printed from the 1970s and into the '80s by *3M Company*. Made from a matte type, adhesive paper until the year 1983. After this date the stickers were made thinner and shinier (glossy paper). It is the earlier thin "Matte" stickers considered more valuable than their counterparts simply because their scents lasted longer. The sticker company- *Trend* Enterprises was popular for creating "Stinky Stickers" from 1980-1984. (I loved the strawberry scent!) In 1984, Trend Enterprises featured over 104 different scents. Watch for these early SNS stickers along with those made by *"CTP"* (*Creative Teaching Press*) and *"Mello Smello"*.

- **Matchbooks**....the older....the better! If a matchbook is dated between the years 1894-1941, it can be very valuable. Of course, as with any collectible field, there are exceptions to the rule. A couple of helpful hints to identifying pre-1938 American matchbook covers: Note a slightly wider horizontal match striker those with elongated covers (called XL's). In the mid-1930s, *Diamond Match Company* manufactured covers in sets and void of any advertisements. These matchbook cover sets (some held hundreds of covers each), featured football and hockey athletic players, movie stars, radio-personalities, dogs etc. Additionally, if you can find the words, "By Colgate" located on the inside of the cover...it is a treasure. *Colgate* was an employee with the *Diamond Match Company* and he designed all covers for these sought-after sets. Other significant collectible matchbook covers are those that feature WWII Navy depictions,

Vintage "Girlie" Matchbook Cover

non-stock pin-up girls (early pre-1960s drawings of woman), trucker themes and covers with President Theodore Roosevelt's images applied to them. Check for early manumarks, which are a line or lines of text found below the striker area on the front covers of matchbooks.

For a better understanding on collecting matchbook covers and a list of sought-after manufacturers, manumarks and matchbook footers; visit the online web page: http://matchpro.org/Treasure.html

TRADE CARDS (TOPPS-Character, Baseball & Football Series), and Cigarette-Tobacco Cards

The Topps Company, Inc. was founded in 1938 and was the preeminent creator and brand marketer of sports cards, entertainment products, and distinctive confectionery.

> **Tip**: If trading cards are borderless and have any handwriting applied to them--they are worthless.

First on the list to discuss are the cards least likely to be thought of as valuable: **The Vintage '70s Bubble Gum Topps Wacky and GPK's (i.e. Garbage Pail Kids) Trading Cards**

Wacky Card Packages contained a series of trading cards and stickers featuring spoofs of North American consumer products. The cards were produced by the Topps Company beginning in 1967, usually in a sticker format. The original series sold for approximately four years. Other known names for these cards were: *Wacky Packs, Wacky Packies, Wackies* and *Wackys.*

Wacky Sticker Cards came out in 1967. These cards were the FIRST sticker cards. The cards were actually punch-outs with gummed glue on the back of each, so the cards could be moistened and applied to surfaces like a stamp. *Wacky Ads* were introduced as *Topps* second experiment with product parody. The ads came out in 1969, which was a year after the original Wacky diecuts.

Each Wacky Ad Pack contained five stickers and a piece of gum, and were sold in .05 cent and .10 cent packages that contained punch-outs much like the original diecuts, however, they have a larger border with artwork depicted also on the border and numbered from 1-36.

Watch for cards and ads with the titles: "Ratz", "Cracked Animals", "Jolly Mean Giant", "Good and Plenty", and "Bandache", which are numbered.

Vintage Topps-Wacky Pack with Stickers-Never Used

For more information on collecting Topps Wacky card packs-go to the online page: http://www.wackypacks.com/beginners.html

Garbage Pail Kids (GPK's)

While card collecting sets/series expanded out from the standard sports cards, it was the funky Garbage Pail Kid cards that became an instant success. Beginning in the year 1985, *Topps Company* produced these comical freaky images, each one having some type of abnormality or suffering of a terrible fate. *Topps Company* introduced these quirky cards in packages with 15 different series. They were released in the United States and became an immediate instant successful collecting series. These packages contained five cards and a stick of chewing gum and sold for .25 cents. Other countries also released various sets of the cards. It is the internationally produced cards that ultimately fetch the higher dollar amounts when trading for resale reasons.

For a complete reference list to the original fifteen different GPKs' series here is an informative link: http://www.garbagepailkids.org/variations.htm.

1980's GPK Pin Series 2 - $8

GPK "Alien Ian" card

The most coveted of all these Garbage Pail Kids was "Adam Bomb", featuring a kid pressing a red button, which ignited a nuclear blast out of his head.

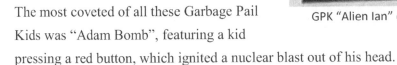 A rare proof "Atomic Bomb" card authenticated by Topps (the company that made Garbage Pail kids), was had an asking price of $4,250 USD on eBay. Additionally, the Japanese released, GPK cards called "Bukimi Kun" sets are incredibly rare and sell in the thousand-dollar-range.

Autographed Sports memorabilia

Collectors have concerns about purchasing forged or fake autographs. Signed sports memorabilia as of recent, have higher values, only if they come with proof of authenticity. Grading verification from an authentication company such as PSA/DNA (www.psaCard.com) or *James Spence Authentication* (www.Spenceloa.com), are top-notch grading companies. This process takes time and money so be certain a card is worth being graded (in fine to very fine condition).

> **Tip**: If you find a particular sports card at an estate sale or auction, ask the owners if they have a photo of the card in question being signed by a particular athletic figure. In the future if the opportunity arises and an athlete signs something for you; have a picture taken of you and the athlete, as he/she is signing. This will definitely guarantee authenticity.

Watch for Topps baseball player trading cards that feature the Hall of Famers: Mickey Mantle, Joe Dimaggio, Hank Aaron, Willie Mays, Honus Wagner and Ty Cobb.

If you've decided to sell trading cards, scan them to your computer instead of snapping a photo-as the image will be more detailed.

Collecting Vintage Cigarette and Tobacco Cards (T-sets) *C, 1870-1940s*

Tobacco companies have used cunning methods for advertising for quite some time. It was in the 1870s when they discovered an exceptional way to promote the public to purchase certain tobacco manufactured cigarette brands. This advertising method came by placing a blank card into a pack of cigarettes, which was used to stiffen that pack. These cards were blank, until a smart businessman thought it would be a smart way of advertising by simply adding encyclopedic photos that depicted—golfing pros, baseball players, glamorous actresses/silver screen actors, unusual animals; soccer stars, motorcars etc. Additionally, companies would add their impressive advertisement information on the backs of these cards—which came in sets. These early collectible cards were called "Cigarette (tobacco) cards." They were designed to be collected (by dedicated patrons) and thus, the cigarette card craze began.

The U.S.A, along with other countries—would manufacture these collectible trade card sets.
The English company of *W.D. & H.O. Willis, (W.D. & H.O. Wills* was a British tobacco importer and cigarette manufacturer formed in Bristol, England.) They were also one of the founding companies of *Imperial Tobacco*. It was *Imperial Tobacco* and *Three Castles* that would place these cards in their cigarette packs. The first Willis series of cards was issued in 1895 and was called "Ships and Soldiers".

In 1887, the United States tobacco/cigarette cards were released by *Allen &*

Ginter and *Old Judge* cigarette manufacturers. These companies featured prominent baseball favorites such as Cap Arson, and the Boxing heavyweight champion, John L. Sullivan. Other card types produced at that time carried photos of famous golf, soccer and billard players; Native Americans and Boy Scouts, which were made by the cigarette companies of, *Goodwin*, *Ogden* and *Ramly*. Another famous tobacco company from America's 19th century (circa, 1880-1910) was *W. Duke, Sons and Company*, which in 1885 had become the largest cigarette manufacturer in the nation.

Here is a tobacco (T-sets) baseball card list with a brief description of each set:

- T-201's- Mecca double folder cards
- T-202's-packed with Hassan Triple Folder cigarette cards which featured multi-player cards
- T204's -came in "Ramly" and "T.T.T" (Turkish) packs of cigarettes.
- T205's- also known as the "gold border" cards. These cards were issued by various cigarette brands.
- T206-was released from 1909 to 1911. These cards were issued in cigarette and loose tobacco packs through 16 different brands owned by the *American Tobacco Company*. They became landmark sets in the history of baseball card collecting, due to their size, rarity, and the quality of their color lithographs. These cards were known as "white border" cards and are highly collectible today.
- T207 -were Issued in 1912, these cigarette cards featured brown backgrounds-the *American Tobacco Company* changed to a drab brown background shade. The cards feature a white strip at the bottom with the particular player's name and team city. The reverse of the card features a biographical write-up on the player and an advertisement along the bottom features the cigarette brand. This set featured the brands of *Broadleaf*, *Cycle*, *Napoleon*, *Recruit* and the scarce-*Red Cross* brand. In total the set had over 200 baseball cards containing several Hall of Famers such as Irving Lewis, Ward Miller, Tris Speaker, Walter Johnson , Louis Lowdermilk and Ralph Works to name a few.

Additional "T" sets produced were numbered-208, 209, 210, 211, 213, 214, 215, 216, 217 and 222.

Boxing Event-Cigarette Card

Tobacco Card-Honus Wagner

For more information on cigarette card sets and collectability; visit the online site: http://www.cardboardconnection.com/t202-hassan-triple-folders-baseball-cards

Did You Know? The T206 cigarette sets held the "Holy Grail" of all the cigarette trading cards. This card featured the major league baseball player 'Honus Wagner" who played for the baseball team the "Pittsburgh Pirates". A Honus Wagner card became the first baseball cigarette card to sell for over $1.26 million dollars on eBay, which made it one of the most expensive baseball cards ever to be sold on eBay. Honus Wagner had decided he didn't want kids to associate him with bad habits such as cigarette smoking, so he had any cigarette packs with his photo on it, pulled from the shelves. It is believed, that roughly 50 to 60 of his cards slipped through the cracks and were sold.

These "T" series, Baseball trade cards from the early 20th century, are quite profitable if found in very good condition and PSA certified and graded.

With paper product rationing and cost-cutting during the WWI, the cigarette card collecting craze was all but over. Their replacement came in 1950 with the debut of Bubble Gum packages which featured trading cards inside each package.

An online site I discovered to be of further assistance on the subject of cigarette trading cards, can be found online at: http://www.cigarettecards.co.uk/value.htm

Cracker Jack's and 1914-1915 Baseball Trading Card Sets

"Take me out to the Ball Game."

"Take me out with the crowd"

"Buy me some peanuts and Cracker Jacks......"

Photo of Sailor Jack

In the year 1893 these favored sweet confections were sold at Chicago's World Fair and mass-produced that same year. The idea for "Cracker Jack" snacks came from a German immigrant named, Frederick W. Rueckheim. He and his brother, Louis experimented and came up with the recipe, which was a mixture of popcorn, molasses and peanuts. In 1899, the wax-sealed, moisture proof box was introduced to keep the mixture from sticking together. Prizes were placed inside the boxes in 1912. The trademarked logo came out in 1918 and featured Sailor Jack and his dog, "Bingo" (modeled after F.W. Rueckheim's grandson, Robert and his dog).

In 1914, the first set of 2 ¼-inch by 3-inch, size thin cardstock- baseball cards were added as prizes in each box of Cracker Jack, caramel popcorn. This set contained 144 subjects. These sets of cards featured the Hall of Famers-Ty Cobb (card # 30), Walter Johnson #37, Honus Wagner #68, Christy Mathewson #88, Joe Jackson #103 and Tris Speaker #65. The second set came out a year later with 176 cards and featured additional players. These cards are so similar that some look like duplicates, but note the numbering as the revere side of the card will have the text "complete set of 144" with the second set of cards text stating "complete set of 176".

People can find the 1915 cards easier than the first set. Additionally, collectors *were* able to acquire cards via the mail by sending in coupons in exchange for them. The Cracker Jack baseball cards are unique because they were the only cards to feature players from the short-lived *Federal Baseball League.*

It is difficult to find the Cracker Jack baseball cards in good condition due to age. They are very collectible, and if they are graded by PSA; they can fetch in the lower-thousand-dollar-range. Demand and condition warrant their values. Furthermore, Cracker Jack baseball, pin-back buttons, can sell in the hundreds.

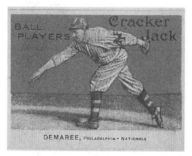

Early 1900's, Cracker Jack Baseball Card,
"Demaree" of the Philadelphia Nationals

In spring of 2015, I saw an eBay auction for an entire set of the Cracker Jack 1915 baseball cards-PSA graded-with a "Buy It Now" price of $99,999.99... Yowza, yowza, yowza!!

HUGE Profits selling Rock Concert Memorabilia and Vinyl Records!

Classic rock concert t-shirts are sought-after by hardcore rock music fans. Promotional concert t-shirts can sell for over $2,000. Watch for vintage 1960s-1980s t-shirts by the musical groups: Zed Leppelin, The Rolling Stones, Nirvana, Iron Madden, John Lennon, Motely Crew, KISS and U2.

Furthermore, similar concert ticket stubs and noteworthy sporting events are worth a high amount of cash.

Did You Know? A 1977 "KISS ALIVE II" (of the Rock band fame) record player by *Tiger Electronics* can sell for over $800! "ROCK ON" KISS!

1980's Rock Group "KISS" Game

Vintage Def Leppard
Concert Tee-Shirt

Vinyl Records (LP's, 78's and 45 rpm's)

Do you still own those bestselling records that were saved from your teenage years, in hopes that in the future, they would become quite valuable?

Unfortunately, because these pressed vinyl discs were mass-produced into the millions, they've lost their values. Furthermore, other factors such as, scratches, loss of their original sleeves, and writing on the record label or cover -will definitely deflate their collectability. Instead, you may want to keep them for reminiscing about past days gone by, and for your own personal listening enjoyment. Even those ancient 1940s' 78 rpm records that your grandparents enjoyed back in the day, aren't considered valuable just because of their age.

No sleeves on your Rock 'n' Roll 45s? *Sorry, send them off to the thrift store.* Exceptions: Autographed releases by noted artists (e.g., John Lennon, Michael Jackson, Elvis Presley, Bob Dylan)

Promo Vinyl Records:

Promotional records were issued by record labels to promote that particular upcoming record's release. They were sent to DJs, radio stations and music media sources before the regular release date in hopes of positive reviews and airplay.

If you find a record label marked, "Promo Only", than my friends, you may have found a true treasure!

Tip: If the music wasn't good-the promos are most likely-worthless. Furthermore, when searching for promo records remember most major record label promos, ceased production in 2008.

This statement meant that the track was only released as a "promo", unavailable to the public. Of course, the value depends on the quality of the track and its rarity. Some "Promo Only" records sell in the thousands-of-dollars range. Promo records may be marked "not for sale", *but* it was not illegal to sell them. Their record labels will have black ink on a white label, with the regular release having color added to the label. The song tracks will be the same though.

Additional information to search in your pursuit to finding "Promo Only" records:

- The label and/or the cover will read, "DJ only, DEMONSTRATION, NOT FOR SALE, Promotional"
- The record label is stamped in ink as "Promo" by the manufacturer
- The cover to the record album may have a corner clipped off to discourage retail sales. The record inside may be identical to the retailed copies, so in this case, the record was not meant for the public.
- Look for any contact information on the label (i.e. phone numbers).

Example of Promo
record LP cover

- Tracks or record labels that are marked, "unavailable on LP"-meaning-it's not part of the particular released album—are collectible.
- Any presence of information included in the track release found inside the packaging, such as color postcards, autographed photos, posters, stickers and DJ feedback form sheets-especially from talented artists (e.g., Elvis Presley, Neil Diamond, Jimi Hendrix).
- If they have a different catalog number, and printing on labels-other than the norm.

Vinyl record tracks that are sought after today will include the following:
- Some 1950s/1960s Rhythm 'n' Blues, and Rock 'n' Roll, 45 RPM records with their original PICTURE sleeve, and in excellent condition.
- 1950s/ 1960s Rock 'n' Roll and Rhythm & Blues (Motown and Detroit) EPS (7" 45 RPM records that were produced with four songs), with original cardboard sleeves covered in cellophane intact; can fetch into the hundreds of dollars range.
- Rhythm and Blue/Rock 'n' Roll records that were played by a radio station that didn't necessarily become hits with its listening audience. Example: The early R & B (e.g. The Flamingos) music-due to lack of money to produce records in large quantities-can fetch in the $500 range.
- Pioneer Rock 'n' Roll groups or individuals with LPs from the 1950s, can sell in the thousand's range.
- Beatles, Beatles, Beatles-Original Beatle's Group LPs, or the records that were made by the Beatles individually, (including foreign copies) have values from $100 to $10,000 or more.

PHOTO BEATLES COVER "Butcher" Cover of "Yesterday" LP

Did You Know?
The Beatles 1966 record album titled, "Yesterday and Today" can sell for over $15,000!

Capitol Records first released over 750,000 of crudely covered album sleeves. The covers featured a photo of the Fab Four appearing in butcher's smocks covered with raw meat and doll body parts-Gross! Most of these albums were destroyed so they are extremely rare to come across. The album was subsequently reissued with a picture of the Beatles sitting on top of steamer trunks.

Here is a partial list of favorite Rock 'n' Roll records that collector's desire: *Jimi Hendrix, Led Zeppelin, The Rolling Stones*, Bob Dylan, Elvis Presley, David Bowie; *RUSH, AC/DC, Madonna, Iron Madden, KISS, The Beach Boys, Bee Gees*, Michael Jackson and Neal Young. Also, Unique Northern Soul - American single records (usually not hits in the USA) that were played by DJs in clubs in Northern England (e.g., Manchester, etc.) in the late 1960s and early 1970s; and Hillbilly Mountain music/songs from early country music (early 1930s and 1940s country artists).

I suggest the reference book: *45 RPM Record Company Sleeves Identification & Price Guide*, 2012- by Shelby Scott, to help with current values of 45 RPM records.

Comic Book Collecting
I am pretty sure that most of America and abroad are savvy to the hobby of collecting famous comic book characters, popular super-heros, their villains- and how valuable they are.

Iconic FIRST's of comic book series, such as *Superman, Batman, Flash, Captain America, Spiderman; X-men, Fantastic Four* and the *Incredible Hulk* are amongst other "super-comic-hero's" can fetch in the thousands. Check out the following comic book list, which was released in the year 2012. This list has the top ten most valuable Golden Age comics in the World, and what they were appraised for that time. (Values will change through the ensuing years)

1. *Fantastic Four* #1 - $279,000
2. *Action Comics* #7 - $404,000
3. *Amazing Fantasy* #15 - $407,000-Introduction for "Spiderman"
4. *Batman* #1 -$440,00
5. All-American Comics #16 - $478,000- Introduction for the "Green Lantern"
6. *Marvel Comics* #1 - $499,000
7. *Detective Comics* #1-$535,000
8. *Superman* #1- $715,000-Solo for the Man Of Steel
9. *Detective Comics* #27-$2.57 million Dollars-Introduction for *Batman*
10. *Action Comics* #1-$2.89 million-There's approximately 100 of these left in the world....SCARCITY!

Vintage Silver Age Super Heroes Comic Books

Some Walt Disney comic books dating from the Golden Age of comics are additionally valuable, selling into the thousands of dollars. Watch for 1940's Dell comics highlighting "Uncle Scrooge", "Mickey Mouse" and "Donald Duck".

Marvel Superhero comics were reintroduced into the public in the 1990s. With the newest remake of the, "Batman" movie in 1990, comic book publishers re-launched the superhero comic books. These newer version comics weren't profitable for collectors. They purchased these comic books with hopes that within 30 years they could resell them for a substantial amount of money. Unfortunately, this didn't happen because their remakes were overproduced. Comics lost values for years, but are now making a come-back from the 1990's crash.

Be careful with selling comic books online-This is an area that necessitates grading similar to grading trading cards and coin collecting.

A comic books condition, will play a major factor in what warrants the value of a rare comic book.

Here are some helpful guidelines on the "Comic Grading System" (CGC). Comic book collectors have a fool-proof way to guard against fraud. CGC, rates the condition and quality of comic books, from 0.5 for extra poor condition to 10- for pristine. (The Superman comic that sold for 1.5 million dollars had a rating of 8.5.) CGC employees--in a temperature/ humidity controlled room, and donning wearing rubber gloves--will inspect comic books for restoration, assign each a grade, and then seal them in hard plastic cases with a "tamper-evident" label. The process of sanctioning by CGC-is *not* priced low. The least expensive current examination fee around $25 for a book valued up to $150, with a forty-day turnaround. For the higher value comic books and the most expedient service-CGC takes 2.5 percent of the fair value, with a cap of $1,500. It is worth checking into grading your comic/comics if you believe they could possibly be rare. (These prices are subject to change with time.)

To view a grading scale for comic books, go to this informative online site: http://www.cgccomics.com/grading/grading.asp

Chapter IX

Casino/Hotel Paraphernalia-Big Bucks!

The early 20th century gambling related collectibles include the garnering of slot machines, casino chips (HOT!!), obsolete casino/hotel ephemera (e.g., pamphlets, ashtrays, souvenirs, room keys-souvenirs of those FUN trips to Las Vegas) also known as the "Entertainment Capital of the World."

So, let's discover how to find some secret Las Vegas Jackpots!

Collecting Casino Chips

If you are lucky enough to open up a box or open an old dresser and find a forgotten, casino chip keepsake...don't toss it away until you have conducted some research to find out if it is, in fact- Valuable!

The following "casino chip" treasure find story is factual.

Who would guess that a $1 casino chip could increase in value to $30,000! A woman from the United States decided that she wanted to make a little bit of pocket money by selling some of her old trinkets on eBay. Ms. Sandy Marbs was a retired *Kwik Kopy* employee, who was living on social benefits, and wanted to supplement her income with some of her possessions. After rummaging through her jewelry box, she came across a casino chip from the Las Vegas-*Showboat Casino*, which had been left sitting in her trinket box for nearly 50 years. She uploaded the necessary information about her casino chip onto eBay to sell it, but because of her lack of knowledge on casino chips, she started the online auction with a low start bid. She decided to set a price of $10 to start the bidding on this particular chip.

Luckily for Marbs, a casino chip collector, who was an expert in the world of gambling memorabilia, spotted her auction. The collector contacted her to warn her not to take the first offer. The collector brought her some wonderful news – the casino chip had a market value of $15,000! The chip had become highly collectible, as it came from one of Vegas's most classic spots – the *Showboat Casino*, which had been open from 1954 until 2001. Key note—the casino was demolished in 2006.

Sandy decided to act on the advice that had been given to her by the *Casino Chip and Gaming Token Collectors Club* individual, and to take more detailed photos of the $1 chip. Within hours, bids were extremely active for the little round gaming piece, and it was eventually sold for a record price of nearly $29,000! The chip was bought by an avid collector.
This is the highest price paid in history for a $1 chip; although, $100,000 was

paid for a "Sahara" Hotel/Casino- $100 chip. This particular chip featured the image of an Egyptian "Sphinx" on it.

| Las Vegas SAHARA Resort and Casino $1 Gaming Chip | Rare Las Vegas 1960s, $100 EL CORTEZ Casino Chip, sold for $4,550 on eBay July, 2015 |

Casino Chip Tutorial

Casino chips are made from specific "molds." The mold identifies the actual maker or distributor of the chip and helps to date the issue. Also, it warrants how collectible it is.

There are casino chips that were used on a regular basis (produced by the casino to play at the table), or limited (LE) editions. The limited editions have specific dates printed on them and were produced in limited numbers (2,000 on average) and this quantity, was usually printed on the chip. The mold of the chip is the most important thing when grading because it identifies the look/manufacturer/distributor of that chip.

> **Tip**: Always keep casino chips out of sunlight and fluorescent light, which will cause deterioration to the chip. This is a great tip in general for all antiques and vintage items because the sun can cause discoloration to fabrics, plastics, furniture, paper products, painted items, and ruin fragrances in perfumes and colognes.

The most collected casino chips are the Las Vegas, Nevada casino chips. The value of the chip will depend on its rarity, grading (condition) and its "aesthetic appeal". Essential to determining the chip's value is the mold type (the Arodie mold is best for collecting), and historical camaraderie. These factors are of utmost importance to the avid collector. A chipped or damaged casino chip won't bring in as much as one in excellent condition. Look for flaws. Are the rims or other parts of the chip worn? Is the hot stamp (center) or inlay faded? You will need a casino chip collector's reference book to learn a bit about grading the condition of the chip due to the large subject matter. I purchased a casino chip reference book titled: *The Official U.S. Casino Chip Price Guide* by James Campiglia and Steve Wells. A very informative book.

Here is an online site I found very helpful in determining the condition of a casino chip: http://www.nevadacasinochips.com/Obsolete.htm

Here is the link to send a casino chip in for value grading: http://www.igsgrading.com/indexchips.htm

An educational reference book for understanding the values, grading and types of casino chips is, "*The Official U.S. Casino Chip Price Guide*", by James Campiglia and Steve Walls.

Tip: When collecting casino chips, don't clean them with soap and water ,or water alone because it can ruin your chips. By using a toothbrush and some "Armor All Multi-Purpose Cleaner," it can do the trick of cleaning a casino chip. Just spray a small amount of the liquid on the chip; brush with the toothbrush and leave on for approximately 20 seconds. Brush again with short light strokes-than wipe with a dry soft cloth. This method is for 'inlay' chips only.

Casino Chip Hunting

If you find a chip that is from the following demolished, or still standing hotel casino's.....PLEASE RESEARCH IT! Furthermore, any chip from a hotel/motel casino that once existed in Las Vegas in the mid-century years, could possibly be worth over a thousand dollars.

Casino chips from Las Vegas imploded casinos are sought-after. Here is a list of Las Vegas demolished casino/hotels along with some interesting facts about each:

- The *Sands*- Once home to the famous "Rat Pack". The *Sands*, "Copa Room" was the birthplace of this creative entertainment group back in 1960. The Rat Pack team consisted of - Frank Sinatra, Sammy Davis, Jr., Joey Bishop, Dean Martin and Peter Lawford. The Sands Casino was imploded in 1996 with the "Venetian" resort replaced it.

Las Vegas Sands Hotel and Casino Photo

In chatting a bit about the "Rat Pack"- vintage 1960's Las Vegas celebrity "Rat Pack" clothing is the latest fashion rage. Frank Sinatra's Fedora-style and "Sharkskin" fabric suits can bring in a lot of dough! Always be sure to do some research on vintage apparel and any of their attached labels.

Frank Sinatra Photo Wearing a Borsalino Hat

Vintage 1950s Fur Felt, Borsalino hat With Feather- selling range $100-$200

Vintage Mid-century Mod Blue Green "Sharkskin" Suit Made in England
by Oxford Street-Listing Price-$298

- *Flamingo*- Is the oldest remaining casino on the Strip. The *Flamingo* first opened in 1946, but the name has flip-flopped back and forth over the years. In 1947, it was called "The *Fabulous Flamingo*", in 1950- The *Flamingo*, 1952- The *Fabulous Flamingo*, 1974- *Flamingo Hilton* and in 2000- *Flamingo Las Vegas*. Casino chips from the Flamingo's earlier days, have sold for over $10,000 each.

For more information on the *Las Vegas Flamingo*, here is an educational online link to view into its past: http://casinogambling.about.com/od/casinos101/a/Vegas-Casino-History-Flamingo-Hotel.htm

- *Stardust*- Was imploded in 2007, the *Stardust* had a colorful past, most notorious for its mob ties. It was also a major source for the movie "Casino."

Famous Las Vegas Stardust Neon Sign

- *Riviera*-Opened in 1955 and is currently- in what began as a rumor- is now official news. In February 2015, the Las Vegas tourism authority is moving forward with plans to purchase the Riviera so it can be demolished to make room for more convention space. I heard this and thought, "No, not the beautiful neon –lit casino!!" "It was by far one of my favorite casino/hotels on the strip."

Riviera Casino Neon Lights before Implosion

- *Dunes*- Was imploded in 1993 and replaced with the $1.6 billion-dollar artsy, *Bellagio* resort.

- *Showboat*-turned-*Castaways* (imploded in 2006): The original *Showboat* bowling lanes was the site for the oldest stop on the "Pro Bowlers Association Tour". Additionally, the *Showboat Sports Pavilion* featured world title boxing matches, professional wrestling, roller derby and billiards.

- The *Landmark*- Built by Frank Carroll, but purchased by eccentric developer Howard Hughes in 1968. In its heyday, the Landmark played host to other celebrities, such as Elvis Presley and Frank Sinatra. The hotel was also featured in a few Hollywood movies prior to its implosion n 1995; most notably "Diamonds Are Forever" and *"Casino"*.

- *Nevada Club* in Reno, Nevada

- The *Silver Slipper*- The signage for this famous Las Vegas casino featured a large, light bulb covered, woman's high-heeled, shoe/slipper, which was placed high on the casino's neon billboard sign. Las Vegas visitors could see it from miles away (What a great marketing gimmick!). The Silver Slipper's showroom once featured a fabulous Burlesque-style show from 1950-1988. It was located across the street from the *Desert Inn*. This iconic, giant sign can still be seen in Las Vegas at the *Neon Museum*.

- *Caesar's Palace*- On August 5, 1966, the 14-story, 700 room, *Caesars Palace* opened with each guest being welcomed by the official greeter- a blonde 40-20-37, *Cleopatra*. The opening included the stage production of

"Rome Swings" with Andy Williams and Phil Richards, playing the character who player "Caesar". Talk about luxurious! Hanging from the ceiling in the Grand Promenade of the resort, was one of the largest chandeliers ever created, costing $125,000, it measured 99-ft by 66-ft and contained more than 100,000 crystals in the 1970s.

- *Desert Inn-*(imploded in 2004)

Desert Inn Hotel-Casino and Howard Hughes

There is no doubt about it, when you mention Las Vegas's now demolished Hotel/Casino; you need to mention the infamous Howard Hughes and his love for the Las Vegas Strip. Howard Hughes had resided on the ninth floor of the Desert Inn along with his aides and personal executives operating on the eighth floor of the resort and casino in the late 1960s -till around the early 1970s. After his first couple weeks of staying at the Desert Inn- Desert Inn's executive, Moe Dalitz told Mr. Hughes, he had to leave. Hughes decided instead, to offer to buy the Hotel/Casino. Dalitz quoted him an inflated price of $13.2 million, but surprisingly Hughes accepted it and took over ownership of the Desert Inn on March 31, 1967. That same year, Hughes continued in what would be an unprecedented buying spree of Las Vegas Strip casinos. He spent $23 million for the Sands Hotel, $3.3 million for the Castaways and $23 million for the New Frontier. In 1968, he spent $5.4 million for the Silver Slipper and $17.3 million for the Landmark. Though, his deal to buy the Stardust for $30.5 million would later fall through. Hughes also acquired the Harold's Club Casino in Reno for $10.5 million. Howard Hughes goal was to rid Las Vegas of its ties to organized crime. I am not quite sure if his plan to rid Las Vegas of the mob worked, but his vision of Las Vegas becoming a huge successful gaming mecca for adults-sure came true.

By the year 1971, it is estimated that Mr. Hughes spent approximately $300,000,000 in purchasing properties and land in Las Vegas. Mr. Hughes knew the potential that Las Vegas and its strip held, and tried to make it a reality. The billionaire entrepreneur had intended on becoming-the largest *single property owner in the gambling capital. He predicted that the state of Nevada would see over a million residents before the end of the 20th century and he was planning to be part of the biggest Las Vegas hotel/casino boom of the latter 20th century. The Las Vegas Strip, is now home to some of Las Vegas's mega resorts/casinos: Excalibur, Luxor, MGM Grand, Monte Carlo, New York, New York, Wynn, Bellagio; The Cosmopolitan, The Venetian, Wynn (The Desert Inn once stood where the resort/casinos "Wynn Las Vegas" and Encore Hotel/ Casino now stand) and so many more.*

Photo of Howard Hughes, "The Aviator"

'50s Magazine Ad for the Desert Inn

Did You Know?

That Howard Hughes had invested so heavily in Las Vegas, Nevada in the 1960s, that local people joked around stating that soon the city of Las Vegas should be renamed "Hugheston"

- *Frontier-* This was the hotel that Elvis Presley made his actual Vegas debut back in 1956. (Presley received a cool reception and was criticized by Vegas entertainment critics.) The hotel was, until its implosion in 2007, the last operating hotel that was once owned by Mr. Howard Hughes.

- *Bally's-* Opened originally as the first *MGM Grand* in 1973 on the site of the former *Bonanza Hotel*. It was the largest hotel in the world at the time.

On November 21, 1980, one of the worst building fires in U.S. history (3rd worst), broke out in the casino killing over 85 people.

Did You Know?
It is said that the halls and stairwells of the old *MGM Grand* hotel (presently owned and operated by Bally's) are haunted by the ghosts of those that died in that infamous *MGM* hotel fire. Apparitions have been seen wandering the halls of the higher floors of the north tower and in the stairwells and elevators.

- *Aladdin*-a property formerly known as *King's Resort* (and before that, the *Tally-Ho*), opened in 1966. The *Aladdin* was so vast that it included 36 acres, a 17-story tower, 1,100 rooms and a checkered past full of financial troubles, legal problems and mob involvement. It was imploded in the year-1998

- *El Cortez*-Originally built in 1941- it was sold in 1945 to infamous mobster Benjamin "Bugsy" Siegel and his business partners for the amount of $600,000. In 1946, it was sold to the next investor which made "Bugsy" over $160,000 richer! Eventually, it sold in 1963 to Jackie Gaughan, and is still run by the Gaughan family today.

- *Sahara*-The striped-down concrete structure that is still standing today was the once renowned "Sahara Resort and Casino"- will now become a new Las Vegas strip resort, the "SLS Las Vegas". The initials "SLS", stand for "Style, Luxury and Service."

- *Tropicana*-The *Tropicana* opening in 1957. The $15 million, 34 acre, 300-room *Tropicana*, called the "The Tiffany of the Strip" by publicist Harvey Diederich.

Opening night festivities were provided by Monte Proser's "Tropicana Revue", a $250,000 musical starring Eddie Fisher in the resorts, "Theatre Restaurant," later renamed the "Fountain Theatre".

The *Tropicana* contained formal gardens surrounding a scalloped-edged, Olympic-size pool in the center courtyard and had tastefully appointed guest rooms with individual lanais overlooking the lush, private tropical setting which were aesthetically placing to the eye.   Mobster, Frank Costello was found to also have some ties with the   casino back in 1957. Speaking of mobsters-The Las Vegas sequel from the movie "The Godfather" was filmed at the *Tropicana.*

Other gaming chips found from areas of the country such as Atlantic City, N.J and Deadwood, South Dakota, aren't worth nearly as much.

Did You Know? Entertainment Director Lou Walters (father of famed newswoman, Barbara Walters), imported the "Folies Bergere Show" from Paris, at an estimated $800,000, for *Tropicana's* main showroom, which became a success.

Vintage Casino and Hotel/Motel Keys

With new technological advances like electronic key cards, old-fashioned keys made in the 19th and 20th century-are no longer needed to open hotel room doors. It's much more convenient to have a key card that fits in your wallet. One swipe is all it takes for you to get into your room. But, what happened to all the old keys that hotels used to use? Like any good collectible that is on the verge of extinction and now, HTF (hard-to-find), they've become a hot collectible.

With the onset of the Industrial Revolution, came increased travel via trains. People leaving home and traveling throughout the country; lead to the popularity of overnight stays in hotels. To discourage guests from mistakenly taking the keys with them when their stays were over, hotels would attach heavy metal tags to the keys (Fobs). Some hotels even had a message imprinted on the tags that they would offer a reward for missing keys if they were returned.

Many of these keys were made of brass and or bronze, and they were often ornate. With the numerous types of tags/fobs attached to them, these small keys started walking away as mementos. Newlyweds would take them home as souvenirs or travelling businessmen would keep them as a reminder of their many journeys.

Many of these earlier keys were skeleton keys, meaning they could fit into most locks. If you had access to the room in the past, then you could have access to any valuables, or belongings for any future guests. As the years went on, skeleton keys were replaced by ones that were a little more complex in their makings. Warded keys, as they were called, were specifically cut keys that would open only one lock. Even later, levered keys were created to fit the heavier locks of hotel rooms.

Some of the most collectible keys today, are those from the early 20th century well-known hotels/motels and long demolished Las Vegas hotel room keys. These keys usually had an engraved or embossed image and logo of the actual hotel on their tags.

Antique Brass Hotel/
Motel Skeleton Key

My Key Story

I was called to conduct an estate sale for an elderly gentleman who was relocating to a nursing home. Inside one of the closets in his home, I found a small trash can filled with old keys obtained from hotels/motels from his many business trips in the United States and abroad. This trash can was put aside by the family to be placed in the dumpster. I decided to go through the can filled with keys, to investigate if they were of any value. I was fascinated to find that some of those keys were worth a good amount of money to antique key collectors. I continued to sort and mildly cleanse them. My rewards for my efforts came to a profit of $600 to the estates profit line.

Vintage Harrah's Resort and Casino
Room Key

Lot of Vintage Hotel/Motel Room Keys

Demolished Las Vegas Casino/ Resort Ashtrays from mid-century Las Vegas ('50s and '60s), can additionally sell in the range of $100-$1000, based on rarity.

Vintage Las Vegas
"Castaways" Ashtray

Of course, we cannot leave this chapter without discussing the famous Las Vegas showman- Elvis Presley and the garnering Elvis Presley related collectibles. Elvis LP's and RPM records, concert ticket stubs, whiskey decanters and miscellaneous items, can be very valuable. For example, a blue vinyl wallet with Elvis's image impressed on it, sold in 2013 for $500 -- a large sum of money for a kid's wallet. Unfortunately, Elvis collectibles are not the hottest collectible trend today. His vinyl records and whiskey decanters in the past would normally sell into the thousands, but currently fetching in the hundreds.

So in closing this chapter I have only one thing to say, "Viva Las Vegas!"

Chapter X

Cultural and Society Collecting Genres

The topic of collecting in particular themes or genres is quite vast. This chapter will bring up some of the more popular items found in those categories.

With trends changing continually, the awe in obtaining merchandise from certain genres may change overnight.

So, what are the current most sought-after items in "Genre" collecting?

With research and experiences I am learning more everyday on objects that are currently garnered; therefore, what to search for to achieve a huge profit. Margin. The next best "Hidden Gem!"

Last year, I came across a box of unwrapped glassware when sorting out items to conduct a customer's estate sale. Inside the box, I discovered over 30 vintage miscellaneous, *Kentucky Derby* souvenir drinking glasses. These glasses were sold at past yearly held, *Kentucky Derby* race events. As I proceeded to remove the wrapping from each glass, I noted some glasses were dated from the 1950s and 1960s. With research, I found that some of these glasses were selling for over $300 each online. Yes, over $300 each! I discovered 1940's *Kentucky Derby* "Mint Julep" glasses can even fetch in the thousand-dollar-range. Why? Kentucky Derby collectors will pay dearly for these souvenirs. The Kentucky Derby race event is a themed event, and so are any souvenirs related to that event are collectible and with time-Valuable.

Kentucky Derby Souvenir Mint
Julep Glasses

1953 Kentucky Derby Souvenir
"Flawed" (Missing Tails on Horses), Mint
Julep Glasses

Hawaiiana

Surf's up! Vintage Polynesian décor is currently heating back up in the 21st century.

Hawaiiana is a term used in reference to history and various aspects of the culture of Hawaii. The term is used especially in reflection of the periods of antiquity and the "Kingdom of Hawaii" Era.

Vintage Mid-century- Tiki-related Objects are Valuable!
Tiki Mugs- Tiki Gods - Tiki Masks - Tiki Totems - Tiki Home Decor - Tiki Huts - Tiki lights and South Pacific Wood Tiki carvings are the latest craze.

In the 1950s and 1960s, Tiki's popularity craze skyrocketed. This Tiki obsession was manifested by the entrance of the state of Hawaii as the 50th state in 1959.

Most Polynesians believe that Tiki was the first man created. In Polynesian mythology, tiki or hei tiki, which is a sculpture carved in the shape of a god, housing a spirit. The creation of the tiki image is known throughout Polynesia.

The Tiki mugs and wood carvings that once collected dust in thrift stores are now hard-to-find. Watch for famous tiki bar/restaurant mugs, such as those found with *Tiki Bob's* of San Francisco, Ca. logos. These mugs can sell for a couple of hundred dollars.

Anything Tiki-inspired, has the center stage in the world of Polynesian culture collecting along with any vintage carved bamboo or teak wood South Pacific sculpture,

Tiki Image

vintage Hawaiian brand or themed clothing, shell tribal jewelry and mid-century tropical beach memorabilia. This is a partial list of some of most notable Polynesian collectible wares:

- PuKa Shell necklaces- Puka is the Hawaiian word for "hole" and refers to the naturally occurring hole in the middle of these rounded and worn shell fragments that are found on the beaches of Hawaii. The original natural puka shells were very easily made into necklaces, bracelets and anklets, because they already had a hole which enabled them to be strung like beads. Puka Shell necklaces became popular to buy in mid-to-late 1970s. The necklaces were made of small round white shells. Worn by surfers, these necklaces were a big fad. Usually worn snug around the neck; they were a status symbol until about 1980. They are back in style again, after their popularity had vanished for over 35 years.

- Vintage 1940s-1960s "Aloha", Hawaiian shirts in tropical motifs applied on silk, cotton or rayon shirts, selling for over $500. Collectible vintage Aloha-Hawaiian brands or labels to watch include: *Alfred Shaheen, Catalina, Kahanamoku, Kamehameha, Kahala, Hale Hawaii, Royal Hawaiian, Duke of Hollywood* and *J.C. Penney's*.

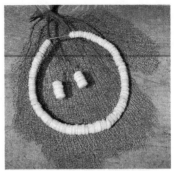

Vintage 1980s Puka Shell Hawaiian Surfer Necklace & Earrings-$125

Vintage Mid-Century Tropical "Aloha" Shirt

Vintage 1950's Hale Hawaii Crepe, Rayon Men's Shirt with Coconut Husk Buttons-listing price-$350

🔑 **Tip**: In your search for dating a Hawaiian print men's shirt, look for any apparent manufacturing labels. If you see any care instructions, it dates the garment to the 1960s or later. If the garment has three to five buttons down the front (not six); larger collars than the recently manufactured shirts; cabana pockets located at the waistline, and buttons made from the shells of coconuts (earliest Aloha shirts)-it's quite possibly a treasure!

- Mid-century teak wood carved home furnishings by *Witco* (*Western International Trading Company)* are sought-after for creating that special mid-century, Polynesian or Tropical Era-atmosphere. The vintage South Pacific home furnishings by *Witco* (*Western International Trading Company*), can sell for over $1,000.

Vintage Mid-century 3-D Danish Witco Kitchen knife fork spoon Wood Art Painting 40" x 30"

Vintage Mid-century Witco Wood "Oceanic" Credenza Cabinet-listing price $2,100

1970's Tiki Bench with Leopard Print Seat 68" x 18" x 12"

Vintage Witco Tiki Bar Stools

- 1940s Animated, Bare Torso "Hula Girl" Table Lamps by *Dodge Company* -sell in the hundreds range.
- Marvel chalkware head busts depicting beautiful Hawaiian women- sell in the hundreds range.

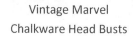

Vintage Marvel
Chalkware Head Busts

- Vintage Asian and Arts and Crafts, Rattan-Woven Wicker and Bamboo patio furniture are presently in demand. The revival of the original 1970's Rattan Peacock/Fan-Back Chairs produced in the 1960s and 1970s, and mid-century designer Paul Frankl- rattan lounge chairs are currently selling in the $300 range.

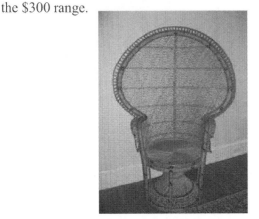

Vintage 1970's Rattan "Peacock" Fan-back Chair

Vintage Mid-century Paul Frankl Lounge Chair

I see these woven chairs every-so-often at garage sales. They remind me of the old 1960's television series, "The Adams Family". One of the main characters, "Morticia," loved to sit in her fan-back Rattan chair.

- Vintage Capiz Shell Pendant Ceiling Lamps and Chandeliers sell in the hundreds based on size and condition.
- Vintage Hawaiian Motif Consumer Products

Additionally, limited edition, 50th Anniversary Disneyland and Disney World "Enchanted Tiki Room" items, and past souvenirs from the park attraction, can fetch a large sum of money.

Vintage Walt Disneyland "Tiki Room" Ephemera

Speaking of Disney? It's time to move on to our next theme of garnering "Disneyana".

Disneyana

Disneyana-is the collecting of memorabilia in a wide variety of collectible toys, books, animation cels, theme park souvenirs, ephemera and other items produced by The *Walt Disney Company*. Examples range from products featuring virtually every Disney character created—such as *Mickey & Minnie Mouse, Donald Duck, Uncle Scrooge, Snow White, Pluto, Goofy and Tinkerbell (of Peter Pan fame)*. Disney memorabilia values have somewhat declined in the last five years, but are still collectible. Here is a list of some of the recent, most-favored Disney merchandise desired by collectors.

- Disney's "Frozen" characters- "Elsa" and "Anna" 17-inch and life-size (38-inch) dolls. Selling in the upper hundreds range.
- Particular Disney classic comic books from the "Golden Age" (late 1930s-early 1950s) are very valuable based on their condition and PGX rating. Introductions to Disney

Walt Disney "Frozen" Dolls- 17" Elsa and Anna-NIB

Vintage Golden Age Disney Scrooge Comic Books

characters and comic book firsts-can bring in thousands of dollars.

- Vintage Disney "Alice in Wonderland" and "Beauty and the Beast" character cookie jars can realize $300 or better.

Any of the Walt Disney items listed below, can sell in the hundreds of dollars.

- Vintage Steiff Stuffed animals-"Mickey" & "Minnie" Mouse and the "Big Bad Wolfe" to name a few.

Tip: Vintage Steiff stuffed animals will have glass eyes and made of mohair fur, and they won't appear to have been recently manufactured and appear dingy -not crisp and new.

- Porcelain Capodimante -*Laurenz Classic* ,Disney character groupings; and LE Disney Resort figurines can sell for over $500 each. This Disney "Beauty and the Beast-Mrs. Pott & Chip Tea Set, can fetch over $150.

Walt Disney's "Beauty and the Beast"-Mrs. Pott and Chip Tea Set- MIB

Disney 1990 "Kit Cloudkicker" Stuffed Plush Toy Animal

- Early Disney character mechanical metal tin litho toys by *Linemar, MARX, J. Chein Company* etc
- The rare Walt Disney-Disney World Park- "Kit Cloudkicker" Plush Stuffed Animal (a character from the "TaleSpin" animated cartoon fame) can sell for over $1,000.
- Any vintage 1960's, Walt Disney, autographed ephemera-park employee checks, brochures; unused Disneyland tickets, and souvenirs from Disneyland Park attractions.

Vintage Walt Disneyland Used ticket &
Miscellaneous Park Memorabilia

Vintage 1930's Lusterware Mickey Mouse
Children's China Tea Set

- **1930s Mickey Mouse Lusterware Children's China Sets-selling range $200-$500**
- Disney Store large character props or displays-Big Bucks!
- Walt Disney original animated production "Cel" art—HOT! A Cel is a transparent sheet of celluloid or similar film material that can be drawn on, and used in the production of cartoons. They were the original cartoon images traced by artists, then colors were applied to each one placed in perfect alignment to create a cartoon. It's hard to find them in perfect condition as the colors may have lifted off the traced image. Disney artists created top quality "cels". Watch for Disney the characters (e.g., Mickey Mouse, Snow White, Alice in Wonderland, Pluto and Goofy.

Alice in Wonderland Cel

- Mint-in-box-*Disney* LE 17" dolls (*Alice in Wonderland, Snow White,* and *Rapunzel*—HOT! Selling for over $3,000--Insanity!
- 1975's Haunted Mansion board game by *Lakeside can sell for $300*

Vintage Mickey Mouse Toy

- *Disney's* Movie "The Black Hole" 1979 toy robot characters B. O. B. (BOB) and S. T. A. R. by Mego GIG. HOT! Selling in the upper-hundreds-range.
- Early Walt Disney themed children's books from the 1930s to the 1940s(1920s'- First edition, Winnie-the-Pooh related storybooks by A. A. Milne-sell in the hundreds.)
- Retired *Disney* LEGO kits----HOT!!! Selling in the thousand-dollar-range.

Vintage 1979 Mego "Black Hole" Set of Four, 12.5" Action Figures

There are so many more items in this wonderful category. This was just a partial list of some of the most notable items.

So, Heigh Ho! Heigh Ho! It's off to Disneyland we go!

Petroliana Collecting

Vintage gas pumps, oil/gas cans (Keep an eye out for *Harley-Davidson* and *John Deere* brands), industrial metal stools, license plates found on cars, advertising thermometers, trucks and motorcycles; vintage vehicle parts and industrial porcelain; and metal hanging pendant and ceiling light fixtures. Additionally, in this category, other items found in the Petroliana genre are, vintage garage/auto signage and roadway map memorabilia. The "American Pickers" (TV Series), are DEFINITELY on to this one!

Here I am standing next to a 1950's Gas Pump

Vintage Garage -Oil Cans

Garage Metal Storage Cabinets

Vintage Champlin Oil Can

Vintage Gas Station, Garage Porcelain Industrial Light Fixture

Militaria

Militaria is the arena of collecting vintage armed forces, war-time military paraphernalia. Here is a partial list of vintage military artifacts and items, in your pursuit for making a profit when reselling them online:

- WWI/WWII Uniforms, apparel and field gear from the Marines-USMC, Navy-USN and USAAF-Army Air Corps/flight, USA-Army, USAF-Air Force; Vietnam, Korean, Gulf and Civil Wars; and foreign troop gear (e.g., German, Japanese, Italian). If a uniform is found with any of its original patches, insignia and chevrons, it will help bring up its resale value. Furthermore, find any information about the original owner-all the better-it will be quite meaningful to the buyer. This information can be located on the uniform itself, or ask the seller if they have any references pertaining to the soldier who once wore it.

- WWII soldier helmets and headgear from American and foreign troops (German)

- WWII Jackets and the 1960's Vietnamese War, such as leather A-2 flight jackets, Bomber Jackets, embroidered Tour-Japan jackets and Army Air Corp jackets are highly sought-after. I recently sold one online for over $600 and it was in good condition-with flaws.

Vintage WWII Bombardier Pilot Jacket

- Vintage Vietnam/WWII winter field coats, hooded real fur collar winter parka's and tiger -striped, outdoor camo-clothing/accessories

- WWII wool USN pea coats, navy military lapel pins and medals, sailor apparel and U.S Navy military, *Longines*-commander watches. Naval ship- deck clocks and lanterns - can fetch a pretty penny!

WWII U.S. Army 14th Air Force Flying Tiger Patch

- Army and aviator leather boots currently

selling for over $200 online if they are in very good condition.

- WWII German uniforms, apparel and head gear from the Third Reich (this term was used to describe the Nazi regime in Germany from January 30, 1933, to May 8, 1945). These original helmets can fetch in the upper-hundreds-range.

Tip: Fake German helmets were, and are-being reproduced. Make sure to look for serial and size numbers on into of helmet on rim. No loose air vents, and plenty of rusted scratch marks versus silver areas wher paint was scratched off and void of any rust.

Vintage WWII German Troop
Helmet

- Military service badges, patches, medals, ranking bar stripes and military pins (gold and sterling silver- wing pins)

WWII Sterling Silver Pilot Wing Pins

WWII Sterling Silver Air Force Army
"Observer" Wings Pin

WWII Sterling Silver Aviator, Pilot Wings, Badge Pin

- Buttons from the state or branch of service in which an ancestor served. It could also be a specific period (e.g., Civil War, Revolutionary War, Mexican War, Spanish-American War etc.). Invest in a quality metal detector if you plan on searching in open fields or landscapes for any odds and ends left behind from past conflicts.

When listing various military items found via digging with a shovel, describe them as being "dug" or "non-dug," depending on whether or not they have been excavated. Military buttons worn by troops and officers in WW I and WWII are also widely collected.

Tip: When cleaning military or other vintage buttons; use a gray eraser to clean rusted metal shanks and keep them in a dry place.

Some helpful online sites in your search to recognizing vintage military buttons:
http://www.lighthouseantiques.net/uniforms/uniforms.html
http://www.civilwarbuttons.com/cscentrlist

The reference book: *Uniform Buttons of the United States 1776-1865* by Warren K. Tice, may be quite helpful on the subject of button collecting. Also, the book titled: *Record of American Uniform and Historical Buttons,* by Alphareus H. Albert

- Canned food rations (unopened) and medical kits from WWII

WWII U.S. Military Field Necessities

- 1940's *Bausch and Lomb* field binoculars
- Compasses and watches-Military wristwatches are also among the most prized watches collected today. There are lots of buyers for vintage military timepieces, and they will go to great lengths in search of them (working or not). These watches were tough and durable. They had diverse roles and can be described as- devices with multiple faces and functions.

  If you happen to discover a WWII Military Pilot/Navigator Swiss *Longines* (made for Czech military) wristwatch-you have found quite the *treasure*! These Chronograph wristwatches (watches with stop-watch capabilities) are selling into the thousands of dollar range, based on condition and styles. Chronograph type wristwatches were very popular with war time aviators, allowing the pilots to make rapid longitude calculations, and conduct precise timing.

Did You Know? The 1932 Longines Hour-Angle Watch was

designed by, and for the famous pioneer/inventor and aviator- Charles Lindbergh. Lindbergh—unaccompanied, crossed the Atlantic Ocean on his airplane "The Spirit of St. Louis" on May 20, 1927.

German and Swiss watches made for the German Luftwaffe (i.e. the Nazi Air Force), are extremely valuable.

Similarly of value, are WWII Era wristwatch brands, such as *Hamilton, Rolex* and *Omega*.

For a better understanding when collecting war era watches; here is a very informative eBay web page I discovered: http://www.ebay.com/gds/WWII-German-military-issue-service-watches-/10000000004657856/g.html

- **Aviator Style Sunglasses (AO ® and Ray-Ban)**

During the early 1930's, *American Optical* (*AO*) once supplied the Air Force with aviator goggles, including the U.S.A.C. Goggle Type B-6 and later the Type B-7 model. The goggles were fitted with several color lenses (green caliber, amber, smoke-gray and clear).

As early as 1940, *American Optical* offered to the U.S military, prescription-polarized sunglasses. They helped reduce the glare that occurred from reflective surfaces radiating from the brightness of clouds, water and snow.

Tip: Watch for 1960's, Vietnam War era, *American Optical* Brand Aviator-style sunglasses. They will be marked on their gold frames-*AO* 1/10 12KGF- and their original cases embossed with -HGU-4/P. The popular, AMC television series "Mad Men" features the character, Don Draper wearing aviator sunglasses. This fact, added to their collectability and demand today. They can sell for over $500 on eBay.

Did You Know?

In 1958, the *AO Company* came out with the Flight Goggle 58 (also known as the original pilot) sunglasses. It was this same type of sunglasses that were honored to be the first ever pair to be part of the landing on the moon, worn by Commander, Neil Armstrong, and the Apollo 11 crew in 1969. They now reside on permanent display in the *Smithsonian Air and Space Museum* in Washington, D.C.

Ray-Ban Aviators

Bausche & Lomb "Ray-Ban", aviator-style sunglasses were made as early as the late 1930s. The prototype for these sunglasses was made of a gold plated metal; and featured dark green lenses made of mineral glass to filter out both infrared and ultraviolet rays. Pilots in the Army Air Corps immediately adopted them, as did pilots in the other branches of the armed forces. The aviator style became synonymous with Ray-Ban. When General Douglas MacArthur landed on the beach in the Philippines during WW II, he was photographed wearing Ray-Ban aviator sunglasses.

1950's Ray-Ban B & L Aviator RB3 12kgf Outdoorsman Green Lens Sunglasses with Case— $550

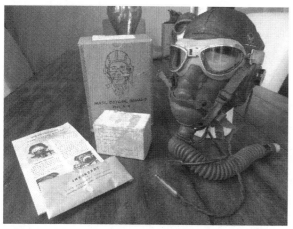

WWII Army Air Corps A-11 Leather Flight Helmet, USAAF A-N 6530 Goggles and A-14 Oxygen Mask

A great online site to view vintage Ray-Bans and their styles can be found at: http://www.vintage-sunglasses-shop.com/designer_ray-ban_display_7.html

A few other types of World War equipment and instructional manuals such as aircraft instruction, flight/pilot, ammunition varieties, German troop vehicle (Jeep and truck) manuals, books, and comic books, such as the *Sub-Mariner*, Comic Books-Mariner was one of *Marvel's* first super-heroes in the 1940s. In near-mint condition, they can sell in the thousands!

CDC- Silver Age WWII Comic
Books

The early 1900s published wartime postcards that exploited war scenes to acquire sentiment from the folks at home (soldier wounded) are among best-selling post cards. Foreign troop postcards (France, Germany, China and Japan), fetch up to a hundred dollars. WWII postcards, were mostly void of photos, but still created sentiment at home with words from American troops.

The above war-related items have revealed only part of the vast arena of militia collecting. Additionally, there are several militaria reference books and online web pages that would be helpful on collecting historic military weapons and ammunition.

The book titled: *Collecting Militaria*, 1976, by Robert Wilkinson –Latham-is an excellent reference book on this subject.

Railroadiana
The arena of collecting all types of railroad memorabilia. Current events, such as railroad mergers, or the abandonment of railroad lines, can spark the interest from collectors to a certain railway line. Your own hometown railroad system may create the need for owning a certain object or artifact from that particular railroad. I

Great Northern Railway Ad.
Holiday Magazine, March 1953

reside in Omaha, Nebraska, which is a major railroad city. Union Pacific Railroad (U. P. R) has its headquarters located here. Omaha is home to the Burlington and Union Train Station (currently the Durham Museum), landmark buildings. Omaha's Union and Burlington Stations were once major depots for several railroad lines connecting and traveling through the state of Nebraska. We have an abundance of local railroad collectors.

Burlington Railroad Depot, Omaha, Ne, ca, 2015

Many railroad hobbyists desire to own particular railroad model train sets, usually of a certain scale (HO and "N" being the most popular), gauge and manufacturer (e.g. *Lionel, Markel, and American Flyer).* Additionally, railroad enthusiasts collect any actual railroad-related relic, which adversely can

Vintage R.R. Crossbuck Signs

promote high prices at local urban auctions (For bargains-search out small town auctions). Collectors will pay a hefty price to possess any model train

Vintage American Flyer Railroad Model Train Cars

239

component or antique railway artifacts from railroad train cars, train tracks and conductors; models and past American railroad-related events. Railroad routes that once existed during the Civil War, the Transcontinental Railroad, early Pullman Palace cars, and the days of those early Western Train Robberies-might generally attract more interest.

Here is a comprised list of collectible railroad-related items:

Vintage Railroad China

Onondaga Pottery (*O.P. Co*), from Geddes (now part of the city of Syracuse), New York started making pieces of dinnerware for the railroad and restaurant-ware for hotels back in 1871. The original company made over 70 percent of the china used on all rail cars. This company is presently called "Syracuse China", and is a leader in making china for the food industry today. You may remember seeing this type of earthenware china, when being served lunch at the local diner back in the 1960s.

There were thousands of china dinnerware patterns created for the railroad dining cars. While most of these pieces of dinnerware can fetch from $50 to $100; it is the top 10 percent of these patterns can sell between- $300 to $1,000 per piece, depending particular R.R. and patterns of dinnerware.

To help the reader understand this vast area of collecting railroad memorabilia; here are the basic three types of patterns or motifs found in railroad china:
- A pattern that was developed for and exclusively used by one railroad.
- A stock pattern that was adopted and modified in some way by a railroad.
- A stock pattern that was used by a railroad, as is, without any special marking or modification.

Here is a list of some of the most collectible dinnerware patterns today and the name of their railroad line:
- Minneapolis St. Paul & Sault Ste. Marie's, *SOO Line's*, "Citation"

- *Union Pacific's* "Columbine", "Harriman Blue" and "Portland Rose"- from the 1930s
- *Chicago, Burlington & Quincy Railroads* "Chuck Wagon"
- *Atchison Topeka & Santa Fe Railway's* (AT & SF)- "California Poppy"
- *Great Northern Railroad's*- "Oriental" pattern.
- *Southern Pacific's*- "Prairie Mountain Wildflower" and "Golden Gate"
- Northern Pacific's, "Garnet"
- *MK&T Railroad*, also known as the "*Katy Lines*" pattern called "Alamo"

Vintage 1920's Southern Pacific Lines, "Sunset Pattern"
Platter by Syracuse-$75

There are many more highly, desired railroad china patterns not mentioned above. The subject of collecting and identifying railroad-dining car china, warrants its own reference book.

Here is a helpful eBay site I found for helping identify and date this china: http://www.ebay.com/gds/Guide-to-Date-Codes-and-Backstamps-for-Syracuse-China-/10000000000132854/g.html

Furthermore, Holloware tableware and flatware serving pieces used in the dining cars are garnered today.

The term "Holloware" relates to the refined and diverse, thicker silver-plated, R.R. dining car table service wares such as bowls, pots, compotes, pitchers, candlesticks and candelabras. Sterling silver was also used for the fancier railroad business cars. Principal silver manufacturers were *Reed & Barton, International, Gorham, R. Wallace,* and *Smith* Silversmiths. They will feature a railroad's specific stamp applied to them.

Here are recommended educational and reference books I found on the subject of collecting railroad china: *Restaurant China: Identification & Value Guide for Restaurant* by Barbara J. Conroy and *Dining on Rails: An Encyclopedia of Railroad China* by Richard W. Luckin

Railroad Ephemera- Search through boxes at auctions for any railcar menus, calendars, train schedules & travel brochures; steam train photos, posters and framed prints. (One of the most remarkable examples of railroad paper artwork is the series of Native American portraits which was done by Winold Reiss (1886-1953) for the *Great Northern Railway*.)

Railroad Wax Seals- These small tool implements were used up until the latter part of the 1940s. They measured 2 -1/2-inch to 4-inch tall and mostly featured a decorative or plain wood handle attached to a bronze or brass head (some were in one-piece in brass or bronze). The wax sealer would be used to imprint the name of whom-ever was sending a message into the wax seal. They were used to make sure letters and packaged contents weren't altered. The sealer will feature its railroad name or information, and the location from which it was used- imprinted on it.

1960's Missouri Pacific Rairoad Line Route Map

Railway Destination Posters-Early 1900s posters depicting railroad lines and their destinations are selling into the thousands range depending on condition.

Railcar Builders Plates-Railroad Builder's plates were made of a cast metal iron, brass or stamped metal plate (later plates); they are affixed to locomotives and other R.R. equipment. They are used to identify the particular origin or manufacturer. This plate gives the builders name, the sequential number of construction, location of the builder and usually the month or year of its construction.

Some plates have information added, such as the classification of the locomotive or certain specifications. Plates can be salvaged from retired and scrapped locomotives frames.

There were three major types of steam locomotive manufacturers in the U.S.A. They are: The *Baldwin Locomotive Works, ALCO (American Locomotive Company)* and *Lima Locomotive Works.* Some smaller locomotive companies included: *Cooke, Pittsburgh, Dickson, Richmond, Vulcan* and *Porter.*

Plates were additionally made in steam locomotive 'Shops'. A few of these shops were the *Juniata Shops of Pennsylvania Railroad, Roanoke Shops of the Norfolk & Western Railway* and the *Paducah Shop of Illinois Central Railroad.*

Vintage conductor railroad employee uniforms (in very good to excellent condition).

R.R. Track and Signage (e.g., crossing buck signs, porcelain reflectors, miscellaneous railroad plaques).

Railroad Crossing Lights

Steam Locomotive Bells made of cast bronze or brass-BIG BUCKS

Railroad Pocket Watches-Pocket watches by *Illinois Watch Company* (Bunn Special), *Hamilton* and *Elgin*-are highly collectible.

Railroad Locks and Switch Keys-HOT! Any railroad lock that is cast or stamped with a railroads initials or title is collectible!

Vintage Adlake Railroad Switch Lock
and Key

Railroad switch keys will usually be stamped with a code that describes what they open, particular railroad initials, and the maker's hallmark. Collectors are on the look-out for unique designs and certain R.R. type which can fetch into the upper-hundreds-range.

Tip: A lock doesn't need a key, to be considered valuable. The most treasured locks are heart-shaped locks once used to secure switches. Early locks were cast from brass that sometimes had some ornate patterns or logos imprinted on them.

Most collectors place a huge value finding a railroad key showing its original patina-not-cleaned and polished. Cleaning them can significantly destroy their value.

Railroad Lanterns and Lamps- The manufacturers of *Adlake, Dietz* and

Dressel-are some of the most desired to collect.

Did You Know? Railroad lamps and lanterns are two different

types of railroad lighting.

Switch lamps were mounted somewhere on the caboose, train or stationary.
Large lenses were used to amplify the internal light source. Switch lamps are
generally larger and most have lenses used to magnify the light-selling range is
over $500.

Antique Adlake Railroad
Switch-Stand Lamp ,4"
Lenses, 16-1/2" H-$350

1920's Arlington Mfg.
Dressel Stationary Railroad
Lamp $249

Vintage Railroad Signal
Lamp with Large Lenses

Lanterns were designed to be portable/in motion, and
were basically globes surrounded by a metal frame
with a fuel source (i.e. conductor lamps). There are
five main types of railroad lanterns: fixed globe, tall
globe, short globe, inspector and conductor. Prices
fluctuate significantly for the colors of the lanterns
globes. Railroad lanterns found in the scarcer colors
of blue, green and amber globes will fetch higher
prices. Additionally, ornate and oil fuel conductors'
model lanterns (i.e. presentation lanterns) can sell in
the thousand-dollar-range. Antique fixed globe
lanterns cemented in, are extremely hard to discover
and accordingly….valuable!

Rare Antique D.L. & W.R.R
Dietz Vesta Railroad Portable Lantern #14812

For more informative information about railroad collecting, I found this online site to be quite informative: http://www.jeffpolston.com/locks.htm

My husband and I once purchased a 1950's Union Pacific train caboose to convert to a travel agency business. Unfortunately, we came across a lot of red tape with the city council members, so regrettably, the project was canceled and we had to resell the caboose.

I hope the section of "Railroadiana" will give the reader a better awareness in the category of collecting railroad items.

Tobacciana

In this section, we will be discussing some tobacco and smoking-related memorabilia collectibles, which can bring in generous profits when reselling online.

Collecting Vintage Packaged Brands of Cigarettes

Vintage unopened packs or cartons of cigarettes are valuable.
A package of 1920s' *Lucky Strike* Cigarettes can sell for over $900 on eBay! Here's a list of some of the more valuable, oldest (pre-1920s) cigarette packs to watch for: *Pall Mall, Chesterfield, Cravens, Sunshine Sweet Caporal, Helmar, Wings, Natural, Mogul, Murad, Hassan; Egyptian- Prettiest, Straights* and *Deities.*

Even well-known packages from WWII's era, such as *Camel, Lucky Strike, Kool, Viceroy* and *Raleigh* can bring in over $200.

Circa -1910-1920, Carton of Ten Packs of "Camel" Cigarettes

Antique Portage, Mild Havana Combination
Metal Sign Advertisement

Vintage Pack of Camel Cigarettes

Women's Rights Movement

Virginia Slims Cigarettes is a brand of cigarette manufactured by *Altria Group* (formerly-*Phillip Morris Companies*). The brand was introduced in 1968 and marketed to young professional women using the slogan "You've come a long way, baby." Later campaigns in the 1990s used the slogans, "It's a woman thing," and "Find your voice". Packages of Virginia Slims from the 1970s sell as high as $150.

Vintage Cool Cigarette Metal
Advertising Display Stand

Important Online Tobacco Selling Regulations

The online auction sites, such as eBay, have strict rules and regulations for selling tobacco online.

You will need to state in your tobacco-related listing the following information:

- The value of the item is in the collectible packaging, not the tobacco itself.

- The value of the packaging is higher than the current retail price of the tobacco in the package.
- While the package has never been opened, the tobacco inside is *not* for consumption.
- The collectible packaging is not currently available in stores.
- The buyer must be at least 18 years old.
- Both the buyer and the seller must follow all applicable laws and shipping regulations for this transaction.

The online site www.CigarettesPedia.com is a free, comprehensive, web-based, cigarette encyclopedia project. It has the largest collection of rare, exclusive, old and new cigarette boxes and packaging with invaluable information about cigarette brands, the history of their appearance, and their manufacturers. Created in 2006, this website features over 30,000 images and articles contributed from avid cigarette collectors from all around the world.

Another online website that specializes in this collecting arena is: http://www.cigarettepacks.ru/index

Ashtrays

Why are ashtrays collectible? One thought is they are small objects produced during some of the most creative periods in history. The fabulous ashtrays from the Victorian, Arts and Crafts, Art Deco and Mid-century Eras, are the most popular. Ashtrays are sort of a snapshot for a certain culture, so it is not uncommon to find ashtrays that were produced to advertise products and events of that day or place of business (hotels, restaurants, casinos etc.).

I have comprised a partial list of some of the most collected ashtrays:
- Vintage porcelain ashtrays made by Hermes of Paris, France. Selling range- between $100 and $500.
- Ashtray stands from the Art Deco and Mid-century Era can bring in over $150. Always keep in mind the items condition and particular design.

- Antique Deco slag Glass and agate smoking stands sell in the $300 area.
- Vintage bronze figural ashtrays sell for over $200
- Ashtrays used for advertising reasons, can sell in the hundred-dollar-range.
- Ashtrays from events, such as the World's Fairs from the early 20th century -selling range is between $50-$75
- Mid-Century pottery pieces in geometric shapes made from ceramic or pottery- "California Pottery" can sell in the hundreds.

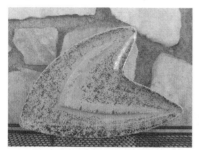

Atomic Age, Shawnee Pink & Gold "Boomerang" Pottery Ashtray-$45

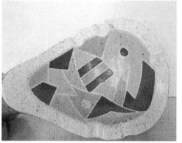

Vintage 1950's Mid-century, Signed, Barbara Willis Ceramic Modernist Ashtray (7.75")- $94.95

- Authentic Italian Murano Art Glass ashtrays
- Crystal ashtrays created by *Baccarat*, *Waterford* and *Lalique* with acid etched signatures or those with their original labeling.
- Airline transportation-themed ashtrays sell in the $300 range

Mid-century Airplane Ashtray

- Edgar Brandt-Art Deco Era, wrought-iron bronze-coated ashtrays are very valuable selling for over a thousand dollars.

Edgar Brandt was born in Paris on December 24, 1880. By trade, was an excellent artist-blacksmith, who combined traditional forging methods with emerging technologies of the machine age such as torch welding and power hammers.

In 1902 he set up an ironworks establishment to create light battle armaments in Paris. Brandt also began producing wrought-iron pieces ranging from gateways, grills, elevator doors, floor lamp bases, consoles and chairs- just to name a few. Chandeliers and lamps were designed and produced in partnership with the glass manufacturer - Daum Freres - in Nancy, France. All were done in the popular Art Nouveau style. His wrought-iron was completed with bronze finishes and incorporated architectural elements with floral motifs.

In 1919, Brandt inherited a machine shop from his father and opened a studio with the help of thirty metalworkers and designers, and the architect- Henri Favier. Around the 1920s, Brandt's style began to shift to reflect the geometric forms and style of the Art Deco years of the 1920s and 1930s.

Art Deco Wrought Iron Edgar Brandt
Polar Bear Ashtray

Chic, Cigarette Cases- a cigarette case depends on its design, age, and the material they were made from. Was it signed by a famous maker, or previously owned by a famous person? These are all important points, when appraising vintage cigarette cases. The factors of rarity, style and fashion warrants the garnering of vintage decorative cigarette holding cases, as well.

Did You Know?

A beautiful cigarette case once used and owned by the famous actress, Rita Hayworth; sold for a whopping $5,720 at auction. Ms. Hayworth, and her own personal cigarette case, was featured on a '40s *Chesterfield* Cigarette advertisement. Her *Chesterfield* cigarette case was fashioned from sterling silver in a trapezoid design and embellished with a simulated ruby, moonstone and green tourmaline floral bouquet wrapped in a yellow gold scroll on the front. It was signed with Rita Hayworth's signature in red enamel.

French jewelers, such as *Cartier* and *Van Cleef & Arpels* created luxurious gold, cigarette cases covered with gemstones, such as diamonds, rubies, and semi-precious stones- sell in the thousands.

Not-so-common cigarette cases are valuable especially if found in excellent condition. A designer from Paris, France from the 1920s, Raymond Templier, created exquisite lacquered cases as well as silver-and-enamel cases featuring colored geometric patterns.

Guilloche cases-can sell in the thousands-of-dollars, especially the cigarette cases designed by George Adam (G. A.) Scheidt.

During the Art Deco Era- *Napier* cigarette cases, sterling silver cases done in repoussé and filigree designs, as well as, enameled cases with bold graphic images of animals and airplane shapes-are sought-after.

Nouveau Sterling Silver Repoussé
Winged Horse Cigarette Case Art

Lot of Cigarette Pack Holders and "Buffalo"
Tobacco Bag

Vintage Premier "Supermatic"
Cigarette Making Machine

Chic-Cigarette Table-top and Pocket Lighters (e.g., *Zippo, Dunhill & Ronson*)

Early *Zippo®* Lighters are prized collectibles.

Some *Zippo* lighters can be found with 14k gold cases, weighing approximately 29 grams and sell for over a thousand dollars. They can also come in sterling silver or solid titanium cases. Watch for the 1950's *Zippo's* Town and Country series, handcrafted painted lighters.

The earliest of the Town and Country lighters had deep etched designs and the artist would apply several layers of acrylic enamel paint. These are the most prized by collectors. Origin models created were the; Mallard Duck, Trout, an English Setter, Geese, Horse, Pheasant, Lily Pad, and the Sailboat. By 1958, the only models offered were the Trout, Mallard and Pheasant. These lighters came in silk-lined boxes to protect their surface paint.

The *Zippo* WWII Black Crackle-heavily painted- four barrel lighters featuring a 14-hole chimney-sells for over $550 if found in their original packaged boxes. Flat-bottomed, *Crackle* lighters are the oldest, which were made in 1942. In 1943-1945, the bottom and top edges of these cases were rounded.

The 1970s *Marlboro* Advertisement-Longhorn Star & Steer lighters- can sell for over $800 in unused condition; and specific *Harley Davidson* prototypes from the 1990s fetch a large sum of cash.

1980's Disney- themed *Zippo* lighters are additionally collectible selling in for over hundred dollars. Keep in mind, finding them in their original labeled boxes--all the better! If you find an old lighter in a drawer, see if you can locate its original box as well.

Vintage Marlboro Advertisement Lighter

Vintage 1982 ZIPPO Walt Disney World Epcot Cigarette Lighter

Early lavish *Alfred Dunhill Ltd* lighters, dating from 1920s - 1950s are highly collectible. The *Dunhill* "Aquarium" and "Aviary" Lucite plastic, paneled lighters that were introduced in 1949, featured reverse-carved; and painted illustrations of fish and bird ion their front sides, sell for over $2,000 on eBay auctions- if found in excellent condition. Other Lucite based cigarette lighters from the mid-century, sell in the hundred-dollar-range.

Vintage 1950's-Skier Evans Clearfloat Lucite Table Lighter with a Chrome Finish -$70

The ornate and famous Art Deco Era "Ronson" table lighters and cigarette cases are valuable. Ronson lighters are also known as the "World's Greatest Lighter". Watch for the Deco cigarette case/lighter combos and Touch Tip table-top lighters.

Vintage Art Deco, Enameled-Table Top Lighter

Vintage 1930's Art Deco Ronson Tortoise Shell Enamel Chrome T132C&E Near Mint—Cigarette Case Lighter—$135

For viewing some of most wanted lighters sought-after, I found an online site devoted to the art of collecting lighters at:

http://www.vintagelighterbook.com/html/all_lighters_.html

"Old West" Memorabilia Mania!

Vintage Western-themed articles bring in Big Bucks!

This section will discuss those western- themed objects that might be overlooked when looking for collectible items to sell.

Every man loves those-oldie but goodie- western movies made from 1930s - 1960s. The western film industry often portrays the conquest of the wilderness, or the seizure of territorial rights from original inhabitants of the frontier lands. Specific settings include lonely isolated forts, ranch houses, the isolated homestead, the saloon, the jail; livery stable, the small-town Main Street or small frontier towns dotted across the western plains.

They may even include Native American sites or villages. Other iconic elements in western films included those popular, Stetsons and spurs, saddles, lassos and Colt .45 revolvers, bandannas and buckskins; stagecoaches, gamblers, long-horned cattle and cattle drives; prostitutes (or madams) with a heart of gold, and more. Let's not forget, the cowboy usually featured his "faithful steed". Roy Rogers favored horse was-"Trigger", Gene Autry's-"Champion", William Boyd's (Hopalong Cassidy)-"Topper", the Lone Ranger's- Silver and Tonto's-"Scout". All these fictional old west cowboys were popularized in books, radio, TV and movies in mid-century America. The demand for owning any of these related items is the latest rage. Vintage wild west-themed character toys, posters, Golden Age comic books, games, school lunchboxes and non-sport trading card sets (1940 Gum Inc.- Lone Ranger and 1950's Topps-Hopalong Cassidy), can bring in hundreds of dollars. Cherished are the tales of Davy Crockett, Daniel Boone, Jim Bowie, Gen. George A. Custer, Wild Bill Hickok, Buffalo Bill Cody, Calamity Jane, Wyatt Earp; Doc Holliday and Bat Masterson. Notorious outlaws, such as the James Brothers- the original "Butch Cassidy and the Sundance Kid"- and "Billy the Kid"- all bring back those fond memories, inspiring many of us to collect a bit of our American western heritage.

So, Yippee-Ki-Yay, we have some fine-e-fied news for you all folks to find that "Bonanza." So what in tarnation are we waiting for? Let's not dilly-dally around. Let's get a wiggle on how to hit the "Pay Dirt."
Let's find some western memorabilia "Cash Bonanza's."

Western Silver Belt Buckles

Belt buckles have been around for years. The most common types of belt buckles include frame-style, plate-style, and box-frame buckles.

Elvis Presley was presented a huge handcrafted gold buckle in 1969 from the *Nevada International Hotel* (Known today as the *Hilton*), for his record breaking sold out performances to a crowd of 2,000 people for 29 days (two shows per day).

1969 Elvis Presley-Style Gold- World Record Attendance 8″ Belt Buckle Replica-selling for over $300

The original buckle was cast in silver, gold plated and studded with diamonds, sapphires and rubies. (I am sure it is worth a grand amount of $$$$$ today.)

For a peak at this unbelievable belt buckle; go online to the website: http://arkhamhaus.com/elvis.html

A great example of a plate-style belt buckle, are the rare, hand-crafted buckles designed by Augustus Owsley "Bear" Stanley and his close friend, Bob Thomas. Owsley's name is synonymous with the heavy rock band, *The Grateful Dead* of the "Steal Your Face" emblem-fame. Owsley made belt buckets from cast silver and bronze , then inscribed with the backs of them with his signature. His original belt buckles can sell for over $18,000.

Vintage 1983, Augustus Owsley Stanley "Steal Your Face" #1
Silver Belt Buckle-sold online for $3,350-

Elaborate, high-quality, western-style sterling silver belt buckles (some with 10k, 14k or 18k gold overlay added), are those specially designed and hand engraved by *Clint Ormes*, *Sunset Trails*, *Comstock Heritage*, *Greg Jensen*; and *R. Schaerlein & Son*, who once to designed buckles for Levi Strauss & Co. and trophy/award belt buckles. These exquisite belts and buckles can also sell over $2,000. Their high-end buckles can feature 14k gold, western-themed icons in the center (e.g., longhorn steer, star, cowboy, fish and bucking horse etc.). The Southwest Native American handcrafted silversmith sterling silver belt buckles with inlaid turquoise, jasper, onyx and mother of pearl semi-precious stones can sell for hundreds of dollars. They are in high demand, with selling prices in the upper-hundreds range.

Cowboy Spurs and *Stetson* Hats

Vintage spur sets by *Kelly* and *J. O. Bass,* sell for over $1,000! Eduardo Garcia, *McChesney* and *Crocket,* can sell for over $500. Watch for sterling silver engraved sets, and pay attention to any noted markings to help identify them.

Cowboy spurs by James Oscar Bass (*J O Bass*) from Atlanta, Georgia-were to become one of the greats amongst the industry because of their rarity and quality.

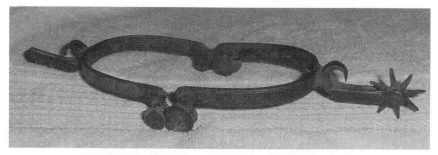

Vintage Sterling Silver *Crockett* Spurs sold for $450

Vintage Pre-1920's, Western Cowboy
McChesney "Bottle Opener" Spurs sold
for $791

Robert John McChesney made spurs for some famous people, such as Will Rogers and numerous other famous rodeo riders. *McChesney Bit and Spur Company* spurs are stamped MCCHESNEY on the outside of each spur-underneath the buttons. McChesney, was also commissioned to make the spurs for the US Army during WWI. Look for the stamped-MCCHESNEY on the outside of each spur, underneath the buttons.

Stetson Cowboy and miscellaneous hats can fetch over $500. Watch for the *El Presidente* 200x & 100x felt hats; the "Open Road", "Whippet", and "Stratoliner" styles.

Vintage Western Stetson Cowboy Hats

***Marx* Brand Toys-** During the 1950's, *Louis Marx & Co.* became the largest toy manufacturer in the world, with the companies tin litho type toys, which are a hot commodity to own currently by vintage toy collectors. *Louis Marx and Co.* was the largest and most successful firm to produce tin litho toys from the 1920s to the 1960s.

1968 Western Marx Fort Apache Toy Set #3681-NRFB

Marx Brothers, Louis and David had a formula for success: To produce a large volume from a large number of designs. This allowed them to keep their prices at a reasonable level. In 1921, they purchased the tooling for two obsolete tin toy dies from toymaker Ferdinand Strauss, a former employee of Louis Marx. They soon became millionaires from the companies success.

Vintage tin litho sets, such as those made by Marx Toys are amongst the leaders with some of these complete toy sets from the 1950s and 1960s selling for over $3,000. Here is a list of some highly collectible western-themed, *Marx* tin litho toy sets:

- Johnny Ringo Western Frontier
- Fort Apache
- Custer's Last Stand
- Wagon Train
- Roy Roger's-Western Town
- Fort York
- Giant Blue and Gray Civil War
- The Rifleman Ranch
- 1950s TV series "Gunsmoke"- Dodge City

History of Tin Litho Toys

Tin Lithograph toys are made from tinplate, which are thin sheets of steel, plated with tin. Toys using tinplate began production in the mid-1800s.
The earliest tin litho toys were made and painted by hand. In the 1850s spring activated tin toys were produced in Germany. Offset lithography, a technique used to print designs on tinplate using a rubber roller, was introduced in the 1880s.

Germany was the major producer of tin litho toys during the early 1900s. Then the countries of France and England joined in. The United States had also started to produce tinplate toys with some smaller manufacturing firms, but experienced real growth after World War I. There was an ample supply, when tin ore mines were opened in Illinois. After WWI, there was a high level of anti-German sentiment, which yielded an overwhelming demand for American produced products. By the 1920s, American firms were the industry leaders of manufacturing tin toys.

The colorful designs on the toys were applied through a process known as chromolithography. Used previously in the printing industry, chromolithography involved making a drawing on special stones using a grease pencil before the printing ink was applied. When wetted, the ink holds fast to the drawing and not the wet stone.

Marx **Western Action Figures**

In 1965, with success in the action figure market with their previous military action figure "Stony Smith"; *Marx* released western action figures with the Daniel Boone figure being the forerunner. This was followed by a 12" cowboy action figure named "Johnny West" from the 1960s, which are selling for over $200 when complete with original accessories and with their original box. The series also included cowboy, Johnny West's horse "Thunderbolt", and the Indian Chief "Cherokee". In 1966, Jane West, and her horse "Flame" was introduced. Over the next few years, Marx introduced several figures to their Johnny West series.

1960's *Marx* Johnny West Action Figures

Vintage Western Wear

Western apparel (jackets with matching trousers or skirts; slacks and shirts from the 1950s-the Rockabilly Era), made from fabric types, such as gabardine and denim, in gingham (check) patterns; plain with lots of fringe, and with fancy embroidered accents--are in high demand for vintage western/southwestern wear clothing lovers.

When envisioning western attire, I think of the fashionable outfits seen in old magazine photos of Patsy Cline, Merle Haggard, Jim Reeves, Hank Williams, Tennessee Ernie Ford, Kitty Wells, Dale Evans and Jean Shepard.

Photo of Country Western Performers

Vintage *California* Ranchwear, Gabardine Western Shirt-$165

Vintage '50s *Karman* Gabardine Western Shirt Green With Gold Piping-$140

Vintage Western *H Bar T* Ranchwear Childs Outfit

Did You Know? Jean Shepard was the first female country music artist to sell over a million records? Jean was born in Oklahoma and was the lead singer of her first group called the "Melody Ranch Girls." Shepard had been a *Capitol Records* recording artist since 1953. Her first hit was as a duet partner with Ferlin Husky called "A Dear John Letter." In 1955, she had her first solo top ten single, "A Satisfied Mind." She joined the *Grand Ole Opry* in 1956 and has been a member for over 50 years. Unfortunately, her husband "Hawkshaw Hawkins" also a honky-tonk singer, was killed in the same plane crash as Patsy Cline in 1963.

Other notable cash-cows in the western category are:

- Native American hand woven saddle blankets created by Navajo artists
- Vintage Cowboy/Cowgirl Leather boots, by brands, such as Tony Lama; Stewart Romero and Lucchese. Alligator and Ostrich skin vintage cowboy boots are selling for over $700 in very good condition. Cowgirls love the boots with intricate inlaid patterns in the leather. (My daughter owns the pair of boots in the left-hand photo.)

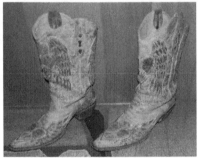 

Designer Leather Cowgirl Boots

Designer Leather Cowboy Boots

- *Brothers*, whiskey barrel style living room and rec-room pieces which feature, sofas, chairs, coffee table, bars, card tables. *Brothers Furniture* of Livermore, KY produced whiskey barrel furniture, which was sold at *J.C Penney's* stores. It was by far, the coolest of the tacky furniture of its time. *Brothers Furniture* literally had an entire catalog of whiskey-barrel furniture made of re-appropriated Jack Daniel's one-inch-thick, white oak, whiskey barrels that were offered for sale through department stores in the Midwest during the late-1960s. While lacking the elegance of other mid-century pieces; these pieces had a fun appearance with diamond-shaped, tufted naugahyde (artificial leather) chairs accompanied with their half-barrel style game table. They were masterpieces in their own way.

Vintage Whiskey Barrel Coffee Table, Sofa, Poker Table and Chairs

Upcycling of whiskey barrels is the latest rage. You can find coffee tables, horticulture containers and much more, created from them.

Vintage western themed furniture made by the *A. Brandt Company,* which includes Ranch Oak Brand Living room pieces sell in the hundreds. The term for this particular style of furniture is considered "cabin chic" style.

Brandt Company, Inc. made its debut with their "Ranch Oak" furniture line in Fort Worth, Texas in 1938, and continued manufacturing the Ranch Oak line into the 1980s. The company's earliest furniture designs depicted images of ranch life carved into their oak home furnishings. Pictorial carvings included:

horses, horse heads and horseshoes, longhorns, campfires, saguaro and prickly pear cactus, and even a western scene of a cowboy riding a bucking bronco. By the 1970s, it looked as though factory catalogs were showing fewer if any, of these western motif-carved pieces; however, some of the longhorn (or steer head) and horse head lamps are still seen in some of the mid-1970s catalogs. During America's mid-century you may have stayed in a National Park Lodge, motel, or on a military base (many pieces were produced under government contract to furnish military bases around the U.S), that furnished rooms with these rustic furnishings.

The *A. Brandt* mid-century furniture sets are trendy currently, and sell for over $1,000 for a sectional set.

A. *Brandt* "Ranch Oak" Mid-century sofa

Vintage *A. Brandt* "Ranch Oak Label

Vintage *A. Brandt* Arm Chair

Vintage Western Dinnerware
Wallace China

The *Wallace* China-"Westward Ho" Pattern by Till Goodan is one to keep an eye out for. Also, Wallace China's wildly popular-action-packed, "Rodeo" pattern, which was introduced in the 1940s, has been recreated by *True West* (per permission from Till Goodan's daughter), for a new generation of western –themed china.

The western art designed pieces by Till Goodan, thrills many today, as it did then. The vintage, as well as the newer pieces produced in 1990; depict rodeo scenes, scenes from a cowboy's life and authentic working ranch brands. From bull riding, trick rope spinning, bareback riding, bronco riding, steer wrestling and cattle herding; this pattern is full of, that long ago American hero, the "Cowboy."

Till Goodan also put a great deal of research into selecting North American brands to surround his artwork pieces. Brands such as the "Running W" from the famous King Ranch in Texas; the "Circle A", which is the official state brand of Arizona; and the "O Bar O Ranch" -- a famous, old New Mexico ranch (once the hide-out of Billy the Kid), encircle each piece of dinnerware. Over 250 brands were used throughout the original pattern. Till Goodan's original rodeo dinnerware was reproduced in 1990 by *True West Chinaware Store*. *True West*'s Store has the exclusive license to signed, Till Goodan artwork.

Just recently, I discovered the high collectability of this dinnerware, but unfortunately the knowledge came too late to help my neighbor to make a hefty cash profit at her sale. My neighbor Julie had held the yard sale for a friend of hers that had passed away, and had requested my opinion about pricing some dinnerware that had been found in a box. The set featured a western themed pattern and the box held at least 25 pieces. Julie knew I operated an estate sales business so she respected my opinion. I suggested that she put a price tag on the box for $60.

After the sale was finished, I asked Julie, "What did that dinnerware sell for?" She stated that the dishes immediately sold. I found out later from a local antique dealer that he had been the buyer of these dishes, and he resold them on eBay for over $1,400. I thought to myself, "The box of western-patterned dinnerware?" I decided to do some research online in hopes of finding what was so special about these unique dishes. I did discover the pattern and discovered a similar set sold for $1,000 on eBay. They were vintage *Wallace* dishes in a pattern called "Rodeo" from their "Westward Ho" line.

I was happy for the dealer who made a profit, but disappointed I had not recognized them as being valuable.

Vintage Mid-Century Wallace China Set

Vintage 1940's Wallace China of California; "Westward Ho" by Till Goodan

Here is a comparison guideline to help when identifying differences from mid-century Wallace China brands, versus the newer-*True West* Chinaware store line.

The original *Wallace* China western pieces included the following patterns:

- Rodeo-very collectible
- Boots & Saddle
- Pioneer Trails (two colors)
- Little Buckaroo child's set
- Longhorn (two colors)
- El Rancho-very collectible
- Chuck Wagon

    Note: These are the "Westward Ho" patterns -- a collection of the first five patterns made for linens, glassware, paper products, etc.

The 1990's, *True West Store* reproduction patterns include the following patterns:

- Rodeo
- Boots & Saddle
- Little Buckaroo
- Longhorn
- Christmas Cowboy (created by True West's Mark Clay from vintage, Till

Goodan Christmas cards)

Any piece marked Wallace China is vintage; however, a "True West" marked piece, is newer. Full back-stamps make the identification process clear, so be careful when identifying these pieces before listing them for sale online.

Wallace China used different back stamps over the years, but if a piece has a Wallace China back stamp- it is vintage.

Wallace Identification Back-stamp Marks:

Wallace China back-stamps won't be found on a piece after 1964. This is when its parent company, *Shenango China* liquidated the company. *Wallace* China was purchased by *Shenango China* in 1959, and *Wallace* back stamps were phased out thereafter. A pattern that was originally introduced by *Wallace* may actually have a *Shenango* back-stamp. A *Shenango* back-stamp on one of the earlier 20th century, western patterns indicates a vintage piece as well. Please note their backstamps for dating details.

For more information, please note the online link: http://www.restaurantwarecollectors.com/forums/showwiki.php?title=True+West+vs+Wallace+China

Moreover, the original vintage *Wallace* China dishes were also very sturdy and useful, thus used in the new American pastime --"The Cookout" the outdoor eating event we all cherish.

The *Wallace* Westward Ho-Rodeo patterns were a tremendous success. Action drawings of rodeo events surrounded by authentic cattle brands appealed to westerners of every persuasion. Rodeo dinnerware graced the tables of restaurants, hotels and ranches. Big names like Gene Autry, Roy Rogers and Bing Crosby-all owned sets of Rodeo ware. Today, the original "Westward Ho" and "El Rancho" lines, made from the Wallace China dinnerware patterns are prized collectibles.

Monterrey Western Ware Enamelware-was introduced in the 1960s and is quite popular to collect. A product of Mexico, they were made with unique western themed transfer motifs, on rimmed plates surrounded by branding iron symbols. Chuckwagon dinner sets sell in the hundreds!

Vintage 1960's Monterrey Western Ware Large Serving Bowl

Vintage 1960's Monterrey Western Ware- Enamelware "Cowboy" Coffee Pot- $65

Roy Rogers **Memorabilia**

The success of the "Roy Rogers Show" (1951-1957), a television series; played a great part in Roy Rogers, Dale Evans and their faithful horse, "Trigger" mania collecting. Items such as lunch boxes with a thermos bottle, in very good condition sell in the hundreds based on their condition. Unfortunately, corrosion will take its toll on vintage metal if not properly cared for. Humidity in the air can really hurt it, so it is when we find these items well kept in a closet away from moisture and sun. d

Photo of Roy Rogers and Dale Evans

Vintage 1950s *Roy Rogers* Gold Foil and Red Jeweled- Gun Holster with Guns, Bullets-sold for $600

Vintage Rare *Roy Rogers* Kilgore Cap Gun
Pair with Leather Holster. Selling range
$450

A bit of trivia about Mr. Roy Rogers and Dale Evans:

Roy Rogers (1911 - 1998) - real name, or name at birth, was Leonard Franklin Slye. In the mid-1930s when he began getting bit parts in movies, he used the name Dick Weston. In late 1937 he signed a movie deal with Republic Studios and in early 1938 changed his name to Roy Rogers. The last name "Rogers" was chosen by the studio of the popularity of the recently deceased Will Rogers. When one of the studio executives suggested using "Leroy" as a first name, Len refused. While growing up he had known a kid that he didn't like with that name, so he refused to have the name assigned to him. After a little consideration Len suggested just shortening "Leroy" to "Roy" and the studio liked it. Although, he began using the name Roy Rogers in 1938, he didn't legally change his name to Roy Rogers until 1942. As Roy Rogers quoted, "It's the way you ride the trail that counts."

Roy Rogers, *Hartland Buttermilk* play figures; guns with holsters and accessories are very collectible. A rare Dale Evans toy cap gun, can sell for over $400, a Roy Rogers holster, cap toy gun and ammo set-recently sold for over $1,200 recently on an online auction.

Vintage Roy Rogers, Hartland
Buttermilk Play Set and Figures

Other nostalgic western-themed

1950's/60's toy cap guns and toy rifles, are also quite valuable in excellent condition, such as Mattel's "Shootin Shell" *HopaLong Cassidy* cast iron toy guns, and Gene Autry's-Kenton Toys, cap guns-just to name a few.

Vintage Time, Ingersoll Wrist
Watch with Original Box. Valued
at $150

A wonderful reference guide to collecting vintage toys and up-to-date values is : *Toys & Prices: The World's Best Toys Price Guide* by Mark Bellomo.

Did You Know?

A rare soda pop can produced in the 1950's (lemon lime) featuring Roy Rogers and Dale Evans, sold for $600 online in 2014.

Here is a great informational online site for collecting beverage cans: https://www.canmuseum.com

Roy Rogers- pocket knives manufactured by *Ulster* of USA featuring a gold horse, can sell in the $200 dollar range.

Vintage 1950's *Roy Rogers* -tin lithograph lunchboxes sell over $200 as well.

Speaking of other valuable vintage lunchboxes to collect, here is a list of some of the most desired: 1950's Superman lunch boxes, 1960's TV series, "Star Trek"; *The Beatles, The Jetsons* and other well-known cartoon characters from the mid-century in excellent condition, can bring in thousands.

Lunchbox collectors will pay a large amount to obtain a revered TV characters or musicians.

"Snoopy" of Peanuts Fame,
Metal Lunchbox

Vintage Pacman Metal,
Lunchbox

Vintage LEVI STRAUSS Denim Blue Jeans and Jackets-Eureka!

The usage of denim fabric in America's history, had a meek start with making tough work clothes, but their evolution and popularization over the years have made them a permanent part of American culture with their popularity spreading throughout the world. Especially desired are denim fabric used to manufacture blue jean apparel by "*Levi Strauss*" and "*Lee*" Companies.

If you are lucky enough to come across the earliest LEVI'S denim shirts, jackets and blue jeans, (known in the earlier 1900's, as waist overalls) "EUREKA!!!"

Denim and the history of iconic Blue Jeans Clothing

In 1853, the California gold rush was in full swing, and everyday items were in short supply. Levi Strauss, a 24-year-old German immigrant, left New York for San Francisco with a small supply of dry goods with the intention of opening a branch of his brother's New York dry good's business. Shortly after his arrival, a prospector wanted to know what Mr. Levi Strauss was selling.

When Strauss told him he had rough canvas to use for tents and wagon covers, the prospector said, "You should have brought pants!" Stating he couldn't find a pair of pants strong enough to last when digging for gold.

Levi Strauss had the canvas made into waist overalls. Miners liked the pants, but had complained they tended to scratch the knees. Levi Strauss substituted a twilled cotton cloth from France called "serge de Nimes", which was a right hand twill fabric with a woven pattern rising left to right. The opposite direction twill (right to left), was used traditionally on "Lee" jeans. This twilled cotton fabric later became known as denim. Denim is woven with a dyed "warp" yarn and a natural "fill" yarn. The pants were nicknamed "Blue Jeans" which started the beginning of the "Blue Jean Hysteria".

Levi Strauss & Company History

In 1873, "Levi Strauss & Company" began using the pocket stitch design. Levi Strauss and a Reno, Nevada-based Latvian tailor by the name of Jacob Davis co-patented the process of putting rivets in pants for strength. On May 20, 1873, they received a U.S. patent. This date is now considered the official birthday of "blue jeans". Levi Strauss asked Jacob Davis to come to San Francisco to oversee the first manufacturing facility for "waist overalls", as the original jeans were known. The two-horse label, brand design was first used in 1886. Just in time for the last great "Alaskan Klondike Gold Rush".

This was great timing for the introduction of denim blue jeans to the numerous prospectors headed for the Alaska and Canada's, Yukon Territory.

Although, Levi's 501® jeans first found favor in the mining and logging communities, they later would become synonymous with cowboys. Blue Jeans became quite iconic with celebrities like, James Dean, Marilyn Monroe, Bing Crosby, the "Duke", John Wayne and Marlon Brando's (a.k.a "The Godfather") role in "The Wild One" for which he wore LEVI'S jeans.

Did you know? Elvis Presley rarely was seen in public wearing denim in the 1950's as he associated the work wear with the poverty of his youth.

Strauss Blue Denim Jacket Levi - Identification Timeline
Pre-1940s
The Mother Lode!!!

The "First Editions" of the *Levi's* jackets-The Mother Lode!

The first Levi's denim jacket had a lot number of 506XX. It had a single breast, left side pocket and had a pleated front. The early version didn't have a pocket flap, which was added on the later jackets. Most of these will *not* have a red-tab and have the buckle-back (cinch-back) fit, with adjustment straps on the center lower back area, much like the denim jeans made in that era. The neck tag (if present) will have a large leather patch, or a pressed card patch (later).

1940s – Late 1950s- This is a highly collectible timeline for LEVI'S, denim jacket fans.

The second edition LEVI's jacket is easily identified by its vertical pleats that run next to the button-down opening. Moreover, it has two exterior patch pockets, but these pockets are definitely more like the rear pockets on a set of jeans (they were constructed from a separate piece of denim that is sewn onto the chest area). In addition, you will also see the "Big E" red tab.

1950s – 1971-These iconic jackets were slimmed down and had a slightly longer silhouette shape with only two pockets. This is generally labeled as the "Type III Edition-70505-0217". The jacket basically may resemble the newer jackets, except for the "Big E" tabs. You will sometimes find these jackets had a quilted blanket lining. Two-tone rows of stitching can be found through-out the jacket. The presence of two adjusting straps on the waistband had replaced the cinch. They were the first Levi's jackets to feature the- now famous pointed pocket flaps. Orange stitching was added later in this period. And they had NO hand warmer pockets.

Vintage Mid-Century LEVI's ®
Jacket

1971 – Mid 1980's-This timeline, has the new small 'e' red-tab on the chest pocket, but solely has only- two pockets. There are NO bottom slash hand pockets within this style. Just chest pockets because they were affordable and only differ from older vintage jackets by subtle features (like the small 'e' red-tab), making this dateline popular with the public. Jackets have a double row of stitching adjacent to the bottom buttonhole.

Other prime vintage denim jackets to search for: **LEE** ®(101's-debuted in 1920s & *401 Riders*-which debuted in 1925) and the "Storm Rider" was introduced in 1933. Levi Strauss also introduced a number of western shirts in 1938. Most collectors like the 1954, "Sawtooth" shirt- named for the shape of the pocket flaps on front of the iconic shirts.

Identifying Fake Levi Strauss, Blue Denim Jackets

When collecting early ('50s) Levi's ® 506 and 507 denim jean jackets and western shirts, identification can be noted by how many pockets are on the front and their side straps. The basic "Rule of Thumb" is two pockets are good and four pockets are bad. Just like the vintage jeans, there are newer replicas being made both here and abroad. There are many subtle clues to search for, when trying to compare the true vintage jeans to fakes, but the best tool is experience and familiarity with vintage types of denim. Is their a care label on the inside of the jacket? If so, it was made post-1970s.

This section will give you some important keys to date a pair of LEVI denim blue jeans, but there are more tips you can find online.

Even a pair of blue jeans with holes in the knees, missing rivets, broken zippers, threads or stitching-broken and patched areas, can still bring in a substantial amount of cash.

A couple of years ago, I sold a pair of damaged 1950's, Levi's blue jean cutoffs for $250!

Where to find these vintage blue jeans?

In someone's garage, a barn and in boxes found in the attic-people kept them around as rags especially people who survived the Great Depression. They saved everything!

I recently had to do a clean-out on someone's garage and discovered in a tattered old cardboard box-a never-worn pair of *Levi's* blue jeans from the late 1960's. I sold the pair for over $1,400 on eBay. Yay!! This pair never made it to the dumpster!

Did You Know? A vintage 1931 *LEE* denim cowboy jacket featuring a *buckle back*, sold for $40,000.

Also, the oldest pair of blue jeans to be found was discovered in a mine at the "Calico Silver Mine" Mojave Desert, California in 1948 dating from the 1890s. It sold on eBay in 2005 for $60,000.

Noteworthy ways to identify a pair of "Levi Strauss" denim blue jeans.

First, When looking for vintage blue jeans, always turn the bottom cuffs of the jeans in question, inside out and look carefully at the fabric selvage edge found on the inside leg seams to of the blue jeans as this selvage has changed through the decades. If the pair is lacking any white selvage-and they have labeled care instructions on the inside-they are *not* old.

If you note a two-toned seam allowance on the inside of the jeans, with white fabric on the outside edge, your jeans may be vintage *Levi's*.

You may have heard the term "Red Line" when talking about vintage *Levi's* blue jeans. This represents the thread that was added to the white selvage after 1927. In 1935, pink colored thread was added to white selvage in early "Lady

Levi's". You may also find a white line of stitching running over this white edge (oldest jeans era), or a blue line of stitching (early 1900's era). Similarly, selvages on the "Wrangler" brand added a gold thread, and white or green threads for Lee jeans.

Vintage 1960s Levi's Blue Jean White Selvage on Leg Inseam

Other Levi's identifying methods:

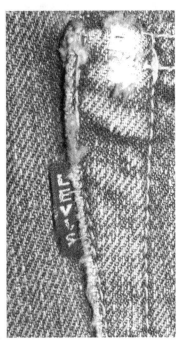

- Levi's "Big E" –this is a term used to describe Levi's clothing before 1971, at which all the upper case "E" Logos appeared on the Red Tab, and were replaced with lower case 'e', after that date. This tab can be found on right back pocket. If the red-tab reads, "Levi's"-the letter "E" is *not* a lower case letter- and the lettering is on both sides of the tab (the side facing forward), than the blue jeans are dated to before the early 1950s.

- Inspect for the presence of a buckle-back. Buckle-backs were introduced before the 1930s. A buckle-back is a buckle that is found on the rear waist of the jeans and was used to tighten the pair of jeans. (Rare to find and

Levi Denim Blue Jeans Pocket- big "E" Red Tab Photo

quite valuable!) In addition, the jeans produced pre-1937 featured a cinched back and a crotch rivet located at the base of the button fly closure. They had belt loops on the waistline during the 1930s, but *no* loops were in place prior to the 1930s. If you come upon a pair of these Levi's blue jeans? You have found a "REAL TREASURE"!

- Examine the rivet button closures. Vintage pairs of jeans that originated before the mid-1970s and prior will have single digits inscribed on the rivet button's back. Most popular, were the numbers 2, 5 and 6 and the letter, "W". The newer pairs of *Levi's* blue jeans, have "501" or "555" stamped on the metal closures.

- If the jeans have "single stitch" back pockets (i.e. lock stitches) and lack of chain stitches on the horizontal double-felled seams on the top of the pockets-it will roughly date the jeans to pre-1976.

- Look at the pocket rivets. Older styles from the mid-1960s to the 1980s, feature flat silver rivets with L.S. & CO-S.F. indented on them. Newer styles feature aluminum or copper

The single digit on the back of the top button on the fly is another vintage LEVI's ID clue. (Hard-to-see)

rivets with circular patterns and L.S. & CO-S.F. indented on them. The circular patterns on the rivets are a sure sign that the Levi's are fairly new.

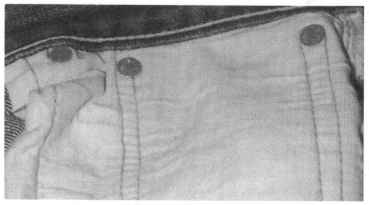

Levi Denim Blue Jean Flat Silver Inside Pocket Rivets

- If the back pockets have hidden rivets (replaced by a bar tack around the year 1966), and if the back plates of the rivets are silver-colored with lowered letters-the jeans date post-1966. Additionally, if the letters on these silver-tone rivets are raised and not lowered, they are pre-1960s.

Vintage '50s/'60s *Levi's* Blue Denim Jean Buttonfly Front Closure

- Zipper-fly closures may date your jeans to post-1947. Button down fronts were used prior to this approximate date.

- Look over the care instruction tags. Older care tags from the 1970s until 1980s used white cloth with dark blue ink. You will also see the instructional phrase "Shrinks about 10%". After 1985, the white care tags have red writing and the *Levi's* emblem placed on the top of the tags. Furthermore, care tags from the 1970s and 1980s have basic washing instructions and the size stamped at the bottom of the tags.

- If a care tag exists inside the *Levi's* jeans, they were made after the 1970s. Care tags don't exist before this date at all, but did feature *Levi's*-stamped care instructions-onto the inside pockets of the jeans.

- During WWII's timeline (1941-1945), the crotch rivet, watch pocket rivets and back cinch are removed to save on fabric and metal. The Arcuate-stitched design on the back pockets is removed and was painted on by the *LS & CO.* factory workers during those years.

- Leather patches found stitched onto the waistline were discontinued in 1955. Stitched on card stock replaced the leather patches. (I sold a pair of Levi's denim jeans for $1,400 on eBay in 2015; the card stock patch lettering, held an indication to their dating because the letter "A" placed above the lot number is only found on jeans made from between 1967-1969, and the digits '0117' in the lot number-only appeared on patches between 1966-1968.)

The ultimate for denim collectors, are 1950s "Big E, Double X Levi's." Meaning, the back patch is marked XX; there are extra rivets at points of wear including hidden rivets inside the pockets; and color is a deep, grainy indigo and are valued at over $5,000 currently.

 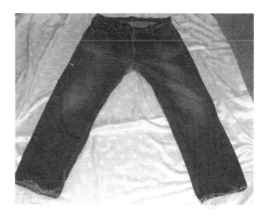

Pairs of 1960's *Levi's* Blue Denim Jeans

Tip: Sizing is important. A 30-inch waist will garner more interest than a 44-inch waist, and a deeper indigo blue pair is more desired more than faded blue jeans.

I found the online video-sharing website called "YouTube", has some helpful videos to help with Levi's blue jean identification methods.

Did You Know?
In the 1950s, denim was banned in some schools, especially on the east coast of the U.S.A., for being a bad influence? With the popularity of the TV and Hollywood-made movies featuring denim-clad "juvenile delinquents" (i.e. James Dean & Marlon Brando), these movies would lead many school administrators to prohibit denim in the classroom. The administration feared that wearing the jeans would lead students to rebel against school authorities. Times have sure changed since blue Jeans are the leading fashion statement in schools today.

LEE Denim Jeans

Henry D. Lee started the "Lee Mercantile Company", in Excelsior Springs, Kansas. His Union-Alls (first coveralls), became very popular in 1913. His first work wear was manufactured in 1911. Lee's "Jelt" denim appeared in 1925. The new coveralls had stronger and longer lasting denim. In 1926, LEE was manufacturing a heavy, 13 oz. jean called the "Cowboy Pant", which was marketed for seamen, loggers, and cowboys. The "Cowboy Pant" was also known as the "Lee 101", and in 1926, LEE introduced the "101Z", the first jean with a zip-fly. LEE was one of the first work-wear manufacturers to use the zipper-which was then a proprietary name; LEE termed its own version, a "Whizit". The "Whizit" zipper was fitted to both Union-Alls and bib overalls in 1928- which became a success.

Identifying Vintage "Lee" Denim
Wording Used on "Lee" Labels

The earlier produced Lee denim used the words: "Union Made" and "Sanforized" with the word "Lee" featuring double "ee's", slanted slightly and facing upwards.

Vintage 1970's Lee Blue Jeans "ee's" on Patch Label, and "ee's" Slightly Slanted

The term "Sanforized" is the mechanical process used for preshrinking fabrics.

One of the oldest LEE jackets from the 1930s features a white background with navy blue stitched lettering. They were called, "housemarks" because of roof shape in the design, along with the "ee's" facing upward.

Here is a list of changes made on Lee Denim blue jeans labels through the years:

- In the mid-1930s, the words, "sanforized," "shrunk" and "Union made", were added.
- In the 1940s, the word, "shrunk" was removed.

- In the 1950s, the word "patented" was added.
- During the 1960s the "R" trademark symbol was added after the word "Lee" and "Made in U.S.A."
- In 1969, the word "Union made" was removed.
- 1970's, the label added "M.R" after the "R" trademark symbol after the word "Lee."

Be careful when in your attempts to identify the date of a pair of LEE and *LEVI'S* blue jeans that you may have found at the local second-hand thrift store or for sale online-fakes/reproductions of vintage *Levi's* denim blue jeans-are worldwide.

Basically, common sense tells us that a pair of blue jeans that are over 50 years old will look tattered in areas. The pair of 1960's *Levi's* jeans I found, had never been worn, you may get lucky, but keep in mind big thrift stores found in the larger cities go through and check for these vintage denim gems before they ever reach the shelves. Check the website www.thecounterfitreport.com.

Other denim companies such as *J. C. Penney's,* came out with their denim work-wear called the "Big Mac" Brand in 1911; and the *Hudson Overall Company*- later to be known as "Blue Bell", creators of *Wrangler®,* opened for business in Greensboro, North Carolina in 1904.

Here are a couple of websites with helpful information on dating *Levi Strauss & Co.* denim blue jeans:

www.vintagemotorcyclejackets.com

http://levisvintageclothing.com/the-historic-501/

https://www.denimhunters.com/2013/05/guide-how-to-date-levis-501-jeans/

A reference book to purchase for helping to identify and date denim: *Vintage Denim & Mens Clothes, Identification and Price Guide: Levis, Lee, Wranglers, Hawaiian Shirts, Work Wear, Flight Jackets, Nike Shoes, and more* by Lucas Jacopetti.

A fantastic online webpage used to help identify fashion labels, fabric and general tips on identifying vintage clothing is:

www.vintagefashionguild.org

$Chapter$ XI

The Popular Iconic Pop Culture called the "Mid-Century Modern Era"

There are several home interior decorating timelines to mention in American History, but I feel the need to converse with my readers, about the iconic "Mid-century Era". Original and replicated mid-century, modern furnishings are in demand. Unfortunately, most items or furnishings from this era are being tossed into dumpsters everyday due to lack of education on current trends in our present day culture. Vintage mid-century and Hollywood Regency style home furnishings and décor--dating from the 1930s through the 1960s--are sought-after. Furniture pieces, such as shelving units, chairs, credenzas, tables and sofas, lead the popularity list. Unfortunately, dining room furniture and bedroom dressers are not as popular with the younger generation. Today, these furnishings are *not* considered necessary to own because the majority of new homes being built offer storage space inside huge closets in the master bedrooms with open kitchens/living room designs (without separate dining rooms). Some mid-century Danish designed dining room sets, are the exception. This generation, *does* appreciate the styles of the iconic, mid-century timeline, to decorate their residences and offices.

Mid-century Modern Era (ca 1945-1972)

The mid-century modern timeline in our history was known for significant architectural changes post-WWII. Pre-war furnishings were more ornate and traditional in their styles. The mid-20th century was a time for the interplay of eccentric curves and shapes, which would mold the current vogue for that era. Scandinavian design was very influential at this time, with a style characterized by simplicity, self-ruled designs and natural shapes. Pieces from this timeline tends to be manufactured with precision and will withstand the test of time. Modernism imaginary and fun styles were excellent for mixing furniture and interior home and office accents with new sleek and smooth dimensioned styles using bright and bolder shades of color.

During the Mid-Century Era, the drab shades from the pre-WWII were done away with. More vibrant, exciting shades came on the scene--colors such as pumpkin orange, turquoise and peacock blues, mustard yellow, pastels of pink, green, blue and yellow. Color schemes also included bright red and blacks and whites. Popular in America more than any other country-these colors were heavily used in the '50s and '60s-to make rooms more cheerful and lively. The usage of steel, molded plywood, teak lumber wood and top quality molded plastics were the major components to manufacturing furniture.

Mid-Century Danish Influence

During the 1940s when manufacturers across Europe and America were busy fulfilling the needs of war, Denmark was busy producing high-end furniture and cabinetry, which had a classical Danish design. Clean lines, modernity, smooth forms, quality wood, architectural influences, shaker like simplicity; were all hallmarks of Danish modern furnishings. Scandinavian/Danish designed teak furnishings are particularly valuable. Teak wood is a quality, beautiful grained wood commonly used to make furniture and designs produced in Denmark. Beautifully carved with smooth finishes-this wood doesn't splinter. Examples are the "Paddle" arm chair; "Whale Bone (i.e. Dog Biscuit)" chairs, office credenzas by Knud Nielsen and Finn Juhl, designed dining room sets are all selling today for thousands of dollars. Danish teak furniture has the best advantage of being constructed of the best woods of old slow growth trees. With a minimum of effort and care, vintage Danish modern furniture can still satisfy daily functional needs and it has retained its beauty for generations.

Teak Credenza

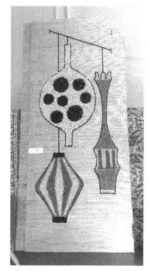

Mid-Century Abstract Arts

MCM Heywood Wakefield Whale Bone Dog Biscuit Captain's Dining Arm Chair- $259

When reselling vintage home furnishings online, please make sure that they are top quality. If not, make sure that all flaws are explained thoroughly in your descriptions. No one wants to confront an irritated eBay buyer who can easily leave you with poor feedback. Purchased furnishings should be examined for any designer and manufacturing labels for origin verification purposes. They should be visually pleasing to the eye (clean), comfortable to seat on and function correctly. Make sure all parts such as screws and hardware are included with the item to be shipped and they are packaged safely and securely. An online showroom for showcasing mid-century furniture décor can be found at: http://www.retropassion21.com/new-items.php

Some Notable Iconic Furniture and Mid-Century Décor Designers
In the early 1940's, Charles and Ray Eames began experimenting with wood molding techniques that would eventually evolve into his creating a plywood dining chair. The scarcity of materials post-WWII- encouraged the use of plywood in designing furniture. In the late 1940s, the *Eames* molded plywood "DCW" Dining Chair" is created and becomes one of the most iconic pieces of 20th century designs. It is instantly recognizable as the work of Eames, with a

"LCW" Bentwood-Eames Chair

Vintage Mid-century Eames Lounge Chair and Ottoman

form that relates directly to the human body. Eames virtually revolutionized furniture construction. Today, some original *Eames* pieces can sell for as much as $20,000, depending on the type of furniture and its design.

I found a vintage Eames Lounge chair and ottoman by *Herman Miller®*, recently at a garage sale. Score! These chairs sell for in the thousands….I was elated to come upon a mid-century treasure, and I only paid $75 for it. SCORE!

Ant chair- (ca 1952) by Arne Jacobsen

Arne Jacobsen by Fritz Hansen
Dot Stools –Set of Four

Charles and Ray Eames and George Nelson (the Architect and Designer); were known as the founding fathers of American modernism. We like to think of George Nelson as "The Creator of Beautiful and Practical Things." Other notable modernist names associated with creating revolutionary changes to home interior furnishings during the mid-century era were: Gio Ponti, Harry Bertoia, Arne Jacobsen who is known for his womb-like "egg" chair, and the three-legged-stackable "Ant" chair; Milo Baughman known for his avant-garde, distinct, and modest designs., and Edward Wormley, for his modern design sofas/couches for the *Dunbar Furniture Company*.

Vintage Herman Miller,
Eames Armchair

The pod style chair was conceived by the Swedish furniture design firm Overman in the mid-20th century and caught on in the U.S.A in the '60s for its futuristic and functional appeal.

Edward J Wormley for Dunbar Furniture Company

Edward J. Wormley was a talented furniture designer who incorporated European and Scandinavian details into furniture. He has hired by manufacturer *Dunbar Furniture Company.*

The Arne Jacobsen "Egg Pod" Chair

During the middle of the 20th century, Dunbar and Edward J Wormley became true icons in American design and furniture history. In 1950, The Chicago Merchandise Mart joined with the Museum of Modern Art to sponsor the Good Design exhibition. The annual exhibition, designed to commend selected home furnishings for their-excellent appearance and progressive performance-was often a platform of recognition for Dunbar furniture. Over a three year period, Wormley's creations for Dunbar dominated the exhibition with an astonishing-thirty unique designs receiving "Good Design" label designations.

Mid-century Wormley by Dunbar Sofa

Some modernist names associated with some of their well-known designed pieces are: Paul McCobb, Peter Hvidt, Florence Knoll, Poul Volther-"Corona" Chair; Ludwig Mies Van Der Rohe a German architect who was the Director of the famous *Bauhaus School (located in Germany)* during the 1930s, and his famous "Barcelona" chair; Hans Wegner who was one of the most prolific Danish designer, producing over 500 different chairs - the "Round chair" and "Wishbone" chair, Marcel Breuer, Gerrit Rietveld famous for his "Red and Blue Chair and "Zig Zag" chairs, Eero Saarinen's molded fiberglass "Tulip" armchair; Verner Panton known for his "Panton" Chair (1960), which was the world's first one-piece molded plastic chair; the "Tivoli" and "Bachelor" chairs, which were both produced by Fritz Hansen, and in Japan-Isamu Noguchi became a giant with his artistic mid-century furnishings for coffee tables.

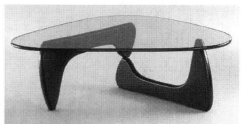

Mid Century Japan– Isamu Noguchi Coffee Table

A "Z" Style chair

This is just a partial list, as there are many more successful iconic home and office furniture designers, artists and engineers from this futuristic timeline. Some unique modern home furnishings common from the Atomic Age/Era were:

The Saucer/Disk Chair

Antique Thonet Rocking Chair

Mid Century "Scoop" Chair

- Fiberglass molded chairs, such as the "Tulip" and "Shell" form chairs, "Slipper" and "Saucer" chairs.

- Black leather and vinyl usage on chairs, such as found in the famous "Barcelona" Chair

- The Vibrating Contour Chair-Lounger

Vintage Vibrating Contour Chair-Lounger

The Barcelona Chair

- Fiber glass hard plastic chairs by *Herman Miller®, Heywood Wakefield's*, "Hey woodite" student chairs commonly used by schools during the 1940s-1960s.

Heywood-Wakefield Company Early Student Classroom Chrome Framed Chairs

Mid-century, Plywood Bent -wood chairs by Thonet

The German skilled craftsman, Michael Thonet's created the original and unique designed bentwood chair styles, which were made from European beechwood in the 19th century. These chairs are still being manufactured today by the *Thonet Company*. Bentwood rocking chairs from the 19th and 20th

century can fetch in the thousand dollar range.

Heywood-Wakefield produced chairs from 1930 to 1960 in Gardner, Massachusetts. Most of the time they used birch wood in a champagne or wheat finish for their simple aerodynamic lines of furniture.

These were some of the well-known modern furniture designers of the mid-century timeline. They helped lead the way in the modernist contemporary movement in our world history. They represented a radical departure from the carved and ornamental wood furniture of the past historical eras.

Highly collectible today as they were in the past, the mid-century modern era style is depicted in the 21st century, AMC channel's "Mad Men," which showcased modern furnishings in Don Draper's office. The TV series brought back attention to the aesthetic appeal from styles from the 1950s and 1960s. Although, this timelines furnishings and apparel has been popular by collectors for years, "Mad Men" did rekindle avid interests in the mid-century styles of clothing and accessories worn during those years, as well as, home furnishings similar to those seen in the American drama TV series. The mid-century modern timeline is also referenced to as the Modern Danish, Eames, Space Age, and Atomic Eras.

Mid-Century Modern Red Sofa

Today's current collecting and decorating trends represent the iconic and unique styles and images from the past mid-century modern architecture. Using the beautifully grained teak wood (an Asian wood), the Danish furniture (e.g. The "Lounge Chair", Selig, "Z" Chair, sideboard cabinetry, shelving units and tables) were created. Molded plastics (acrylic, lucite, plexiglass, and fiberglass) furnishings were used to make chair styles like the "Mushroom" and "Shell" chairs.

Mid-century molded Fiberglass Chairs

Mid-century FIberglass Shell Chairs

The popularity of the Plastic Substance Called "Lucite"

Mid-Century translucent lucite wares are very sought-after currently. Home furnishings and accessories such as tables, chairs, lamps, tissue containers, handbags home decor and jewelry from 1950s-1960s can be made of lucite. Here are some examples of vintage lucite items sold recently online.

Mid-century Mod- Lucite chair

Vintage 3-Tier Lucite Bar Cart-$500

1950's Clear Carved Lucite Purse/
Handbag-$325

Vintage Mid-Century, Rotating
Asian Table Lamp with Lucite
Set

Lucite is also known as acrylic, plexiglass and perspex. Lucite is a clear high grade plastic made primarily from petroleum is the synthetic polymer, polymethyl methacrylate. In essence, it is plastic, but with advantages in appearance and strength. Some may use the phrase "vintage Lucite" to refer to any clear plastic substance- that is not new; however, a closer look at vintage mid-century clear Lucite wares, provides clarity on why it has become extremely collectible. It's simply amazing!

Notable Mid-century Manufacturing Companies Labels
Mid-century modern furniture has a distinct look defined by thin-legged teak furniture, low seated chairs and sofas with the usage of clean, steam-lined shapes and flowing curves.

Chromcraft
The *Chromcraft Corporation* had its beginning in St. Louis, Missouri in 1908. It was originally known as *American Fixture and Showcase Company*. The typical tradition of ingenuity and ambition carried this newly founded company through various stages of expansion from a humble beginning to a fine operating corporation. Dining room sets with the *Chromcraft* name, are very valuable selling for over $1,000.

Broyhill Furniture Company-America's Leading Home Furnishings

Manufacturing Company

Vintage *Broyhill Furniture* (currently known as the *Heritage Home Group)* lines have made their revival in the home today, they are: *Brazilia, Sculptra, Premier Saga* and *Emphasis.*

Drexel Company's lines *-Declaration* and *Plus One (c, 1970s)*

Kofod Larsen-Danish Furniture; Ethan Allen's *"Custom Room Plan"* (CRP) from the '70s, and the *Kroehler Company* who sold sofa sets and sectionals in various colors and sizes with the usage of the indestructible 'Frieze" fabric, are sought-after brands.

Henredon- The name is synonymous with beautiful high-quality wood furnishings and upholstery designed pieces used for dining room, living room and bedroom furniture sets.

Herman Miller®Furniture Company- The *Herman Miller* name is known for innovative and comfortable mid-century chairs and furnishings for the home and office, and under the guidance of Design Director- George Nelson, it was likely the most prolific and influential producer of furniture of the modernist style. *Herman Miller* is credited with the invention of the office cubicle most of us at some time or another, have spent some time in our past or present. Some of Herman Miller® classic designed furniture pieces are the Eames "Lounge Chair" with matching ottoman and executive chairs; the Aeron chair and the "Noguchi Table" (designed by Isamu Noguchi in 1948). The company has had the talents of a large number of well-known modernist designers work together to produce their line of iconic industrial and home furnishings designs.

George Nelson Associates- In 1947, *George Nelson Associates* was established. George Nelson's post-WWII building furniture and lighting designs led the way into the 20th century's most iconic modernist era. For decades his designed mid-century modern creations such as the "Ball" Clock, the "Marshmallow" Sofa and "Coconut Chair, are one-of-a kind treasures. Nelson was also known for his "CSS" storage and shelving unit systems. These units were designed for *Herman Miller* and sell into the thousands of dollars.

Sunburst and Starburst Clock Designs

George Nelson also developed over 150 iconic clocks which resembled fun, whimsical modern shapes in bright bold colors. If you come across a "Sunburst clock" designed by George Nelson, you will have found a treasure. Other designers and manufacturers of this era to be inspired by the sunburst shape include *Seth Thomas, Lux, Westclox* and *Elgin*. The contemporary sunburst (or starburst) shape remains as popular today as it did fifty years ago, making starburst clocks desirable to acquire. They can sell for over $500.

Vintage Sunburst Wall Clock

I often come across these retro treasures at garage sales, selling for only $10. When I find bargains such as this I feel that magical "Treasure Hunter Rush" come over me.

H. G.Knoll Furniture Company (1938)*-Currently known as the *Knoll Group Inc.*-The *Knoll

Company was founded in 1938 by Hans Knoll of New York, who was the son of a skilled German furniture maker. Hans also was a skilled furniture craftsman. Mr. Knoll found a willing local market for his high-quality furniture designs during the late 1930s and early 1940s, but it was postwar that Knoll benefited from spiraling needs for office furniture in the economic business market boom.

Throughout the 1950s to the mid-1970s, corporate America built and furnished billions of square feet of office space throughout the country. Knoll's design philosophy was heavily influenced by the famous *Bauhaus school of design* that was becoming dominant at the time. The school held the notion that modern art and architecture must be responsive to the aesthetic and engineering needs of the industrial world. His primary goal was to produce furniture that was elegant and functional, yet affordable. During the 1950s and 1960s, *Knoll* became known for its innovative designs and high-quality office furniture. Besides its good reputation, *Knoll* benefited from escalation in office furniture markets during the post-WWII economic and population boom. Well-known designers that worked for *Knoll* included- Vico Magistretti, Kazhuhide Takahama, Warren Platner, and Tobia Scarpa.

It's very important that you remember to look for manufacturer and designer labels or markings on mid-century furnishings. Copies were and are reproduced. When you think of listing a vintage mid-century piece of furniture online, don't use the phrase, "in the style of" or the other descriptive words 'Like' and 'similar to'. In your title make sure to make every effort to identify it's authenticity when reselling the piece. I conducted an estate in Omaha, NE, and I made a notation on my website one of the items for sale, would be an Arts and Crafts Era- William Morris (1934-1896)- Mission reclining chair. After a few of my dedicated vintage furniture dealers showed up to perhaps purchase the chair-guess what?....They didn't. I later discovered from an antique dealer, it was a version of the chair-not an authentic Morris chair—the first recliner. This necessitated lowering its price, and we ended up selling the chair for a fraction of what it would have sold for if it had been an authentic Morris chair. Always check under each piece for manufacturing information or design particulars!

Mid Century Home Décor and Accessories
One-of-a-kind Space Age shaped sculptures, Op Art wall décor and home accessories; and contemporary oil on canvas paintings- all played a very important role in achieving this

Antique Arts and Crafts Era, Mission William Morris Reclining Chair-$1,000 Range look in the home during this time. The traditional knick-knacks were replaced with modern art and handmade objects prized for form and feeling.

Mid-century metal wall sculptures

Abstract Metal Wall Décor from the 1960s-70s, designed by the sculptor, C. Jere can sell for thousands of dollars today.

C. Jere, mid-century metal works attract the admiration of leading dealers throughout the world. Curtis Freiler and Jerry Fels, were the founders of the *Artisan House Company*. Their metal sculptured works were marketed between 1963 -1972. The *C. Jere* team, created a variety of metal works realistic- to highly abstract. The *Artisan House Company* business was sold in 1972, but Jerry Fels continued to work designing for the company. The sculptures are still produced today, but some of the older techniques, such as enameling, usage of resins and bronzes-haven't been used in decades. Here are some examples of elaborate wall-mounted metal sculptures by *C. Jere.*

C. Jere Signature

C. Jere "Flock of Birds" Metal Wall Sculpture selling range $1,500

C. Jere Metal Wall Art Village Scene

C. Jere 1971 Brass "Rain Drops" Signed Wall Art Sculpture—$2,850

Notable other 1960s-1980s, metal sculptures were William Bowie, Bijan, and "Marc Creates"

Did You Know? Many are under the impression that *C. Jere* was a metalwork artist of wall sculptures and household accessories. Their designer signature, *C. Jere*, is in fact, a fictional combination name that the artists Curtis Freiler and Jerry Fels, had put together.

Mid-century, Metal Hairpin Leg Furniture

Wrought iron, Hairpin leg home furnishings were invented by Henry P. Glass in 1941. Oddly enough Henry didn't obtain the patent on his invention. The steel wire legs were used to create industrial designed and functional tables, chairs, plant stands, patio furnishings and sofas. They were part of the *Russel Wright, American-Way Collection* and were produced in limited numbers. This may have been to create a limited collection, or if it was because of limited materials due to the war. The *American-Way* "Hairpin Group" was manufactured by the New York based company, *Molla, Inc*, which was known for their high-quality patio furniture. Glass designed two separate *American-Way Collections* that featured hairpin legs: The original "Hairpin Group," featured five different tables, three types of chairs and a settee. The iconic mid-century modern furniture designers, Knoll; and Eames- the husband and wife team- used hairpin legs on some of their furnishings, so it probable that they are the most recognized designers for these furniture leg types.

On Feb 12, 1954, Richard G. Reineman filed for a patent on the three-rod hairpin leg design (not the two-rod), and the patent was granted on May 8, 1956. The object of the invention was to provide a new and improved furniture leg.

From the original description on the patent, it seems the original intent of the three-pin hairpin leg was for tables and the appearance of added stability would make it a more obvious choice for furniture that needed to support a significant amount of weight. The invention relates to a furniture leg construction and more particularly, to a table leg construction having a leg secured to a mounting plate, and a U-shaped reinforcing brace connected to the leg and mounting plate for reinforcing it.

Vintage Metal Hairpin Leg,
Wood Slab-Top Coffee Table

Vintage Metal
Hairpin Leg Plant
Stands

The Op Art-Abstract Movement of the Mid-century

Op Art is also known as "optical art". It is used to describe some paintings and other works of art which use optical illusions. Op art is also referred to as "geometric abstraction" and "hard-edge abstraction," although the preferred term for it is "perceptual abstraction." The term "Op" bears similarity to the other popular movement of the 1960's, "Pop art" (catchy name, but not the same style). Op Art works are abstract, with many of the well-known pieces made in only black and white shades. When the viewer looks at the art, the impression given is of movement, hidden images, flashing and vibration, patterns, or the image having been significantly distorted to the eye.

The optical illusion creates these different responses from observers through patterns, flashes, contrasts, movement, and hidden imagery. The viewer is basically pulled into the pictures image. Renowned mid-century artist Victor Vasarely was regarded as the father of Op Art.

For examples of Victor Vasarely's art, visit the Victor Vasarely image gallery on Google, or for more information on his life, visit the online website: http:// http://www.vasarely.com/site/site.htm

Op Art Design

Op Art Record Holder

Op art sculptures, serigraphs, prints, paintings and bold and brightly colored op art fabric used to cover padded chairs and sofas. In the clothing department, Psychedelic Op Art garments created by mid-century designers, Emilio Pucci, and Jean Paul Gaultier, are highly desirable.

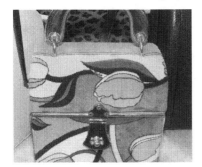

Emilio Pucci Designer Handbag

Emilio Pucci Designed
Ladies Dress

Emilio Pucci Tag

Mid-century Silversmith and Danish Designer: Georg Jensen

With a history that spans more than 100 years, the designer name of *Georg Jensen*, represented quality craftsmanship and timeless aesthetic design, producing lifestyle products ranging from hollowware to watches, jewelry and home products. The son of world famous jewelry designer, Georg A. Jensen became a successful sculptor and silversmith producing many iconic works displayed in and around Copenhagen, Denmark. His furniture designs focused mainly on round coffee tables and easy chairs. There are numerous other mid-century Danish teak furniture pieces he designed; his book only highlights a few of his many talents.

Georg Jensen's son, Søren Georg Jensen, also had his father's talents with sculpturing with silver during the mid-century. His architectural pieces were more abstract and geometric in shape.

Mid-Century barware signage and bar souvenirs: martini shakers (Sterling and silver plate sorts, Skyscrapers, and Art Deco Zeppelin shapes), paper napkins and glassware can be quite valuable.

The mid-20th century is considered the golden age of cocktails, so seek out popular, high-quality brands from that era. Cocktail glasses with designs and signatures by *Dorothy Thorpe, George Briard, Couroc* and *McKee,* are all great names whose pieces are relatively easy to find in most thrift stores or garage sales. The mid-century line of *Culver Ltd* barware is collectible.

George Briard Signature on Mosaic Glass End Table

Early Culver Ltd glassware was decorated in 22-karat gold and can fetch in the hundreds. Watch for the company's early production line (1950s-1960s), which featured acid etch, hand-painted features, decalcomania, and sand-cut monogramming; done in various unique designed themes. They will be marked with the "Culver" signature in script from the '40s-'50s, and block lettering during the '60s and '70s. If found with their holding racks….all the better!

Mid-Century, Dorothy Thorpe Signed Silver-Rimmed Barware/Glassware

Vintage Culver Red and Gold Paisley Barware Set with Caddy-$193

Vintage 1960's Culver, Rare New Orleans, 22K Jester Rhinestone Highballs 4 Gold Dancing Harlequins, Jeweled Bar Glasses Set-$269.99

Collectible Mid-century- Blenko Glass
What is Blenko Glass look like?

Simple answer: A genie's bottle!

The original *Blenko Glass Company* begun in 1893 when founder William J. Blenko came to America with the intention of starting a company to produce the glass used in stained glass windows. At that time, all stained glass panels were only produced in Europe and he could see a future market opening up in the United States. The company had to close after ten years in 1909, but reopened again in 1921, still creating stained glass. Sales were a bit slow, so William Blenko decided to add art glass to his line. In 1930, the company name was changed to the "Blenko Glass Company".

Using striking Modernism geometric shapes, exquisite color, skilled craftsmen, and imaginative designs have made *Blenko* famous in the time-honored craft of hand-blown glass and stained glass. With forms and designs of its hand-crafted products that are unique and inspiring, one of the first in-house designers was Winslow Anderson from 1947 to 1954. His revolutionary Scandinavian free-form designed pieces are very collectible. His 1950, bent-neck decanter (#948), is a price-winning example. These particular pieces of blown glass, sell upwards of $200.

Vintage Mid-century Blenko,
Tangerine Glass Pitcher

Vintage Mid-century Blenko,
Tangerine Decanter

Vintage 1960's Blenko Foil Label

Vintage Blue Blenko Bottle with Stopper

Another glass form designer for *Blenko* was "Wayne Husted" (circa, 1952-1963), who came out with three-foot-tall, architectural floor pieces, prized by avid mid-century glass collectors. Likewise, Joel Philip Myers, who was a designer from 1963-1970 created some striking pieces. Primary colors for vintage *Blenko* glass are; lime, aqua, lilac, rose, gold, tangerine, mulberry and Nile green.

Identifying these beautiful pieces of glass artwork can be difficult. *Blenko* has used foil labels over the years which are metallic silver and read, "Blenko Handcraft," (except for a short time when a sandblasted mark BLENKO was used from 1958-1961). Be sure to look under any colorful glass pieces dated to the time period from 1950s through the 1980s, to see if they have any tell-tale markings. (See foil label on page 303.)

Other methods of identifying *Blenko* characteristics-other than the original given labels-will include:
- Rough pontil marks on the bases because the pieces are free-blown, rounded and slightly uneven fire-polished rims with thick walls.

Don't always assume that if a piece of glass has a rough pontil, then it must be a *Blenko* piece. Most glass collectors have also been taught that if it doesn't have a pontil, then it can't be *Blenko*. Sorry to disappoint the true believers, but this theory is incorrect as other American glass companies located in West Virginia left the rough pontils on the majority of their designs. Bischoff, Pilgrim, Rainbow glass, are always found with a rough pontil. Ohio's Erickson Glass pieces have mostly polished pontils, but are sometimes found with a rough pontil.

A Pontil mark, or punt mark is the scar where the pontil, punty, or punt was broken from a work of blown glass. The presence of a scar indicates that a glass bottle or bowl was blown freehand, while the absence of a punt mark suggests either that the mark has been obliterated, or that the work was mold-blow.

The majority of *Blenko* designs *can* be found with rough pontils. Just as with everything else, there are always exceptions to this rule.

Some *Blenko* designs were designed to have a polished base. Furthermore, some pieces had too large of a pontil making the piece wobbly. The piece was then taken to the grinding shop to be ground and polished.

- Coloring is another method of identifying these pieces. Mid-century shades used were turquoise, sky blue, amethyst, chartreuse, ruby, tangerine and sea green. Color schemes will play a factor in discovering the date of a *Blenko* glass creation. The first thing a *Blenko* collector looks at is color, so learn color timelines via online or printed resources; worry about how to identify *Blenko* glass rough pontil pieces, and polished pontil pieces later.
- *Blenko* glass *doesn't* have carved or cut designs.
- *Blenko* glass bottom rims are thick (approximately ¼")-not thin.
- Rims can be rounded and uneven from fire-polishing.

Blenko glass reference guidebooks, or catalogs with identification numbers on

---

Tip: When buying and collecting *Blenko* glass, keep in mind, "Bigger is better," for resale intentions.

Blenko pieces created from their specific designers, is also helpful when IDing *Blenko* Glass.

Cleaning *Blenko* Glass Creations

Crackle appearances on the glass; and its clarity, are important, as mineral deposits left from water can be problem-some to *Blenko* Glass, because it is very soft and porous.

Follow the bottle cleaning directions stated earlier in this book to clean *Blenko* glass art pieces of stained water deposits. I mentioned using a denture cleaner, such as Polident or Efferdent. To make a bottle cleaning solution, add these products to the inside of the bottle and let it soak. This can be done two or three times.

If stains are still present —clean with warm soapy water containing one cup of uncooked rice, or decanter cleaning beads and swirl around the inside of the bottle, drain and then rinse clean with clear warm or hot water, mixed with a small amount of rubbing alcohol and let dry. Make sure to let any *Blenko* bottles with stoppers, dry for over 24 hours before covering them with that stopper.

There are several other collectible types of mid-century glass and crystal that are collectible- I mentioned some of these brands and types, earlier in chapter five of this book.

Here is an informative webpage I discovered to help educate the reader on Identifying and cleaning , vintage *Blenko* glass: http://www.vmglasshouse.com/

Venetian, Murano Art Glass-Lamps and Home Décor Accessories

From lamps to paperweights, Italian *Murano* Art Glass is favored for its magnificent beautiful hand-blown glass creations made by glassmaking artisans. Some of the most well-known 20th century Venetian master glassmakers from Italy's, Murano Island — glass furnace factories are: *Ercole Barovier, Angelo Vittorio Mazzega, Archimede Seguso, Gio Ponti, Paolo Venini; Vincenzo Nason, Alfredo Barbini, Carlo Scarpa and Giovanni Seguso.*

Italian Murano Glass Fish Sculpture

Italian Murano Art Glass– Venini

Murano Glass Sculpture Label

Murano Art Glass is an area of collecting that is vast. I would suggest that if you are interested in buying and reselling Murano designed glass, it is of utmost importance to study Murano Glass 20th century catalogs and reference books.

Here is a suggested reference book on the subject of collecting Murano glass: *Murano Magic: Complete Guide to Venetian Glass. Its History and Artists (Schiffer Art Books) by Carl T. Gable*

A Vintage 20th century Italian Murano Abstract Art Glass Vase-Wedding with Clear Glass & Seven Colored Art Ribbons-$759

An educational online site I discovered for helping to identify mid-century glass items can be found at:

http://www.20thcenturyglass.com/glass_encyclopedia_home.htm

Murano Glass Reproductions and Fakes:

First thing to look for on potential *Murano* glass designs is the presence of any engraving or signatures, or evidence of any original attached *Murano* labels. Unfortunately, there are far too many reproductions and counterfeit *Murano* glass pieces in the market place today. Be careful if you are planning on purchasing what is advertised as being- original *Murano* art glass pieces on eBay, and other ecommerce sites.

Mid-century Light Fixtures and Lamps

Lighting (light fixtures and lamps), from the mid-century can encompass a vast array of varieties, so this book will refer to some of the most notable styles produced between the years: 1945-1970.

A notable innovative lighting designer was Gino Sarfatti, who created over 600 different lighting designs during the mid-century timeline. Popular today and yesterday, his eccentric "Sputnik" shaped chandeliers.

The *Lightolier Company,* became synonymous with mid century architectural lighting during the twentieth century with leadership under William Blitzer. Since 2007, it has become decision of the *Phillips Royal Electronics Comp.*

Gino Sarfatti's "Sputnik" Ceiling Light Fixture

Vintage Articulating Arm Desk Lamp With Cube Base

1960's Designer Castiglioni Brothers Vintage Arco Arc "Eyeball" Spot Light with Rotating Arm Lamp, asking price-$250

Robert Sonneman was a modernist lighting pioneer. His desk-top "Articulating Arm Lamp" was an iconic mid-century style of light.

Today, there are many reproductions on the market of styles from this time period and during the Art Deco Era. How can a person recognize a vintage lamp from the newly made versions? First, search the light/lamp for the manufacturer's name; second, does the electrical cord seem aged in appearance? If a vintage table lamp is found with a Drum-style, lampshade—made of a fiberglass and resin parchment material, usually whip stitched to its metal frame—than you probably have a true vintage lamp.

Some of these parchment shades of that iconic era were also geometric in shape and featured two-tiers. These lamp shades could feature lace edges and were decorated with everything from geometric lines and designs- to splatters and squiggles, evoking the drip paintings of Abstract-Expressionist artist, Jackson Pollock.

Another notable mid-century lighting company was *PH* (Poul Henningsen) *Lighting.*

Mid-Century, Poul Henningsen (1894–1967), *PH Lighting*-Lamps and Ceiling Fixtures

Authentic lighting designs by Poul Henningsen (*PH Lighting*) can sell for hundreds--and up into the thousand dollar range.

Poul Henningsen was a true Functionalist from the *Danish Modern School* not for furniture, but for Danish mid-century lighting designs. He was actually known to have been the world's first lighting architect. Henningsen's efforts to prevent the blinding glare created from the electric lamp bulb, succeeded in 1926 with a three-shade lamp- known as the **PH** lamp. The curving of the shades allowed his hanging lamps to illuminate both the table and the rest of the room. He designed many similar lamps, some with frosted glass, including desk lamps, chandeliers and wall-mounted fixtures. Poul Henningsen and Arne Jacobsen, designed lighting for the *Louis Poulsen Lighting Manufacturing Company* during the mid-century. Famous light designs by Henningsen are the **PH-5** and "artichoke" pendant lamps, which were designed in 1958.

Futuristic Lamp types from the Mid-Century

Vintage mid-century modern lamps were characterized by simple lines and Space Age technology, and where used to transform the ambiance of any room to retro-modern atmosphere. In general, light fixtures had shapes that were sleek, spherical, saucer-like and geometric in nature.

Cone-shaped shades were made to turn light downwards or in various directions to highlight preferred artwork. The cones were mostly made from metal in shades of black, white or in polished spun metals, such as aluminum, brass and a fiberglass material.

Vintage Saucer Desk Lamp

Vintage 23" Double Spun Metal Cone-Shaped Desk Lamp-
$100

One of the most notable shapes of shades from this period was probably the "Bubble" lampshade, produced in 1952 (see page 312). Shaped roughly like a mushroom's cap, the lamp was made of translucent plastic pulled tight over a wire frames.

Vintage Mid-Century,
Laurel "Mushroom"
Lamp

Another groovy-shaped lamp was called the "Gumdrop" lamp. This one was made by *Laurel Lighting Manufacturing Company*. Additionally, many variations of this type of lamp came from the William Curry's Stemlites designer line. Selling in the hundreds-- Oh! Goody, goody gumdrops!

The latest vintage craze for lighting resources in the living room are the mid-century, Hollywood Regency style, corner "Swag" hanging lamps. These corner hanging lamps were made with a single globe or in multiple tiers. The most popular globes are made of glass, acrylic, or glass caged in wrought iron, or a gilt metal in shapes of spheres, globes or orbs (influenced by Sputnik or Space Age saucer and satellite shapes), and Mediterranean, Gothic styles.

Vintage Mid-Century
Gumdrop Table Lamp

Vintage hanging "Spaghetti" lamps from the 1950s, were crafted from a spun-like acrylic, lucite resins in strands wrapped, or swirled around a globular shape created to resemble "Spaghetti". These swag hanging lamps can fetch in the hundreds of dollars range.

Vintage Swag Lamp

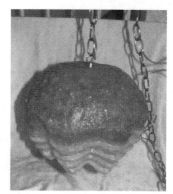

Vintage Acrylic Lamps

Yet another popular vintage hanging swag corner lamp style, were those that resembled giant bunches of purple or green grapes. These lamps were made of acrylic or lucite balls that were glued together. I remember my Grandmother had one of these in her den. Guess what? They are selling for over $100 today. Polished chrome lamp bases were prevalent during the Mid-Century, Modern Era. The architecturally influenced, column form table lamps, were sleek and tubular and the lamp bases were composed of alternating chrome and brass, or just brass/chrome alone. Watch for modernist designer/sculptors names, such as Robert Sonnemon , Milo Baughman and Paul Evans.

Vintage Grape Swag Lamp

Vintage George Nelson's Iconic Bubble (Saucer) Light Fixtures

Vintage Danish Mid-Century Hanging Pendant Lamp

Mid-century designer George Nelson's soft diffused illuminate, shaped Bubble lamps (e.g., Ball, Saucer, Cigar and Criss-Cross types) sell in the hundreds.

Corner- pole tension lamps with cone shades are selling for up to $350.

Vintage Animated, Motion Lamps from the 1930s-1950s, are hard to find in good running condition. These clever rotating light devices are quite collectible. Look for the brands of Econolite, L. A. Goodman Corporation (later known as Lacolite Industries), National and Scene-In. They operate by heat generated from a center light bulb, which causes inserted cylinders to rotate around the bulb and create motion to the image on the cylinders. These pleasurable lamps sell for over $400 in very good condition.

Vintage 1955 Econolite "Niagara Falls" Motion Lamp-$200

Mid-Century-Tension-Pole-Lamps

Oh, I can't forget to mention those iconic 1970's Goddess, motion, oil-dripping "Rain" Swag Lamps from the '60s and '70s. These lamps worked by using a pump that would run dripping lamp oil, or mineral oil gently over several tight heavy nylon line strands to create a slow motion rain effect. They were quite relaxing and fun to watch as a teenager while visiting my aunt's house. It is important to change the oil in the lamp and pump clean every year, or the oil becomes rancid. These lamps were even more captivating to watch when using a soft color light bulb. Most were sold by *Johnson Industries* of Los Angeles, California. These lamps sell from $200-$350 based on aesthetic factors, size and working condition.

Remember those ceiling pull-down pendant light fixtures found in a dated, 1960s kitchen hanging over the kitchen table-Treasure! Any vintage saucer shaped lighting fixture or shade, are popular currently to acquire. These sell for over $150 based on condition and style.

1960's Pull-down Saucer, Ceiling Light Fixture

Vintage 1970's Goddess, Oil-Dripping "Rain" Motion Light, Table Lamp-$250

The 1940s decorative art, table lamps, such as those called "Blackamoor" lamps, have had a revival in popularity and collectability today.

Blackamoor figural pieces (Italian moretto, moretti) are depictions of black Africans used in sculptures, jewelry, armorial designs and decorative art. The 20th century pieces were made from different companies during the Art Deco and mid-century period. Most antique Blackamoors were carved out of wood, covered in gesso and covered in a polychrome paint. Some are made of bronze and other metals. The mid-20th century Blackamoors were made of ceramic, chalkware and porcelain. Blackamoor lamps shapes featured Nubian (mostly male) Genie, or Aladdin-like, symmetrical figural poses or head busts. Most valuable, are the sculpted and hand painted Blackamoors created in Italy during the Rococo Revival of the early 20th century. Some of these earlier types would feature electrified candelabra's on their tops. These earlier lamps can fetch in the thousands of dollars range.

Collectible lighting sources that were popular in the earlier 20th century and Victorian Eras were the "Gone with the wind" (GWTW) kerosene style lamps-named after the iconic movie of that name; Art Deco and Art Nouveau Era ceiling lighting fixtures; and wall lighting, glass slip shades.

Art Deco and Art Nouveau Era lighting is highly sought-after with exquisitely styled fixtures and lamps. I hope to discuss these eras more in detail in my next book.

Vintage Mid-Century "Blackamoor" Table Lamp

Vintage GWTW Porcelain Hand Painted Table Lamp

Vintage Art Deco, Ornate Caged, Slag Glass Pendant Chandelier

Vintage GWTW Crystal Table Lamp

Mid-Century Airplane Theme
Ceiling Light Fixture

Vintage Art Deco
Chandelier Glass
Slip Shades

Vintage Art Deco Blue
Glass Table Lamp

It's so disheartening when an old house or building is torn down as many of the lavish and stylish light fixtures are being destroyed. I have started contacting demolition companies with hopes of purchasing some of the salvage from a home, or building that is about to be destroyed. Real cash to be made here!!

Designers today are copying the styles of yesterday for creating lamps, lights, furnishings and appliances, but at a much higher cost. Have you observed some of the newer electric or gas stove styles or porcelain sinks? Yes, they are replicas of the past. Their hopes are for bringing back that old-fashioned flair back into today's home.

Modernism in Jewelry-1930's-1970's

Here is a brief summary of Modernism styles used in creating exquisite jewelry designs. Thinking of those mod, mid-century years, what comes to mind is art… wearable art. Much of it is inspired by the unusual and dynamic whimsical shapes of the Atomic Age. Most fine silver artisan created pendants, rings, bracelets and necklaces will be marked with that particular artist/silversmith's initials or hallmark. The majority of mid-century pieces were geometric, and biomorphic in shape. Other types of metal alloys were used to create exquisite pieces, such as gold, copper and brass. Pieces may also have wood, bone and stones inlaid or infused into the metal of choice in their works of art. Some of the leaders of these exquisitely designed, one-of-a-kind pieces of art originated in the Greenwich Village a suburb of lower Manhattan, New York City, but also in the Scandinavian countries and Mexico. Some of most notable silversmith artists names were Georg Jensen-mentioned earlier- Nanna Ditzel, Henning Koppel, Betty Cooke, Sam Kramer; Will Smith, Ed Wiener, Paul Lobel, John Bryan of North Carolina, and Bjorn Weckstrom of Finland- who added chunks of acrylic to his creations.

Metal-smith jeweler Margret Craver can be given much of the credit for starting this jewelry creating period in the United States. In the 1940s, she worked tirelessly to set up hospital service programs sponsored by *Handy and Harman* (a metals refining company), to rehabilitate army veterans through wire working (1947-1951). The veterans were taught by experienced metal-smiths from Europe, to train other American teachers in the craft of silver-smithing. These workshops played a vital role in the expansion of metals programs at American colleges and universities. Many attendees became influential teachers who set up long-lasting, seminal metal-smithing departments at their respective schools.

A fantastic online site about silversmiths, jewelry styles and hallmarked jewelry can be found online at: http://www.modernsilver.com

Vintage Signed and Taxco, Mexico Silver Pieces

Pieces of mid-century silver jewelry signed by the artisans- Los Castillo, Hector Aguilar, Margot de Taxco and William Spratling are prized for their modernist styles. Similarly, mid-century silver jewelry crafted in Taxco, Mexico- can fetch a good amount of cash.

Los Castillo Taxco Sea Star brooch / Pendant (2-3/8"), Sterling silver & Mozaico Azteca Stone Inlay -$120

Silver Mark/Stamp

Vintage Modernism Sterling Silver
Brooches/Pins

Taxco is a small city located in the Mexican state of Guerrero. The cities municipality's coat of arms is an Aztec "Glyph." A Glyph is the shape of a Mesoamerican ball court with rings, players and skulls. Taxco is most noted for its vast mining of silver and local crafted silversmiths. William Spratling, an American who moved here in 1920s, created silver workshops and exported silver items mostly in the U.S.A.

Taxco Markings - The 'Eagle" shaped mark was instituted by the Mexican government in 1948, therefore, the eagle symbol can help to date a piece. The number inside the Eagle's chest indicates assay city or an individual maker. For

318

example, the number (3) stands for Taxco. This was changed in 1979 to the letter "T" for Taxco, with the silversmith's initial featured at a later date. There are a number of different marks or stamps for silver from Mexico; to view some of these jewelry markings and maker's hallmark stamps of other countries, visit the online web page:

http://www.925-1000.com

Always carry a quality jeweler's magnifying Loupe to search for engraved markings or artisans/maker's marks, and metal purity markings that where were applied to fine gold, platinum and silver pieces. These marks were placed on the backs of pendants, brooches, bracelets, earrings, or inside jewelry rings. It's **not** unusual to find an antique ring missing artisan and metal markings. It may have been worn off with usage over the years. With careful examination, you may find a trace of a jewelers stamp mark. Also, if a rings mark was originally placed on the bottom inside lower area, the mark may have been lost if the ring was resized.

Most recently I found a half-inch round vintage religious, Catholic medallion gold charm that depicted Jesus and the Virgin Mother. The back of the charm had a tiny stamp which featured initials and the number "750". This mark was extremely tiny and the gold charm was soiled. Without the use of the jeweler's loupe, the naked eye couldn't identify its gold content.

When searching for fine gold jewelry and markings are not visible-here are some helpful tips to help in identifying a jewelry piece's gold content:

The Vinegar Test

- Clean off any soil on the gold piece with water and a soft washcloth, than soak the jewelry piece in question, in white vinegar-no more than 15 minutes. Fine gold will shine; fake gold will change colors when exposed to the vinegar. (Keep in mind that if the piece turns colors, there is no way of changing it back.) Gold plate will turn black when exposed to vinegar so I would not try this method on vintage signed costume jewelry. Gold is a stable metal and does not react with oxygen corroding. Because it is stable, it will not change colors when exposed to vinegar. Run the gold piece under cool water or spray it with a water bottle to remove any of the vinegar. Rub the gold piece with a clean soft cloth to dry it.

- **Nitric Acid Test-** Put the suspected piece of gold in a stainless steel bowl and add a drop of nitric acid on top of the piece-If there is a green color reaction, the piece is gold plated. If it has a milky appearance-it is gold-plated sterling silver; a gold reaction indicates your item is gold-plated brass and has NO reaction....if it is gold. Simply feel the gold piece in question. Is it soft and malleable? Gold is heavy- but soft.

- **The Scratch Test-**Rub your gold item gently across a piece of ceramic like pottery, a plate, or even certain types of ceramic tile. If your item is real gold it will leave a gold streak. If it's false gold it will leave a dark grey or black streak.

- Use a magnet. Gold and silver are not magnetic. So if it's magnetic it can't be gold or silver. (Keep in mind that copper and some steel alloys- are not magnetic either.)

- Gold does not tarnish, so if your piece is discolored-it is not fine gold. Consider the shade of the gold jewelry and its style. Examples of gold from the Victorian Era often have a reddish tinge because they are made from rose gold (gold with a mixture of copper). Rose gold and the style/design to a piece of jewelry, are strong indicators of age.

Vintage Victorian Edwardian 14K Hollow Yellow Gold, Bohemian Garnet Seed Brooch

- Look for official gold markings, or karat stamps, such as the following: The letter "K" placed after specific numbers (e.g., 10K, 14K, 18K, 22K or 24K). The number 999, which denotes that the piece is 99 percent gold or pure gold. "PT" stamps followed by a number, means a platinum metal. European gold stamps - 750 denotes 18 karat, and 585 is 14k gold. Further gold stamps used to denote gold types: "GP"-meaning- gold plated; "GF" is gold filled, and "EP" stands for gold electroplate.

Tip: Purchase a gold testing pen or kit. These kits will identify the amount of gold in the alloy; whether it is 24K Bullion, 22K, 18K, 14K and 10K gold. They will additionally identify fine silver (Sterling and Coin), and to differentiate platinum from white gold. Most gold collectors have a gold testing source available on them at all times. A much needed tool to invest in - considering the price of gold presently.

Gold and Diamonds Discovered in a Barn?

One of my personal gold find stories took place a couple of years ago while attending a large farm auction. I found a woman's diamond accented, 14k gold wristwatch. The watch had placed inside a dilapidated box, and had been found by one of the auctioneers in the barn's loft. This box came out during the last 10 minutes of the auction when most auction attendees had departed. I stayed to the end of the auction, along with a handful of other people, and ended up purchasing the box for only $14. I sold the watch for $450 online. Due to the auctions time restraints, I only had a fraction of a chance to view the contents in the box. With a quick glance, I spotted the wristwatch, which appeared to have a fine gold setting with real diamonds, but I wasn't sure. I decided to make a quick decision and purchase the box. After all, the box had only cost me $14.

I had lingered around to the end of the auction, and ended up walking away with a treasure, not to mention a nice assortment of vintage costume jewelry pieces signed- *Kramer, Miriam Haskell, Vendome, Lisner,* and *Schiaparelli,* which had also been placed in the same box. Obviously, someone had placed this box in an inconspicuous location-in a barn's loft close to a bale of hay? You never know where you will find treasure!

Identifying Vintage Jewelry

Identifying vintage jewelry can be as simple as looking at its clasp. The most familiar clasp is the circular clasp. This type of clasp dates the modern necklaces back to post-WWII. Before this, clasps had a variety of shapes; some screwing together and common vintage clasps would feature a pin that fit into a cylindrical chamber. The presence of this type of clasp will date a necklace no later than pre - 1940s.

Check the pin closure on the back a brooch. As with clasps, pins were updated in the post-WWII era with modern safety fittings. A brooch that features a pin that slides under a simple hook will be dated pre-1940s at the latest. Another method for dating a bauble is to note the age of the box it came in (if present). The fabric content found on the inside of the display box along with any information printed on the box cover, can say a lot about its age as well. I found a fantastic online reference site for helping in identifying jewelry signed pieces:

http://www.morninggloryantiques.com/

Rings, Necklaces, wristwatches, earrings and brooches that appear to hold diamonds or cubic zirconia stones, may be identified by its setting by finding the letters, "C.Z." engraved on the backside of the piece, or inside a rings band -C.Z. stands for cubic zirconia. Learn to identify and spot the differences between real and fake diamonds. Real diamonds have unique characteristics; here are a couple of tell-tale ways to identify a real diamond:

- Breathe on a clean diamond. If the fog clears immediately, it's probably real.
- Check for tiny diamond imperfections called inclusions. They're often missing from fakes. Use a high-magnifying glass lens jeweler's loupe for

this form of identifying.

- View the underside of a diamond to sight any bright orange rays generated from light hitting the stone, if so-it is a fake. An authentic diamond reflects brilliant gray shades, rather than rainbow shades.

- Check the mounting or setting. An imposter stone may be set in an inferior setting.

- **The Newspaper Test:** Use a small sheet of newspaper. Lay the newspaper down on a flat surface- preferably a solid, dark colored surface rather than a clear glass counter. Make sure the light in the room is bright and coming from above your head not from a table lamp. This way, the stone you are testing, or other objects in the room, will not cast a shadow that might throw off the results of your this test. Handle the stone carefully, and try not to smudge it with your fingerprints. Turn it upside down so the flat face is toward the newspaper-covered area with the point side facing up. Lay the stone on a column of letters, which you would normally find fairly easy to read. Can you see the print clearly? If yes, than it's not real.

There are several supportive online videos aimed to help in identifying a fake diamond.

I personally have a local jewelry store examine any undecided diamonds and precious gemstones. For a minimal fee, they will check for a piece's authenticity.

The mid-century timeline is quite vast and there are several published reference books in the marketplace, about this iconic era. Knowledge on any collectible subject is very important when selling for profit online. Now, let's discuss some facts about the fab, mid-century clothing styles.

Iconic, Mid Century, Retro Fashions and Accessories

Its mid-century revival time! Yes, wearing those mod-high-fashioned and brightly colored clothes from the '60s and '70s are the latest rage!

There has been a major upswing in our generation for mid-century textile prints and styles from the "Mod" or "Retro" Era. Today's young generation is enthusiastic about the styles and quality of apparel from the past. Simply "Mad Men" hysteria!

Fashionable clothing from the mid-century, were transformed by new concepts emerging from the London, England pop scene. The British rock 'n' roll, music invasion Britain, had tremendous influence through-out Europe and the U.S.A. This era brought modernism styles to the clothing arena with simple geometric shapes typical of the 1960s. The flared A-line was in style for dresses, skirts and coats in short-above-the-knee lengths. The guys wore slim -fitted, bright-colored garments were sold cheaply in boutiques all over London, England.

Let's face it, vintage clothing is in demand! The stylish and quality garments once fitted with metal zippers and buttons of yesterday, have been replaced with Velcro and plastic closures in our current clothing market.

Take a close look at the stitching on apparel made in today's world. Buttons, if present, fall off easily and stitching is inadequate; fake pockets, and clothing shrink after laundering for the first time. These facts — along with style, add to the appeal of finding and obtaining the stylish clothing of decades gone by.

The 1960s became the beginning of the "Hippie" look, which originated on the west coast of America. This was a time when designers of dress and textiles tested with vivid bright colors, patterns and textures. Most fashionable people from the 1960s wore long layers of loose clothing with those wild clashing colors. Designer, *Pacco Rabanne* dresses laid the way for plastic discs and metal links, which looked more like sculptures than clothing.

At the beginning of the decade, the market was dominated by Parisian designers of expensive haute couture garments by *Dior* and *Balenciaga.* Formal suits for high-society women also underwent a structural change resulting in looser lines and shorter skirts.

Present-day designers are now imitating the mid-centuries funky fabric patterns when creating their current clothing lines to sell for high-end boutiques and major department stores.

1960s Fashion Designers

Among the iconic 1960's era, was the couturier fashion designer *Emilio Pucci* (see page 300), who is known for his bold colors and graphic and geometric patterns. Pucci's fashions were psychedelic and exciting. Similarly, Hubert De Givenchy is known for creating fashions for the Hollywood movie star, "Audrey Hepburn." He created most of her wardrobe, which was simple, yet elegant. An example could be seen with Audrey wearing a simple "Shift" dress being worn with bold accessories.

Did You Know? Givenchy, created, "The little black dress" as worn by Ms. Hepburn in the hit, "*Breakfast at Tiffany's.* This dress sold at *Christie's Auction House* for a whopping $920,000 in 2006. Audrey Hepburn's refined glamorous figure made way for slender, less bosomy fashions that were the rage for the prior 1950's Marilyn Monroe "bombshell" style.

Mini-skirts and more legs were popular and 1960's British fashion icon-Mary Quant gave the miniskirt its name, but miniskirts are said to be have been invented by Andre Courreges who is also known for "Go-Go Boots" fame. Mary was also known for the ever so popular, "Hot Pants". I used to

Vintage 1970'S Multi-Colored, Patent Leather Go-Go Boots

have a black patent leather pair of Go-Go boots I wore with some hot pants back in 1972.

Other notable designers from the 1960's were: *Pierre Balmain, Yves Saint Laurent, Christian Dior, Coco Chanel* and *Ossie Clark. Clark* was known for his fashions for "Twiggy," The Beatles, The Rolling Stones and Liza Minnelli; Yves saint Laurent, for the return of the Navy Pea Coat and safari jacket style; and *Bonnie Cashin, Christian Dior,* and *Pierre Cardin,* who was noted for starting the thigh-high boots and collarless jacket.

One of the first super models of the decade was "Twiggy." *Twiggy* was featured on the covers of Vogue time after time in the 1960's. *Twiggy*, was the world's first "Supermodel." She was a skinny kid with the face of an angel who became an icon instantly. "She'll last a couple of weeks," a bystander quipped in 1967 when she

Photo of *Twiggy*

took New York City by storm. Fact is, *Twiggy* was a top paying model for over 35 years.

Magazines such as *Glamour, Seventeen, Vogue, Life* and *Harper's Bazaar* set the newest fads and fashions using the Super Models of the 1960s. A February, 1968 issue of *Glamour* magazine, featured an article about 19 models who were considered "Super Models". They were: Cheryl Tiegs, Verushka, Lisa Palmer, Peggy Moffitt, Susan Murray, Twiggy, Susan Harnett; Marisa Berenson, Gretchen Harris, Heide Wiedeck, Irish Bianchi, Hiroko Matsumoto, Anne DeZagher; Kathie Carpenter, Jean Shrimpton, Jean Patchett, Benedetta Barzini, Claudia Duxbury, and Agneta Frieberg.

Additionally, our famous and glamorous first lady, Jackie Kennedy helped set clothing trends during the '60s, while in the *Presidential White House* with the help of her favorite designers' *Oleg Cassini* and *Anne Cole Lowe. Anne Cole Lowe* is also known for creating Jackie's wedding dress. Some of Jackie's suits were made from a fabric type called "Boucle." Who can forget the famous "Pink Suit" and her "Pill Box" style hats she loved so much to wear. Jackie also would become a lifelong fan with wearing designer, *Coco Chanel* fashions.

Jacqueline Kennedy's famous pink suit ironically made its debut in a photo essay about *Chanel* in the, Sept. 1, 1961 issue of *LIFE* magazine, which featured Jackie on the cover wearing yet another designer - *Oleg Cassini* outfit.

Jackie wore her pink suit several times from 1961 to 1963. She sometimes wore a matching blouse underneath the jacket, or just open with her famous pearls. It was at President Kennedy's request that she wear the outfit in Dallas. President Kennedy had stated to a mutual friend, Susan Mary Alsop-that Jackie, his wife of ten years, looked "ravishing in it.

1960's Jacqueline Bouvier Kennedy (First-Lady) Photo, Wearing Her Famous Chanel, Pink Suit

The suit is now stored out of public view in the National Archives. It will not be seen by the public until at least 2063, according to a deed of Caroline Kennedy, Jackie Kennedy's sole surviving heir. At that time, when the 100-year deed expires, the Kennedy family descendants will renegotiate the matter. (I guess I won't be viewing it in my lifetime.)

Paper Dresses of the 1960s

The "Paper Dress" fab was started in 1966 by *Scott Paper Company* (of toilet tissue fame) and was actually worn by Jackie Kennedy as well as other famous woman. It had a simple 2-D shape ideal for the bold graphic prints that were so fashionable for the mod '60s era.

The 1960's Space Age had launched a number of futuristic fashion fads, but none was a bigger craze than paper dresses. The original "Paper Caper" mini dress (5-7- inches above knee), sold through a chipper ad campaign in *Seventeen* Magazine for sale at $1.25 and came with .52 cents of coupons. The colorful A-line frock (dress) was meant to be thrown away after one use. *LIFE Magazine* got on board and sold half a million of the paper outfits in the first five months without any notable effort.

The *Scott Paper Company* had been initially chasing after an idea for a new market – using paper- garments for hospitals and other places where disposable clothing, could be more cost effective than doing endless loads of laundry. *Scott Paper Company* was about to introduce a line of paper table linens, and predicted a promotional paper house-dress would be a cute gimmick. The dress was sleeveless, collarless and had two big patch pockets. It was splashed with black-and-white Op Art or a bright red paisley pattern. Made of layers of cellulose and nylon, the crunchy, waffle-textured mini-dress resembled a piqué woven fabric.

Vintage 1960's Paper Dress (Campbell Soup Company—Souper Dress)

Very soon after, other brands, such as *Mars, Hallmark, Dove, Lux* and *Lifebuoy*, jumped on board and offered their own version of the paper mini dress. The Campbell Co. even created the funky "Souper Dress," printed in a pattern with rows of tomato cans -taking a bit of the success from Andy Warhol's Pop-Art paintings. In 1968, presidential candidates George Romney, Robert Kennedy and Richard Nixon handed out promotional paper campaign dresses, and graphic designer Harry Gordon created a line of paper dresses covered in rock 'n' roll poster art. Vintage paper dresses are very collectible, so don't forget to look in those closets and dresser drawers!

Did You Know? New York's grooviest boutique
"Paraphernalia", invented a Chia Pet–style paper mini- dress embedded with

flower seeds that apparently blossomed after it was misted. We need one these creations today…..definitely organic. Also, *Whippette Sportswear* produced "Le Canned Dress," three dresses that were sold in a brightly colored can for $25.

When listing vintage clothing, I found this very informative online site to be quite helpful, when sorting out and dating, those vintage clothing fashions. It is literally chalked full of photos assist in identifying vintage fashions: http://www.fashion-era.com

Who Was, "Andy Warhol"?

Who was Andy Warhol: Andrew Warhola, (August 6, 1928 – February 22, 1987), or Andy Warhol as he is known to the world, was an American renaissance man. Known primarily for his innovative paintings and artistic achievements, Warhol made a name for himself in the world of avant-garde film, music, publishing, writing, and acting. He helped to found and define the cultural Pop art movement that hit America during the 1950s. Though, he is best remembered for his paintings of Campbell's soup cans, he also created hundreds of other works including commercial advertisements and films. He was controversial, revered, and always daring.

Warhol was a creative and talented child who showed artistic talent early on. After high school he went to study commercial art at Carnegie Mellon University in Pittsburgh. He graduated in 1949 and immediately moved to New York City, where he became a successful magazine illustrator. He created his own style of art called "blotted ink" and soon became one of New York's most sought after illustrators.

His first exhibit was at the Hugo Gallery in 1952 and was titled, "*Andy Warhol: Fifteen Drawings Based on the Writings of Truman Capote.*" From 1956 to 1959 his works were featured at the *Bodley Gallery* along with one show at the *Museum of Modern Art*. By 1962 he was doing art shows in California. In the 1960s, Warhol moved into a studio which he named "The Factory" (the building used to be a factory). The "Factory" was lined with tinfoil and silver paint and was located in the heart of the city. It was from here that he made his assault on the New York art scene. When he wasn't at the "Factory" he was hanging out at "Serendipity 3" or "Studio 54."

Warhol's works began to revolve around one main concept—Americana and American popular culture. His paintings were comprised of money, food, women's shoes, celebrities, newspaper clippings and everyday objects. His music, his writings, and his films all represented American culture and its values.

Warhol forged his way to fame with his famed paintings of Campbell's Soup can labels-which he ate for lunch practically every day. He created 32 canvases for each type of Campbell's soup. His exhibit of these cans became a huge hit in California.

Andy Warhol's "Marilyn Monroe" Pop Art Framed Artwork

Did You Know? An unfortunate fact about Andy Warhol: When he was a child when Warhol was in the third grade, he contracted St. Vitus' disease which is thought to result from complications brought on by scarlet fever. Warhol suffered greatly from the attacks of this disease, which caused involuntary muscle movement on his nervous system. Warhol's appearance altered greatly and he became very self-conscious of his looks.

Enid Collins handbags selling in the hundreds range!

1960's Enid Collins created handbags are whimsical hand-painted handbags (wooden-box and canvas-bucket) made with unique themed folk art designs with a mixture of leather, brass findings with applied rhinestones and sequins.

The "EC" handbags were of good quality and made with silk screened themes of whimsical glitz and fun; this drew the attention of high-end retail stores. Each handbag had a title. (Over 100 themes were designed.) Here is a list of a few of the highly collectible names or themes:

Glitter Bugs Bags (I & II), Horseplay, Wise Guys, Carriage Trade, The Money Tree, Daisy Buckets; Jewel Garden Buckets, Pineapple Boxes, The Roadrunner, Sea Garden Buckets and *Sophistikits (I and II).*

These were do-it-yourself kits, manufactured in the late 1960s by the original *Collins Company.* Because these kits are hard to find unassembled, the kits bring in a premium dollar amount to their sellers.

Themes to watch for: Cats, owls, horses, dogs, peacocks, birds, fish, "the signs of the zodiac and "flower power".

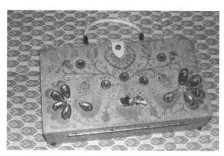
Vintage Enid Collins Wooden Box-Handbag, "Pavan II"

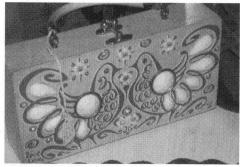
Vintage Enid Collins Wooden Box Handbag, "Love Doves"

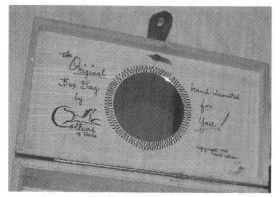
Enid Collins Signature Handbag Markings and Logo

Here are some Enid Collins handbag identifying tips:

- Signatures are important. Early box bags are fully signed under the Enid Collins name or initials or possibly both.

- The '60s handbags were also dated by year (particularly with the box types).

- The bags most often will have their themed names on the outside of the handbag.

- Many bags are also signed in lower case letters "ec" or simply with a "c". This represents the year in which Enid Collins actually owned the company. The bags that are marked with a capital "C" or "Collins of Texas" were made by the *Tandy Leather Corporation* in the 1970s. You won't find the name of "Enid Collins" printed on the inside or outside, of the Tandy manufactured handbags.

- The original bags were usually marked with "Enid Collins "Original" and "Collins of Texas". Often, there is the Enid Collins, galloping horse logo.

- There is a small round mirror or full square mirror on inside.

- They have quality brass findings and "twist latch" fasteners.

Tip: If the handbag is marked, "Japan", anywhere on the bag, it's a fake. Enid Collins' handbags initial selling prices will fluctuate based on its condition and theme. Even one missing stone or embellishment-will definitely effect profits.

Judith Leiber Handbags

Another valuable vintage handbag to watch keep a watchful eye out for is the lavishly designed handbags by "Judith Leiber." Judith Leiber created some exquisitely designed evening clutches, miniaudieres and purses that are so unique that some of the world's most prestigious museums have deemed them to be "works of art". Founded in 1963 by Judith and her husband, the artist Gerber Leiber, Judith Leiber has outfitted celebrities, socialites, princesses and queens with some of the most luxurious accessories on the market. Today her collections also include: sunglasses, belts, fragrances, and a bridal collection.

Ultra Rare Vintage 1981 JUDITH LEIBER Chinese Hand Warmer Purse with Swarovski Crystals Minaudiere Handbag

Vintage Judith Leiber Black And White Crystal Jeweled Minaudiere Handbag

Judith Leiber was born in Budapest, Hungary and was a Holocaust survivor. During World War II, she trained with the *Hungarian Handbag Guild* and was the very first woman to be recognized as a master of the bag-making craft. In 1998, Judith and Gerber sold their company and retired. Since 1953, nearly every presidential wife (First Ladies of the Whitehouse) has carried a Judith Leiber handbag to the presidential inauguration ceremony. If you're ever in East Hampton, New York, visit the *Leiber Museum*. The museum was built in 2005 by the Leiber's as a gallery and showcase for Judith's creations and Gerber's modernist paintings and sculptures. Mrs. Leiber states that she created at least 3,500 glorious styles of handbags. The Swarovski crystal beaded bags Judith created had each and every crystal inserted by hand.

There is so much more to discuss about mid-century merchandise. Hopefully in the future we can discuss this subject further. You can find some interesting online blogs and articles about the Mid-Century Era, or purchase some reference books to further your education on the styles of the mid-century decades.

Chapter XII

Vintage Vanity Treasures Found in the Home

Toiletries, Perfumes, Colognes and Cosmetics....

And Please Don't Throw Away That Old Gillette Safety Razor!

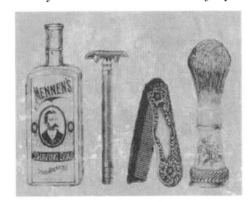

In this chapter we will discuss some of the most neglected cash-cows found in the medicine chest of the bathroom, a hall closet, and on top of bedroom dressers.

The values of vintage perfumes, colognes, toiletries & personal hygiene products, men's razors and ladies cosmetics, can be very misunderstood. When a family member decides to clean out a cabinet in the home, this is one of the first areas with items condemned to a trash receptacle.

Let's talk diligently about these misunderstood consumer products, and how valuable they can be in today's society.

Perfumes (Vintage Fragrances and Designer Labels)

Oh, the allure of vintage fragrances and Parfums! Vintage parfums such as those created for the designer labels of: *Gucci, CoCo Chanel's* (No 5), *Christian Dior*'s (Diorama, Miss Dior), *Guerlain*'s (Lavande, Champs-Elysees and Shalimar), *Calvin Klein's*- Bvlgari; *Hermes, Givenchy, Versace, Schiaparelli's* (Shocking), *Jacques Fath's* (Iris Gris) and parfums from France-are all very valuable, and sought-after for their luscious scents.

Vintage Hermes Perfume

Other famous authentic designer fragrances to watch for are: *Fendi, Emanuel* Ungaro, YSL (*Yves Saint Laurent*), *Jovan* -1970's "Musk Oil", *Laura Ashley, Faberge's* ("Tigress", "Aphrodisia" and "Woodhue"); *Oscar de La Rente, Jean Patou's* ("Moment" and "Joy"); *Giorgio Armani* and *Ralph Lauren*- just to name a few, can fetch a huge amount of cash from their clothing, accessories and jewelry lines.

Vintage Coco Chanel's "CHANEL No 5"-Perfume

If you discover vintage perfumes in exquisite crystal bottles by *Lalique* and *Baccarat*.....Major Treasure!

⚷ **Tip**: Anything marked with the large "CC" logo (Coco Chanel) is an extraordinary treasure. The logo has two c's interlocked with each other. However, be careful! Imitators/fakes, such as handbags are found everywhere, and are can be very hard to distinguish from the actual authentic items.

It doesn't matter if they are empty bottles, they can still be quite valuable. Furthermore, make sure you list them as authentic vintage scents (new-old-stock or NOS), since there are a lot of counterfeit perfumes being reproduced today.

Vintage collectible perfume bottles that were manufactured under the company names of *Guerlain, Coty, Van Cleef & Arpels* and *Gres* date between the 1920s-1980s, and can bring in, huge cash profits. Highly collectible and valuable are the bottles from the Art Nouveau and Art Deco Eras.

Of course, these perfume bottles are hard to find, but they are out there, waiting to be discovered.

Vintage Miscellaneous Perfume and cologne Fragrances

Those large bottle displays once found in the local pharmacies or corner markets---valuable! Large displays used to advertise perfume/cologne brands are called factices or dummies.

A great reference book I discovered for learning about perfume notes is called: *Perfumes: The A-Z Guide by* Luca Turin and Tania Sanchez.

An informative perfume bottle guidebook with beautiful illustrations is the, *Antique Trader Perfume Bottles Price Guidebook* by Kyle Husfloin.

An online reference guide quite educational on this subject can be found at: www.basenotes.net. This site lists over 20,000 perfumes, and is a guide to the world of fragrances.

Perfume, Cologne, Eau de Toilette or Splash?

Mademoiselle/Monsieur, it's time to chat about a couple of those fabulous one-of-a-kind fragrances and their manufacturers. Fragrances have been around for centuries, but the latter part of 19th century was the first real era of perfume as we know it now. This is because of advances in organic chemistry knowledge, which made it possible to create numerous scents. Some of the major fragrance categories are-floral, fruit, oriental, and green marine, each area contained certain natural oils derived from Mother Nature. Perfume is made by of mixtures containing denatured ethyl alcohol (78 to 95 percent) and essential oils. Some perfumes are stronger than others. Here are some of the different types of scents produced: Perfume-has 22 percent essential oils and is the costliest; Eau de Parfum-is 15 to 22 percent essential oils; Eau de Toilette (EDT) is 8 to 15 percent oils; Eau de Cologne has four percent essential oils added and Splash, has only one to three percent essential oil added. This explains why perfumes (French-"Parfums") are more expensive than colognes.

The countries of Italy, France and Germany lead in the creating luxury Parfum fragrances. France has created some of the most desired and collected of all perfumes made in the world. The designer name *Christian Dior*-created the title for its first perfume "Miss Dior", which was ever-so-popular and a top seller for years. The fragrance was created by the French Perfumer's, Jean Carles and Paul Vacher.

The *Dior Corporation* launched "Miss Dior" its first perfume in 1947. Miss Dior parfum was named after Catherine Dior-*Christian Dior's* sister. In 1948, a New York City Christian Dior Parfums branch was established. The modern Dior corporation also notes that "a luxury ready-to-wear house was established in 1948 at the corner of 5th Avenue and 57th Street, New York — which was the first of its kind. In 1949, the "Diorama" perfume is released by *Christian Dior*.

These two original *Christian Dior* pure Parfum scents came in beautiful *Baccarat* crystal bottles. Accordingly, this makes them very collectible, especially if find a bottle with its original contents, still retains a strong scent (not weak), and found inside its original presentation box.

Another perfume found in a *Baccarat* crystal flagon (i.e. perfume bottle) is "Shalimar". "Shalimar" is a women's fragrance originally created by *Jacques Guerlain* in 1921, as a classic soft amber (Oriental) parfum. It is currently produced by *Guerlain*.

1940's Christian Dior "Miss Dior" Baccarat Perfume Bottle

"Shalimar" was created in 1921 and re-released in 1925 in a bottle designed by

---

Tip: Vintage Deco Shalimar bottle labels simply have the word "Shalimar" surrounded by a gold border, while on newer bottles there is also the name of "Guerlain" underneath. Additionally, the recent bottles are flatter and non-fluted.

Vintage Guerlain Shalimar
Perfume with Baccarat Bottle

Raymond Guerlain and made by *Cristalleries de Baccarat* (bottle design # 597) the new bottle was launched at the *Decorative Arts Exhibition* as an antidote against The Great Depression. These sell in the hundreds of dollars.

Did You Know?

The name *"Shalimar"* was inspired after the "Gardens of Shalimar", which was located in Lahore – which is present day, Pakistan.

Vintage figural bottles by designer Elsa Schiaparelli--found with contents intact--are very collectible and quite valuable. "Shocking" Schiaparelli perfume bottles came out in 1937, and shoppers could find them in most department stores. The "Shocking" bottle shape was an inspirational idea between Schiap (as she was known), Jean Carles, who made the perfume, and the Surrealist drawings by artists Marcel Vertes and Salvador Dali. The design was in the shape of a dressmaker's mannequin.

1930's Schiaparelli
"Shocking Pink",
Mae West Perfume
Torso Bottle-$350

Note: A Flacon is a small perfume bottle: a small, often decorated, stoppered bottle used especially for holding perfume.

People collect perfume bottles for different reasons. The perfume aroma that came in the original bottle may be desired, or because the bottle that the fragrance came in had its own unique individual beautiful shape and design. Collectors seek out, and often pay high prices for past and present bottles used by perfumers. Among the most sought after are beautiful bottles made by *R. Lalique, Baccarat, J. Viard, Brosse, A. Jollivet, Cristal Nancy, Wheaton, C. K. Benda,* and *Lucien Guillard.* Whether one of these bottles is full, empty, or in between, it could rake in hundreds to thousands of dollars to its owners. That said, you can find these beautiful bottles in the most simplest of places.

Early 1900's perfume bottles made by *Renè Lalique* for *Frances Coty of Paris* are highly collectible from all parts of the globe. It is a fact, each *Lalique* bottle is a piece of art handmade by master glass workers. During the Art Nouveau period, *Lalique* was well known for creating a wide variety of objects including perfume bottles for *Coty, Guerlain* and many others--over 250 perfume bottles total. The companies of *Lalique* and *Baccarat* crystal, created exquisite flagons for the perfume/fragrance industry.

Vintage Lalique Crystal Nina Ricci L' Air du Temps Parfum Bottle Dove Stopper— $125

Vintage Miniature Lalique, Eau De Toilette Bottle

One of the most famous perfume bottles created during the mid-20th century was "Lalique L'air du Temps". This bottle featured one or more frosted doves on top of the bottle. It's not uncommon to find these exquisite bottles in boxes at auctions or estate sales.

Did You Know?

The *International Perfume Bottle Association* (IPBA) holds a convention every year. In May of 2013, the convention was help in Jacksonville, FL. (The IPBA operates one of the largest specialty perfume bottle auctions held each year in different cities.) Several countries attend this huge auction. The attending patrons showed strong interest for 18th and 19th century scent containers. The auction was highlighted by a continental figural perfume brooch of enameled sterling silver in the form of a rose, which sold for a whopping $20,400. In the Czech category, a beautifully-jeweled bottle in black glass and a red figural stopper, in the form of a butterfly sold for $6,600. The commercial category featured over 25 bottles designed by glass artists *Julian Viard* and *Rene Lalique*. A *Viard* figural bottle with a blue patina, created for the *Ramses* perfume "Sphinx D'Or", sold for $19,200 and the *Lalique* bottle, "Flausa", made for *Roger & Gallet*, sold for $6,600.

Some of the highest prices went to rare *Baccarat* presentations created for commercial perfumers. The figural bottle of an elephant with rider created for *Lubin* and the scent "Kismet", sold for $13,200. The centerpiece of the auction was also a *Baccarat* design for *Patanwalla* containing the perfume "Bhagwan". A figural bottle of an Indian male deity with enameled detail and being housed in its original luxury box that has only been known to exist through the drawings in the *Baccarat* archives. When bidding was finished, this bottle sold for $63,600. A 1917 Baccarat bottle in box for "Toute l'Egypt" for Monne reached $38,000, at IBPA's convention in 2014.

I have mentioned the convention event to simply show my readers how perfume bottles can be extremely valuable!

Vintage Personal Hygiene Products
Vintage Shampoos from the 1960s-1980's
Remember the original 1970's Herbal Essence or 1960's *Prell* shampoos? Well, you guessed it—collectible.

I admired the clean herbal scent from 1970's *Herbal Essence* Shampoo-I would purchase it today just for that reason alone.

1970's Herbal Essence Shampoo-which I totally loved-sells for over $150 for a full bottle.
Dippity-Do hair gel from 1960s selling for $45

1970's Clairol® Herbal Essence

Believe it or Not! Vintage KOTEX (The delicate rose graphics on the KOTEX boxes are admired.) Modess, hospital-size feminine pads from the 1950s-1960s, can sell for over $300.

The nostalgic men's grooming product called "Old Spice" by the *Shulton Company*, is sought -after for their aftershave, cologne-splash, and deodorant scent.

Discontinued brands or shades of nail colour by *Chanel le Vernis*, are selling for over $200.

Women's Home COMPANION,
December 1952

The list can go on and on. Any vintage discontinued consumer products can be valuable if keep in pristine condition.

Farrah Fawcett Merchandise
Past iconic stars promoted certain merchandise lines such as 'Farrah Fawcett's hair care product line. Farrah was a sex symbol of the 1980's. She starred in the 1970's hit television series, "Charlie's Angels." Farrah Fawcett posters broke sales records, making her an international pop culture icon. Her layered hair-style went on to become an international trend, with the ladies, called a "Farrah-do," or a "Farrah-flip.

Other valuable Farrah collectibles are magazines and TV Guides that feature Farrah Fawcett's photo on the front covers; the BARBIE "Super Star-Farrah Fawcett" doll; and the 1977- Farrah Fawcett Styling Head Glamour Center toy by the *Mego Corporation*.

I recently spotted a vintage unopened box of 'Farrah Fawcett' hairspray, sold for over $325 on eBay. They don't manufacture the product anymore—its dead-stock.

Vintage'70s Farrah Fawcett/Charlie's Angels Tee-Shirt

Vintage Men's Aftershave

"There's something about an Aqua Velva Man!"
Everyone remembers that iconic TV commercial phrase, as well as, the commercial slogans for "King's Men Aftershave", "Mennen Skin Bracer". Yes, these men's cologne and aftershaves are all sought-after if stored correctly; **kept in dark cool area,** and their scent is still strong.

Some notable collectible vintage male fragrances that fetch a fair amount of cash are:

- "Nine Flags" Set of 9 (selling as high as $470)
- "Eau Sauvage by Christian Dor-$150 selling range
- " Egoiste" by *Chanel* - $300 selling range
- *Revlon* "Pub" aftershave - $200 selling range

Vintage "Aramis" After Shave 4 Fl Oz

- "Chaps" by *Ralph Lauren-$100 range*
- Men's "Aramis" cologne-$130 range

It's just a matter of research as to what is trendy in today's consumer market.

Vintage Hai Karate Cologne

Vintage cologne is the rage today and people want the original, not the repro-duced - imitators of the original product. (Unused and sealed preferred.)

Vintage English Leather Men's Splash

Yardley of London, England

"Oh behave!" As Austin Powers, the International Man of Mystery would say! Women's Yardley Colognes from the mid-century such as, "Oh! De London," takes us back to the 1960s Pop culture decade. Vintage 1960's *Yardley* fra-grances, such as "Oh! de London" and "Sea Jade", can sell for over $200 de-pending on quantity volume of the cologne, and if it has been kept away from damaging elements that are caused from exposure to the sun and heat.

Recently, a vintage bottle of "Oh! de London" *Yardley* cologne sold for $199 on eBay. Watch for *Yardley* Perfume Gift Sets (MIB), valuable, because of their very distinct floral notes and production was "discontinued".

Other popular fragrances that are in demand and bring in a good amount of profit from the '60s and '70s are:

- *Fabergès* Sexy, 1970's "Tigress" cologne
- *Fabergè* "Woodhue" and "Babe" cologne and cologne sets

Vintage Men's Woodhue Cologne Gift Set

Vintage 1950s Full- 6 Ounce Tigress Cologne Extraordinaire By Faberge In Original Box.

Vintage Gift Set of Faberge Ladies Fragrances-Tigress, Aphrodisia and Woodhue

- *Prince Matchabelli* empty perfume or full perfume bottles like this, "Queen of Georgia" Blue flask and other ornate early 1950's bottles, fetching a sweet $350.

1950s Prince Matchabelli 1/2 Oz Crystal Blue Opaque Enamel Gold Maltese Cross & Crown- Perfume Bottle-$135

Vintage Prince Matchabelli Stradivari *SEALED 1 Fl. Oz. Perfume Crown Bottle with Presentation Box-$189

- Estee Lauder's solid perfumes in figural shaped compacts, sell up to $300
- Estee Lauder's vintage perfume "Youth Dew" fragrances can fetch $45 if in mint condition.

My Perfume Treasure Trove Story

About a year ago, I attended a local estate sale. In the home's basement I found a closet and filled with over 50 unopened boxes of vintage 1970s and 1980s perfumes and colognes. The estate sale company conducting the sale had wanted $5 to $8 for each unopened box, so I decided to purchase ten boxes of these unused per-

Estee Lauder Enameled 1990's Blue Fish Sea Stars, Lucidity Powder Compact-$339

fumes. I researched my perfume purchases on the Internet and was thrilled to discover that they were quite valuable. I rushed back to the sale and purchased what they had left. I spent a total of $100 on all of the perfume boxes, resold them and made a profit of $1500. Not a bad investment for the initial $100 spent.

These perfumes were kept in a dark cool place, thus, their fragrance notes had been preserved –not to mention- their boxes had never been opened. The homes previous owner had once worked behind the perfume counter at J.C. Penney's back in the '70s and '80s, and had retained these boxes to give away as gifts. Glad I found them before they were tossed into the trash!

Men's Safety Razors

Although, there are many types of antique straight razors; I want to share some information on the hidden values found in vintage "Safety Razors." At present, we have seen a revival in men's personal hygiene practices with "wet shaving". Past grooming methods using 50-year-old vintage safety razors, is the latest trend.

Collectors today are searching for those unique hard-to-find vintage razors dating from the early and mid-20th century-both safety and straight razors. Some are worth thousands of dollars —while others just a few dollars. Safety razors were reminiscent of our ancestor's times; they are keepsakes of a lost era.

> **Tip**: When purchasing vintage razors to sell online remember to clean and sanitize them first, and be careful when handling, as the blade may still be in the shaving device.

Vintage safety razors come in many styles and makes, but the most popular type desired is *Gillette Company's* "Fat Boy" razor, and the "Adjustable 1- 9" setting- safety razor.

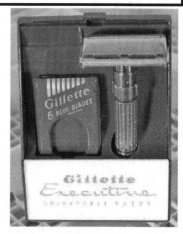

Vintage 1958 Rare D3 Gillette-
Executive, Adjustable Safety
Razor with Partial Case-$167

Antique Shaving Mirror

Vintage Safety Razor Lot-Sold for $375

Vintage Gillette Ad

Vintage Gillette Razor
Display With New-old-stock

History of the Gillette Razor

From 1904 to 1974 the *Gillette Safety Razor Company* of Boston, Massachusetts created a razor empire when introducing the disposable blade, double edge, safety razor. This revolution in shaving technology brought the barbershop into people's homes for the first time, and helped to create one of the world's most prominent consumer product companies of all time.

In the United States, *Gillette* (the company was founded by King C. Gillette in 1903), is the most familiar manufacturer of safety razors and blades. He wanted to create a razor that was thin and disposable, and didn't need to be constantly sharpened. The *Gillette Safety Razor Company* would make safety razors for the government and were issued to the armed forces during World War I. By the end of the war, some 3.5 million razors and 32 million blades were put into military hands, thereby converting an entire nation to the *Gillette* safety razor.

Another one of the most collectible of the *Gillette* razors is the 1952-53, "British Gillette"- #66. The #66 is one of several razors manufactured and sold by *Gillette* in Britain (the #16 and the #58 are two other popular razors of that line). The #66 should be considered one of the best *Gillette* safety razors manufactured. It was plated in rhodium, which lasts over 50 years. The weight and balance meet in a razor that provides a superb shave. It is a razor that is the epitome of form and function in a device. Pay attention to the razor's handle and end-cap design. In addition to the heavier version of the *Gillette* #66 razor (approx. 82 grams), they also made a lightweight- aluminum version of the #66 (weight-approx. 37 grams).

Photo of Safety Codes Found Underneath the Razor Guard

Tip: British razors at this time did not use date codes, the only way to estimate the date is by their case.

Dating a Gillette Razor

Razor Serial Numbers were impressed on all *Gillette* razors from 1904 until 1921, and on deluxe models from 1921 — 1931 (except for a period in 1927-28). This corresponds to the time King Gillette was directly associated with the business and may have been at his insistence. These serial numbers were located on the top of the guard, or sometimes the inner barrel. Lack of serial numbers also occurred from 1931-1951, so it may be a bit more difficult to identify razors from this timeline.

Other *Gillette* razor dating methods:

*   1903-1929 (serial numbers) will be present on the razor.
*   1930-1949 (the "NDC" years) razor blades were stamped with a date code.
*   1950-1988 (letter codes) were used. After the year 1950, *Gillette* made it much easier to identify razors. The date codes are found underneath the guard on each safety razor. The code identifies the year (with corresponding letters) and calendar quarter of manufacture (number 1 representing January, February, March & number 2 for the months of April, May and June etc.). Date codes on blades (see above) also continued through this period.

This should help you get started in dating those old safety razors.

For more information for dating Gillette safety razors, the following online website has more details: www.razorarchive.com/gillette-date-codes

Similarly, vintage Schick Safety razors like the, *Personal Touch Twin Blade Shaver* and the *Dial, 1-8,* Adjustable Razor- can fetch over $100 if found unopened in original packing.

In the electric razor category, the German-made rechargeable men's *Braun* razor is in demand based on quality, and condition of the product.

Safety razor collecting has become a most recent hobby most notably for design, history and engineering. With so many varieties produced, it would be worth your time to invest in a razor collector's guidebook.

Here are some suggestions:

The Razor Anthology, by Knife World Publications; *1000 Razors Priced and Illustrated, by Bill Schroeder;* and the *Safety Razor Reference Guide from Ace to Z* by Robert K. Waits (1990...xerographic reprint in 1992).

Vintage Ladies Facial Cosmetics

If you're ever lucky enough to find 1960's Mod, "Yardley" cosmetics found in there "London Look" product line; you will indeed have quite the find, unused or used.

1960's Yardley "Silcker" Lipstick-Used

Yardley's Colorful 1960s Make-up Line

Yardley's "Slicker" Lipstick and Lip Polish- Unlike a traditional lipstick, Slicker was designed not to change the color of the lips, but simply to provide them with an attractive sheen. The sheerness of Slicker meant it could be worn alone, on top of regular lipstick or underneath it. A well-known slogan for the product was "Slicker under...Slicker over...Slicker alone! "Lipstick Slickers" were packaged in mod, striped cases with funky shades. Here is a list of some of their zany titles: "Helpless Pink", "London Luv Pink", "Sunny Slicker", "Surf Slicker", "Piccadilly", "Nippy Beige"; "Tan-Tan", "Good Night", and "Nectaringo". These vintage lipsticks (unused) can fetch over $150 because of demand and quantity of lip color in the tube.

Along with the Lipstick slickers, other makeup types in this group where- "Sigh - Shadow" eye shadows; London Lashes, English Eyeliner, "London Fluff" Face Pressed Powder, and "New to Nothing" Foundation. All these vintage Yardley cosmetics can sell for over $100 if found unused or in lightly used condition.

Unused Yardley of London, Glimmerick Water
Color Eye Shadow sold for $89

Vintage Cosmetic, Lipstick holders are also valuable. If you find one that seems to be gold metal, check to see if it could be gold plated-it could sell for around $200 online. Furthermore, mid-century compact and lipstick duos with rhinestones such as "Charles of the Ritz" sell in the hundreds of dollars.

Ladies Pressed Powder Compacts

When collecting a bit of beauty essential products from the past; one of the most adored for collecting is the "Compact", which held the original buyers own personal, favored facial pressed powder-make-up.

Back in the 1920s, it was of utmost importance to apply or touch-up our facial make-up because it was somewhat of a social statement. It was acceptable for a woman to groom herself in public, and take out a mirrored compact containing a pressed powder make-up and while sitting in a restaurant table, glance at her face and apply the powder to her nose.

Vintage ladies compacts and Minaudieres (mini evening bags) have become very collectible for their styles and designs (Art Deco, Nouveau and Mid-Century). Some of the most collectible are under the famous names of *Estee Lauder, Stratton, Kigu, Tiffany & Co, Cartier* and *Evans; Judith Leiber* and other designer names.

If you happen to come upon an 18K gold compact case or compact by *Cartier* or *Van Cleef & Arpels*-Merveilleux!! You are talking values near the $10,000 mark!

1960's Stratton England Astrology/
Zodiac Powder Compact - $240

If a vintage compact discovered, seems to be made of a fine silver alloy- search to find any type of hallmark on the compact. A silver hallmark will denote the purity of the silver. Some notable fine silver hallmarks found on compacts are Sterling, 925, 800 (80% silver). Foreign countries used symbols and makers names to denote silver, such as those by *Kigu* and *Tiffany & Co.*

What is a Hallmark? There is a common misunderstanding about what a hallmark really is. Many people confuse hallmarks with makers' marks. A hallmark is nothing more than an indication of metal content, a guarantee of purity or quality, which may include a maker's mark and other marks. Makers' marks alone are not considered hallmarks. Hallmarks are most often found on precious metal objects. Jewelry is exempted from hallmarking under certain circumstances. However, when a piece of jewelry is hallmarked, the marks can yield clues to country of origin, and sometimes the date of manufacture; and indications of the metal content of the piece.

Guillioche Type Compacts

The French word, "Guilloché," which is pronounced "gee-oh-SHAY", does not refer to a *type* of enameling on a compact or charm, but rather it is actually the process applied to the material used. Guilloché is a symmetrical pattern engraving technique which is produced by a mechanical engine-turning table. The patterns that were created were plentiful and closely resembled those created by the popular "Spirograph" child's kit made in the 1970's.

The rose-engine - as the machine is named - have been used for plate engraving in the early 1800's, these plates however, were never used to serve as a base for enameling. It was Carl Fabergé who first combined the technique of guilloché with enamel during the fin-de-siècle. It is therefore, not a distinct enameling technique. Furthermore, this technique is used also in jewelry making which involves carving a design into a base metal. Guilloche can be made with, or without enameling. The Guilloché pattern may then be filled with different colors and opacities of enamel paint. Here is an example of a vintage compact with Guilloche enameling.

Vintage Sterling Silver "Fairy" Compact

Vintage Guilloché Pattern- Compact

Did You Know? Machine types used to create Guilloché patterns include the rose engine and geometric lathe. These machines, which were used to create Guilloché patterns-are no longer manufactured. So, if a "Guilloché" piece is marked "made in China", than it is *not* a true Guilloché pattern.

A great source of information on the subject of collecting powder compacts can be found in the book: *Miller's Powder Compacts-A Collector's Guide* by Juliette Edwards.

Vinatage AVON Products

Most vintage Avon products are NOT currently considered valuable, but I wanted to mention some of Avon's products that can fetch a reasonable profit if found for a low cost:

- Early promotional *Avon Company* items
- New in box (NIB,) vintage Avon Half Round, 8" hair brushes. This brush is white with clear nylon bristles. These can sell for around $200 in unused condition. Additionally, their "Pink Flair" hair brushes can fetch around $130 if unused.
- The *Avon* for Elizabeth Taylor line included the "Elephant Walk" earrings and brooch set; "Egyptian Cleopatra" (named after Elizabeth Taylor's 1963 Cleopatra Film); and "Sea Shimmer Koi" sets- all sell for over $150
- Unused Original "Moonwind" fragrance, cologne sets, sell for around $75
- Specific jewelry pieces (e.g. *Jose Maria Barrera, Kenneth Cole*) sell in the hundreds
- Stuffed 20" Blue Plush Monkey, pattern #123, with long arms and legs- $100 range
- "Kerby Loves"- A Plush Brown Stuffed Animal Bear wearing a red shirt sells in the $100 range.

> **Tip**: Particular vintage plush stuffed animals from the 1970s-1980s are HOT! You can find these at Yard/Garage Sales. Example: The original 1986, "My Pet Monster" by *Amtoy* can sell for over $250.

There are so many vintage consumer goods that should *not* be considered worthless or discard-able, but these are a few found in the personal vanity and grooming area.

Valuable Architectural Salvage Found in the Bathroom?

You bet, if I had the time, I would definitely think about opening my own vintage architectural store!

When I hear of a house being torn down in an established neighborhood that was built before the 1980s, I think to myself, "Oh my, their goes some misjudged treasures off to the local dump!"

They're collectible because of their style, functionality, rarity and being high-quality made. Here is a list of valuable and much sought after architectural items to be found in the bathroom:

- Mid-century toilets and tank covers-in colors of blue, green, brown, peach, pink and white, selling in the $300 -$500 range. Think of it this way, "GAUDY IS TRENDY!!!"

Vintage 1960's Blue Colored Toilet

- Bathtubs-Clawfoot and early 1900s bath tubs are selling over $1000. In addition, mid-century bath tubs in the colors mentioned above-are in demand.
- Vintage early 1900s' porcelain kitchen and bathroom sinks/basins are HOT!
- Art Deco style bathroom light fixtures used on each side of a medicine cabinet selling up to $200
- Vintage water facet fixtures (single tap)-$200 range
- Vintage medicine cabinets (e.g., metal with etched glass and Hollywood Regency gold ornate edged mirrored)-over $125
- Antique Metal Robe/Door hooks and bath tub caddies sell in the hundred-dollar-range
- Vintage door knobs-Dating from the early 1800s into the 20th century, can sell for over $250.

Between the years 1830 -1870, there were more than 100 patents granted for door knobs.

Some of the most desired vintage door knobs and their timelines are:

- Pressed glass was popular from the 1820s to the 1850s
- Vintage crystal and glass knobs from 1860s -1950s
- Wooden knobs dating from 1885 -1910
- China-porcelain knobs imported from England and France through the 1850s
- Ornate cast metal from around the mid-1840s

Antique Ornate Metal Door Knobs

Antique Art Deco Purple Glass and Brass Door Knobs-$140

In 1870, a method for compression casting allowed the Victorian society to obtain the more detailed metal hardware that they adored so much. These very ornate bronze, brass carved designs are very valuable.

Antique Art Deco Drawer Pull

Additionally, vintage towel racks, grab bars, toilet paper holders, brass metal door and window hardware, and soap dishes are selling between-$50-150.

Salvage, Salvage, Salvage!!!

Repurposed Antique Claw Foot Bath Tub

Another untapped treasure to be found in the bathroom, are the whimsical ceramic wall plaques that depict mermaids, fish, bubbles and seahorses. Companies that produced these adorable wall plaques were *Ceramicraft, Norcrest, Lefton* and *Enesco*….especially the sets with the lusterware sheen applied to them, can be quite valuable.

Old 1929 High School Wood Door I Paid $25 for and resold for $200

Vintage Enesco Glazed Mermaid and Dolphin Bathroom Wall Pocket Plaque (5" H x 5-1/2" W)-$145

Vintage Ceramicraft Bathroom Brown, Green and Pink Fish Wall Pocket

Lusterware pottery or porcelain is created with a metallic glaze that gives the effect of iridescence.

Some unusual medicine cabinet or bathroom closet items can sell for $200 or more.

- Old aspirin tins, medicine bottles from the early 20th century (opium, early antidepressants).-selling in hundred dollar range.
- Personal hygiene items-the *Davol* Enema Fountain Syringe and hot water bottles, selling for over $150-in excellent or never used condition.
- Vintage Matson, Hollywood Regency style; mirrored vanity trays with gold gilt ornate edgings, and felted bottoms-selling range $80-$150
- Vintage "cottage chic"- tole hand-painted small trash cans with fantastic floral motifs and wicker hampers-sell for over $50.

Vintage Chic Hand Painted
"Roses" Motif Trash Can

Vintage Hand Painted Trash
Can With a Sailing Carrack/
Ship

- Yes, even those 1960's crocheted/knitted, Poodle toilet paper holders are selling for over $50. Don't forget the vintage '60s "Aurora" soft, beautiful, and delicately- scented toilet tissue rolls that sell for the same amount!

Did You Know?
Jim Henson—of the "Muppets" fame--was hired to film a series of 30 second ads for the comfy "Aurora" tissue brand by the *American Can Company*, which featured a feminine gloved- hand made up to resemble a ballerina. The beautiful hand would elegantly slide across the tissue paper explaining how soft it was in the commercials. The voice used in the ads was Jane Henson's (Jim's wife). In 1966, Lisa Henson's (their daughter) voice was used….The rest is Muppet history.

This is just an example of the many unnoticed items that can easily be tossed into the rubbish, that are indeed worth just as much as a diamond wristwatch. It's time to conclude this chapter on the hidden treasures waiting to be discovered from vintage personal vanity/ hygiene products and items found in the house to consider selling for extra cash!

Closing-Happy Treasure Hunting!

In closing, I hope this book will help you in your endeavors to find hidden treasures in your own home, or in your search for treasures among another's estate. This easy-to-read book will definitely help get started on the right path to finding those unknown cash cows!

There are so many more of those hidden vintage valuables to mention. Vintage clothing (ca 1890's—1990's), antiquity books, Christmas and Holiday memorabilia, sewing room articles, electronics, vintage costume jewelry were just a few areas that need exploring and hopefully another book will follow on those subjects.

Remember to keep in mind the following tips when searching for hidden treasures:

- Watch current collectible market trends. By observing what other potential buyers are searching for, and what   they are willing to pay for these items.
- Keep in mind, appraisals can only give us a clue to whether an item is valuable by its description and rarity. Appraisers preach what an antique is valued at; this doesn't dictate what a buyer will actually pay for that particular item. Appraisals to your wares can definitely change in the blink of an eye, so keep them up-to-date.

I attended an auction a few years ago that had some fabulous oil on canvas paintings and signed LE (limited edition) prints. At one time their resale values may have brought in a larger dollar amount than what they were selling for that day. A relative to the family whose possessions were being auctioned- attended the auction and became very concerned that the oil paintings, prints and a

1990's queen bedroom set with solid oak wall headboard; were only going to sell for a fraction of what the owner had originally paid for it. I explained to this woman, "Unfortunately, 1990's huge shelved bedroom units/sets similar to the one being auctioned off; are not a hot commodity in today's market, despite the original price the owner had paid for the set." The mattress only to this set, ending up selling for $150, sadly the unit was left behind for donation. The original price paid for the bedroom unit back in the 1990's had been $6,000.

Home owners who are attempting to downsize in their home will be disappointed when selling larger furnishings, such as wood entertainment centers, 1970s-'80s dining room and living room sets, artwork, and large 1990s' pottery lamps. They are just NOT desired with the younger generation of today.

What did sell at this particular auction was a closet full of new or lightly used Chico's® Women's Clothing Store apparel. Selling for over $3,000! Although, considered a high price to pay for a closet full of clothing, it was not a large sum to pay considering a new shirt at Chico's® store, which sell for approximately $70. There had to have been over 300 pieces of clothing in that closet. If you do the math, the buyer will obtain quite a profit in the long run. She did her research!

Research, hunting for collectible merchandise, and a computer with internet access, and a little time and patience is all it takes to make an extra income of $25,000 a year or more.

When hunting for garage and yard sales, remember when an item has a set marked price, it doesn't necessarily mean the seller won't negotiate with you-the buyer. I have been to garage sales and estate sales where items seem to be marked on the high-side, but vendors will deal!

- Never set prices on your second hand merchandise based on what its original purchase price was, or what its cost had been in the past.
- Don't hoard your purchases. Remember you're trying to make money!

So let's keep the **cash from going into the trash,** and channel it into your pocket instead!

Happy Treasure Hunting, My Friends!!

Photo Contributors by Chapter

Introduction

Rick Keema@NWMercantile. (n.d). *Vintage Aluminum Halliburton Centurion Zero 22"Suitcase.* [photograph]. Retrieved from www.etsy.com

Chapter I

Debbie Lambert@Brittany4209. (n.d.). *Mattel, Francie Doll (ca Pre-1973) "Miss Teenage Beauty"- #1284 Ensemble.* [photograph]. Retrieved from www.ebay.com

Samantha Syoen@prettyeve. (n.d.). *1959 Mattel "Roman Holiday" Barbie Doll TM Tagged Outfit, #968.* [photograph]. Retrieved from www.ebay.com

TheIvoryMannequin. (n.d). *Vintage '60s Red NylonVanity fair Panties With Pillow Tab.* [photograph]. Retrieved from www.etsy.com

Sue Knight@Plantdreaming. (n.d.). *1950s Bakelite Bangle, Injected, Random Dot Bracelet.* [photograph]. Retrieved from www.etsy.com

Chapter II

Betty@StitchesByElizabeth. (n.d.). *Bucilla Christmas - "Shopping Spree" 18" Maria Stanziani Stocking Kit 2007 NIP.* [photograph]. Retrieved from www.etsy.com

Jeshua@toytrekker. (n.d.). *1986 Playskool Jammie Pie "Pitty-Pin"- Plush Doll in Purple.* [photograph]. Retrieved from www.ebay.com

Kelly@treasurecoveally. (n.d.). *1979 Fisher Price Bunny Rabbit-Security Blanket Puppet in Original Box.* [photograph]. Retrieved from www.etsy.com

De la David@deladavid. (n.d.). *Vintage Custom Air Jordan Retro 1-Green Shoes/ Sneakers.* [photograph]. Retrieved from www.etsy.com

Poppy@ LittleRedHenVintage. (n.d.) *Vintage Set of 2 Paint-By-Number Pictures with Ballet Dancers (E4963).* [photograph]. Retrieved from www.etsy.com

Judea Zander@Gumgumfuninthesun. (n.d.). *Vintage '50s Rushton Star Creation Rubber Face Duck Stuffed Plush Toy.* [photograph]. Retrieved from www.rubylane.com

Clancy Johnson (n.d.). *1980's Kenner Care Bear's Cousin "Proud Heart Cat".* [photograph]. Retrieved from www.ebay.com

Natalie Kunow@WooVintageClothing. (n.d.). *Rare '40s Salvador Dali Silk* Tie-Woo Vintage Collection. [photograph]. Retrieved from www.etsy.com

Ruth Weston@AntiquesAndTeacups. (n.d.). *Margaret Keane's 1963, Big Eyes "Circe" Framed Print (34" x 22").* [photograph]. Retrieved from www.etsy.com

Chapter IV

Beth@Nouveauqueen. (n.d). *1950's Wilendur "Lobster-Clam" Print Tablecloth.* [photograph]. Retrieved from www.ebay.com

Pam Peterson@VintageCocobytheLake. (n.d.). *Vintage Vera Neumann Kitchen Tea Towel-Lady Bug Symbol (ca 1950s-1960s).* [photograph]. Retrieved from www.etsy.com

Emmelin Golling@EmmelinesWorld. (n.d.). *1958 Holt Howard "Pixieware" Jam & Jelly Condiment Jar.* [photograph]. Retrieved from www.etsy.com

Renee@reneed8383. (n.d.). *1960's Holt Howard "Cozy Kitten" Jam & Jelly Condiment Jar.* [photograph]. Retrieved from www.etsy.com

Kimberly Ryan@rustfarm. (n.d.). *Vintage '40s-'50s Chalkware "French Clown" Ball String Holder.* [photograph]. Retrieved from www.etsy.com

Christina@TheWhitepepper. (n.d.). *Vintage 1960's Mid-Century, Gold Cosco Step Stool.* [photograph]. Retrieved from www.etsy.com

Denise@StrangeBeauty. (n.d.). *Vintage 1950's Boscul White and Yellow Columbine (Peanut Butter) Drinking Glass.* [photograph]. Retrieved from www.etsy.com

Marty@gasman201. (n.d.). *Vintage Burger King Fire King Restaurant Ware Mug HTF.* [photograph]. Retrieved from www.etsy.com

Brianrobinjones. (n.d.) *Antique Griswold Cast Iron Skillet/fry pan-#13.* [photograph]. Retrieved from www.ebay.com

Jay Kaye@planettutopia. (n.d.). *1960's Cathrineholm "Lotus" Pattern Coffee Pot from Norway.* [photograph]. Retrieved from www.etsy.com

ThePapers. (n.d.). *Cathrineholm , Blue on White 'Lotus" Enamel Bowl-5.5" (14cm).* [photograph]. Retrieved from www.etsy.com

JCR@LovesPastel. (n.d.). *Vintage Mid-Century Pink Metal Cosco Utility Cart.* [photograph]. Retrieved from www.etsy.com

Matthew Seip. (n.d.). *Antique 1900s "Sharples Tubular Cream Separator" Advertisement- Metal Pot Scraper, Metal Sign Graphic.* [photograph]. Retrieved from www.ebay.com

Amber Foster@TheReasonls. (n.d.). *Black & Decker Spacemaker, Under-the-Counter Can Opener-NIB.* [photograph]. Retrieved from www.etsy.com

Welovelucite. (n.d.). *Four-Piece, Mid-Century Pyrex "Dots" Nesting Mixing Bowl Set-Size-#401, 402 and 403.* [photograph]. Retrieved from www.etsy.com

Martin and Melanie@SecondWindShop. (n.d.) *1950s Pyrex Pastel Custard Cups With Rack-Made in England -Very rare.* [photograph]. Retrieved from www.etsy.com

Skyler@LarkPaperCo. (n.d.). *Vintage Pyrex Vision Corning Vision Amber Ware Cookware Set.* [photograph]. Retrieved from www.etsy.com

Suzanne@Onmykitchentable. (n.d.). *1960's Atomic Age- JAJ (made in England) Pyrex, Red "Gooseberry" Pattern Serving Dish with Lid (Cinderella Model 443) and Warming Stand.* [photograph]. Retrieved from www.etsy.com

Vintage Golden West, Closset & Devers, 2 lb Coffee Can With Cowgirl Advertising. [photograph]. Retrieved from www.etsy.com

Sally & Marty Smith@buckeyeantiques. (n.d.). *Antique Tiger Chewing Tobacco Tin…Vintage Primitive Folk Cigarette Advertising Historical Country Store- Pipe Storage Container.* [photograph]. Retrieved from www.etsy.com

Chapter V

Becka@BechasPlace. (n.d.). *Rare (ca 1953-1971) Spode "Irene" Pattern, Scalloped-Rim Dinner Place Setting.* [photograph]. Retrieved from www.etsy.com

ShoponSherman. (n.d). *Vintage 1950's Aynsley JA Bailey Teacup and Saucer China Set -Handpainted Rose Motif W gold.* [photograph]. Retrieved from www.etsy.com

Shelly Moore@BluebirdCreekVintage. (n.d.). *Vintage Wallace, Rosepoint Pattern, Sterling Silver Flatware.* [photograph]. Retrieved from www.etsy.com

CottageAntiquesLTD. (n.d.). *Mid-Century, Dansk, Jens Quistgaard Teak Handled Steak Knives-Fjord By Dansk Set.* [photograph]. Retrieved from www.ebay.com

GalaxyReborn. (n.d.). *Vintage Filet Lace, White Tablecloth.* [photograph]. Retrieved from www.etsy.com

Majka MAChic@MAChic (n.d.) *1950's Italian "Point de Venise" Floral, Handmade Needle Lace Tablecloth.* [photograph]. Retrieved from www.etsy.com

Jolanta@cloudberry123. (n.d.). *Vintage 1900-1909 Hand Embroidered, Circular Tablecloth with Reticella Lace.* [photograph]. Retrieved from www.ebay.com

Kakki Smith@KIS Originals. (n.d.). *Vintage Italian Reticella Needle Lace Place Mats Set.* [photograph]. Retrieved from www.etsy.com

Robin Linn Reynoir, New Orleans, LA@Nolacottage. (n.d.). *Vintage 1940's Italian Alencon Lace and Linen Napkins Place Mats-Unused Set.* [photograph]. Retrieved from www.etsy.com

mollymsquires@TheGreenDoorGallery. (n.d.). Large (25-Inc), *Blanc de Chine Reticulated Lamp.* [photograph]. Retrieved from www.etsy.com

Mel & Teresa@Appletree Junction Antiques. (n.d.). *Vintage 1930-36, Macbeth-Evans, "American Sweetheart" Pattern, Depression Glass Cup and Saucers -Monex Color.* [photograph]. Retrieved from www.rubylane.com

Modern To Vintage Furniture & Design@Vintagefurnitureetc. (n.d.). *Vintage 20th Century L. C. Signed Tiffany, Favrile-Vase (10-1/4" H).* [photograph]. Retrieved from www.etsy.com

Christie@ChristiesCurios. (n.d.). *Vintage Tiffany Iridescent Favrile 5.5" Tumbler-Signed.* [photograph]. Retrieved from www.etsy.com

Gary Germer & Associates, Portland, Oregon. (n.d.). *1930's Lalique Opalescent St. Francis, French Art (Birds), Glass Vase (7" H x 6-3/4" W x 2-1/4" W at Base)-Signed*

R. *Lalique France.* [photograph]. Retrieved from www.etsy.com

EyeScandi. (n.d.).*Vintage 1960's "Sunflowers" Candle Holders by Kosta Boda-Design by Ann & Goran Warff-Rare 7-1/4" H , 4-3/8" H and 3-1/2" H-3 Set of Three.* [photograph]. Retrieved from www.etsy.com

Chapter VI

Erinscloset. (n.d.). *Vintage "Peacock" Pattern Chenille Bedspread 92" x 96".* [photograph]. Retrieved from www.ebay.com

Elaine Frazier@buffalogalsgallery. (n.d.). *Vintage Chenille Peacock Bedspread 92" x 98".* [photograph]. Retrieved from www.etsy.com

Sewbuzyb. (n.d.). *Vintage Hofmann Chenille Bedspread-Daisy Pattern Example. [photograph].* Retrieved from www.etsy.com

Linda Pearson@SnowyCreekDesigns. (n.d.) *Green White Hofmann Chenille Bedspread -96" x 109".* [photograph] Retrieved from www.etsy.com

Leslie Sturt@LooLuu's. (n.d.). *Vintage Cowboy Chenille Bedspread. [photograph].* Retrieved from www.rubylane.com

Marsha Beaton@The Loft Antiques. (n.d.). *Gorgeous Vintage "Hearts" and Flowers Motif Chenille Bedspread.* [photograph]. Retrieved from www.rubylane.com

Brenda Anne@RiversideMills. (n.d.). *Vintage 1950's Bates Blue and White, Matelassé-Americana Bedspread (112"L x 96" W).* [photograph]. Retrieved from www.etsy.com

Danielle Tideberg@AntiquesandVaria. (n.d.). *Historical 1910. Textile Camp Trade Indian Blanket (70" x 80") -Joined Robes/Shawl Blanket.* [photograph]. Retrieved from www.etsy.com

PaintitBlackVintage. (n.d.). *Vintage Pendleton Westerly, Cowichan- Big Lebowski "Dude" Shawl Collar, Sweater.* [photograph]. Retrieved from www.etsy.com

TobyJames@ElevatedWeirdo. (n.d.). *Vintage 1960's Peter Max Inspired, Psychedelic Set of Bed Sheets.* [photograph]. Retrieved from www.etsy.com

Chapter VII

HollyDale@lilypondvintage. (n.d.). *Vintage 1940's Carre Sunburst Spring Iron Garden Chair.* [photograph]. Retrieved from www.etsy.com

Jacqueline Flansburg@idaseyeantiques. (n.d.). *Vintage Salterini Hoop Mid-Century Tete-A-Tete Radar Patio Table and Chairs.* [photograph]. Retrieved from www.etsy.com

Susan@PinstripeVintage. (n.d.). *Vintage Large Samsonite, Bermuda Green Marble Suitcase With Key.* [photograph]. Retrieved from www.etsy.com

Susan@PinstripeVintage. (n.d.) *Vintage 1940's-1950's, Samsonite Colorado Brown Round Train Case.* [photograph]. Retrieved from www.etsy.com

Christine@CollectandRecollect. (n.d.). *Vintage 1940's Aero Pak Stripe Hard-Shell Suit Case-26" x 16" H x 8.5.* [photograph]. Retrieved from www.etsy.com

Lana@Sovintagepatterns.com. (n.d.). *1970's Vogue American Designer Dress Pattern - Diane Von Furstenberg Wrap Dress.* [photograph]. Retrieved from www.etsy.com

Chapter VIII

Amber Otten@Santashauntedboot. (n.d.). *Vintage Halloween Decor, Large 1920's German Embossed Black Cat, Moon, Stars Die Cut.* [photograph]. Retrieved from www.etsy.com

Deb@Whimzythyme. (n.d.). *Vintage Halloween Tin Litho Toy Noisemaker.* [photograph]. Retrieved from www.etsy.com

Jeff Baron@vintagebaron. (n.d.). *Famous Monsters of Filmland 1966 Yearbook Magazine.* [photograph]. Retrieved from www.etsy.com

MISS 5000@MISSVINTAGE5000. (n.d.). *Vintage Topps-Wacky Pack With Stickers-Never Used.* [photograph]. Retrieved from www.etsy.com

Mel@ApplePickerVintage. (n.d.). *1980's Topps GPK Series 2-42a42b Pin Card.* [photograph]. Retrieved from www.etsy.com

Huff Jones@blackfedora541. (n.d.). *Rare Las Vegas 1960s, $100 EL CORTEZ Casino Chip, sold for $4,550 on eBay July, 2015.* [photograph]. Retrieved from www.ebay.com

MisterBibs Vintage@MisterBibs. (n.d.). *Rare Las Vegas 1960s, $100 EL CORTEZ Casino Chip, sold for $4,550 on eBay July, 2015.* [photograph]. Retrieved from www.etsy.com

Kristine Anderson@LoungeActVintage. (n.d.). *Vintage Mid-century Mod Blue Green "Sharkskin" Suit Made in England by Oxford Street.* [photograph]. Retrieved from www.etsy.com

Chapter IX

Krista Morrison@StarShineVintage. (n.d.). *Vintage 1980's Puka Shell Hawaiian Surfer Necklace & Earrings.* [photograph]. Retrieved from www.etsy.com

Jasja Boelhouwer@Cavemanteeks. (n.d.). *Vintage 1950's Hale Hawaii Crepe, Rayon Men's Shirt with Coconut Husk Buttons.* [photograph]. Retrieved from www.etsy.com

Carrie@Mymodfun. (n.d.). *Vintage Mid-century 3-D Danish Witco Kitchen knife fork spoon Wood Art Painting 40x30".* [photograph]. Retrieved from www.etsy.com

Urban Americana@UrbanAmericana. (n.d.). *Vintage Witco Tiki Bar Stools.* [photograph]. Retrieved from www.etsy.com

Elizabeth Leffler@BoughWowsFleaMarket. (n.d.). *1970's Tiki Bench with Leopard Print Seat 68" x 18" x 12".* [photograph]. Retrieved from www.etsy.com

Michael@RECAP Restoration-RecapRestorations. (n.d.). *Vintage Mid-century Witco Wood "Oceanic" Credenza Cabinet.* [photograph]. Retrieved from www.etsy.com

Tinasdolls1993. (n.d.). *Walt Disney "Frozen" Dolls- 17" Elsa and Anna-NIB.* [photograph]. Retrieved from www.ebay.com

Kathy@DKCollectibles. (n.d.). *Walt Disney's "Beauty and the Beast"-Mrs. Pott and Chip Tea Set-MIB.* [photograph]. Retrieved from www.etsy.com

Brandi S.@twinklelotsVintage. (n.d.). *Disney 1990 "Kit Cloudkicker" Stuffed Animal.* [photograph]. Retrieved from www.etsy.com

Volunteer816. (n.d.). *Vintage 1979 Mego "Black Hole" Set of Six, 12.5" Action Figures.* [photograph]. Retrieved from www.ebay.com

Krystian & Mary@SameKVintage. (n.d.). *1950's Ray-Ban Bausch & Lomb, Aviator RB3 Mini Outdoorsman 12KGF-Green Lens, Sunglasses.* [photograph]. Retrieved from www.etsy.com

Tolly in Gilroy (WW2MILITARYITEMS)-(Tolly4-eBay user name). (n.d.). *WWII Army Air Corps A-11 Leather Flight Helmet & USAAF A-N 6530 Goggles With an A-14 Oxygen Mark.* [photograph]. Retrieved from www.etsy.com

Cheryl Sundberg@cherylanngoods. (n.d.). *Vintage 1920's Southern Pacific Lines, "Sunset Pattern" Platter by Syracuse.* [photograph]. Retrieved from www.etsy.com

Ric@RicsRelics. (n.d.). *Antique Railroad Signal Light Adlake Switch Lamp, 4" Lenses, 16-1/2" H.* [photograph]. Retrieved from www.etsy.com

Stuart Levy@DesperadoesEmporium. (n.d.). *1920's Arlington Mfg. Dressel Stationary Railroad Lamp (three yellow lenses and one red).* [photograph]. Retrieved from www.etsy.com

Linda@TheArtifactAttic. (n.d.). *Rare Antique D.L. & W.R.R Dietz Vesta Railroad Portable Lantern #14812.* [photograph]. Retrieved from www.etsy.com

Eddie@collectofanatic. (n.d.). *Circa -1910-1920, Carton of Ten Packs of "Camel" Cigarettes.* [photograph]. Retrieved from www.ebay.com

Brian and Ross@ModernJelly. (n.d.). *1950's Atomic Age, Shawnee Pink & Gold "Boomerang" Pottery Ashtray.* [photograph]. Retrieved from www.etsy.com

Nancy@TheGrooveVintage. (n.d.). *Vintage 1950's Mid-century, Signed, Barbara Willis Ceramic Modernist Ashtray (7.75").* [photograph]. Retrieved from www.etsy.com

Marjolein van der Slikke@DECONAMIC, Antwerp, Belgium. (n.d.). *Art Deco Wrought Iron Edgar Brandt Polar Bear Ashtray.* [photograph]. Retrieved from www.1stdibs.com

Gloria Rogers@Mendocino Vintage. (n.d.). *Nouveau Sterling Silver Repoussé Winged Horse Cigarette Case Art.* [photograph]. Retrieved from www.rubylane.com

Jeff@RetroCot. (n.d.). *Vintage 1982 ZIPPO Walt Disney World Epcot Cigarette Lighter.* [photograph]. Retrieved from www.etsy.com

Victorandmargie@LitttleGypsyVagabond. (n.d.). *Vintage 1950's-Skier Evans Clear-*

float Lucite Table Lighter with a Chrome Finish (3-3/4"H x 2-1/8" W x 2-5/8" D. [photograph]. Retrieved from www.etsy.com

Ed & Carolyn Sunday@SundayandSunday. (n.d.). *Vintage 1930's Deco Enamel and Chrome-Ronson T132C&E Cigarette Case Lighter-Unused.* [photograph]. Retrieved from www.etsy.com

Curt Butterfield@ELVISCOSTUMES. (n.d.). *1969 Elvis Presley-Style Gold- World Record Attendance Belt Buckle Replica* [photograph]. Retrieved from www.etsy.com

Pap1ka--eBay User Title. (n.d.). *Vintage 1983, Augustus Owsley Stanley "Steal Your Face" #1 Silver Belt Buckle.* [photograph]. Retrieved from www.ebay.com

Ron Bowers@spuranch--eBay User Title). (n.d.). *Vintage Sterling Silver Crockett Spurs.* [photograph]. Retrieved from www.ebay.com

Gooser2012—eBay User Title. (n.d.). *Vintage Pre-1920's, Western Cowboy McChesney "Bottle Opener" Spurs.* [photograph]. Retrieved from www.ebay.com

Bkwilley—eBay User Title. (n.d.). *1968 Western Marx Fort Apache Toy Set#3681.* [photograph]. Retrieved from www.ebay.com

Bernie McMahon@cowpunkabilly. (n.d.). *Vintage '50s Karman Gabardine Western Shirt Green With Gold Piping.* [photograph]. Retrieved from www.etsy.com

Marc Joseph@Wonderama. (n.d.). *Vintage California Ranchwear, Gabardine Western Shirt.* [photograph]. Retrieved from www.etsy.com

Ruthie Polyard@RuthiesThisandThat. (n.d.). *Vintage 1960's Monterrey Western Ware-Enamelware "Cowboy" Coffee Pot.* [photograph]. Retrieved from www.etsy.com

Krispy2eric—ebay User Title. (n.d.). *Vintage 1950s Roy Rogers Gold Foil and Red Jeweled- Gun Holster with Guns, Bullets.* [photograph]. Retrieved from www.ebay.com

Jonasmaggie12850—eBay User Title. (n.d.). *Vintage Time, Ingersoll HOPALONG CASSIDY, Wrist Watch with Original Box.* [photograph]. Retrieved from www.ebay.com

Chapter XI

Drawing by Harry Richardson (page 283). 1953, *Holiday Magazine*

Chris and Heather White@StudiobySerendipity. (n.d.). *MCM Heywood Wakefield Whale Bone Dog Biscuit Captain's Dining Arm Chair.* [photograph]. Retrieved from www.etsy.com

Millea Bros Ltd. (n.d.) *Mid-Century, Edward Wormley Sofa by Dunbar.* [photograph]. Retrieved from Auctions@LiveAuctioneers.com

E.G. Valentine@PoshPicker (n.d.). *Vintage 1970's 3-Tier Lucite Bar Cart.* [photograph]. Retrieved from www.etsy.com

Delonna@BOBBLESnBLING. (n.d.). *1950's Clear Carved Lucite Purse/Handbag.* [photograph]. Retrieved from www.etsy.com

Nickie Noel@SPUNKvtg. (n.d.). *Antique Arts and Crafts Era, Mission William Morris Reclining Chair.* [photograph]. Retrieved from www.etsy.com

Amanda Fox@20cmodern.com. (n.d.). *Vintage Mid-Century, C. Jere. Signer, Brass "Raindrops" Wall Art Sculpture.* [photograph]. Retrieved from www.etsy.com

Patti@PattiandCo. (Vua de' Federighi, 10/r-Florence, Italy) (n.d.) *1960's Emilio Pucci Designed Ladies Dress. [photograph].* Retrieved from www.etsy.com

Barb Goodwin@EmptyNestVintage. (n.d.). *Vintage Culver Red and Gold Paisley Barware Set with Caddy.* [photograph]. Retrieved from www.etsy.com

Eli White@LightlySaucedRetro. (n.d.). *Vintage 1960's Culver, Rare New Orleans, 22K Jester Rhinestone Highballs 4 Gold Dancing Harlequins, Jeweled Bar Glasses Set.* [photograph]. Retrieved from www.etsy.com

Ian & Barbara Janes@TouchstoneVintage. (n.d). *Vintage Murano, Venini- Blown Art Glass Hollow Paperweight.* [photograph]. Retrieved from www.etsy.com

Deb Suwala@ZeeJunkHunter. (n.d.). *Vintage 1960's Mid-Century, Chrome Arc Floor Lamp "Eyeball" Spot Light with Rotating Arm on Heavy Steel Base.* [photograph]. Retrieved from www.etsy.com

Janet@BooksShop. (n.d.). *Vintage 23" Double Spun Metal Cone-Shaped Desk Lamp.* [photograph]. Retrieved from www.etsy.com

Raymond@collectors-row.com. (n.d.). *Vintage Mid-Century, Laurel "Mushroom" Lamp.* [photograph]. Retrieved from www.rubyland.com

Katherine M@FunkyJunkMarketplace. (n.d.). *Vintage 1955 Econolite "Niagara Falls" Motion Lamp.* [photograph]. Retrieved from www.etsy.com

MollyFinds. (n.d.). *Vintage 1970's Goddess, Oil-Dripping "Rain" Motion Light, Table Lamp.* [photograph]. Retrieved from www.etsy.com

Teri Goodson@tigvintage. (n.d.). *Los Castillo Taxco Sea Star brooch / Pendant (2-3/8"), Sterling silver & Mozaico Azteca Stone Inlay.* [photograph]. Retrieved from www.etsy.com

Krista@FinickyForager. (n.d). *Vintage Victorian Edwardian 14K Hollow Yellow Gold, Bohemian Garnet Seed Brooch.* [photograph]. Retrieved from www.etsy.com

Stacy LoAlbo@IncogneetoVintage (Somerville, N. J.). (n.d.) *Ultra Rare Vintage 1981 JUDITH LEIBER Chinese Hand Warmer Purse with Swarovski Crystals Minaudiere Handbag.* [photograph] Retrieved from www.etsy.com

Ann Mills@CollectionsbyAnn2. (n.d.). *Vintage Judith Leiber Black And White Crystal Jeweled Minaudiere Handbag.* [photograph]. Retrieved from www.etsy.com

Chapter XII

Fx2452-eBay User Title. (n.d.). *Vintage Christian Dior, "Miss Dior", Baccarat Crystal Perfume Bottle.* [photograph]. Retrieved from www.ebay.com

Movieguy1920-eBay User. (n.d.) *Vintage Nini Ricci, "L' air Du Temps Parfum-Sealed With Lalique Bottle, Frosted Doves Stopper.* [photograph]. Retrieved from www.ebay.com

Veronica@VintageMeetModern. (n.d.). *Vintage 1930's Schiaparelli "Shocking Pink" Mae West- Nude Torso Shaped Perfume Bottle.* [photograph]. Retrieved from www.etsy.com

Bea@Retiredhungarian. (n.d.). *Vintage 1960's Faberge Gift Set-Tigress, Aphrodisia & Woodhue Colognes (1.5 Ounce each).* [photograph]. Retrieved by www.etsy.com

Debra Webb@Time Portal. (n.d.). *Vintage Original 1950's Tigress Cologne By Faberge 6 oz With Faux Fur Cap.* [photograph]. Retrieved from www.etsy.com

Dazedandvintage.com. (n.d.). *Vintage '70s Farrah Fawcett/Charlie's Angels Tee-Shirt.* [photograph]. Retrieved from www.etsy.com

Coveted Castoffs. (n.d.). *1950s Prince Matchabelli (Deco Nouveau, 1/2 Oz Crystal Blue Opaque Enamel Gold Maltese Cross & Crown- Perfume Bottle.* [photograph]. Retrieved from www.etsy.com

Susan@MyVintageBowtique. (n.d.). *Vintage Prince Matchabelli Stradivari *SEALED 1 Fluid Ounce Perfume Crown Bottle with Presentation Box.* [photograph]. Retrieved from www.etsy.com

Susan@MyVintageBowtique. (n.d). *Estee Lauder Ultra Rare 1990's BLUE FISH Sea Stars Collection Lucidity Powder Compact.* [photograph]. Retrieved from www.etsy.com

Dave D.@VintageBlade. (n.d.). *Vintage 1958 Rare D3 Gillette-Executive, Adjustable Safety Razor with Partial Case.* [photograph]. Retrieved from www.etsy.com

Susan@MyVintageBowtique. (n.d.). *1960's Stratton England, Horoscope/Astrology Powder Compact.* [photograph]. Retrieved from www.etsy.com

Bewitched1981-eBay User Title. (n.d.). *Vintage Yardley of London Glimmerick Water Color Eye Shadow-Unused.* [photograph]. Retrieved from www.ebay.com

Ken & Karen@RedlandsVintage. (n.d.). Antique Art Deco Purple Glass and Brass Door Knobs. [photograph]. Retrieved from www.etsy.com

Angela Henderson@filigreefairy. (n.d.). *Vintage Enesco Glazed Mermaid and Dolphin Bathroom Wall Pocket Plaque (5" H x 5-1/2" W).* [photograph]. Retrieved from www.etsy.com

Chris Franklin@vintagewonderforever. (n.d.). *Vintage Ceramicraft Bathroom Brown, Green and Pink Fish Wall Pocket.* [photograph]. Retrieved from www.etsy.com

Bibliography

Marsh, Graham and Paul Trynka. *Denim- From Cowboys to Catwalks, A Visual History of the World's Most legendary Fabric*, London, England: Aurum Press Limited, 2002.

Pages 31, 36-37 & 45, 66

Aronson, Joseph. *The Encyclopedia of Furniture Third Edition.* New York, NY: Clarkson Potter Publishers, 1965.

Pages 308-309, 311

Aronson, Joseph. *The book of furniture and decoration: period and modern.* New York, NY: Crown Publishers, Inc, 1937.

Pages 308-309

Simonds, Cherri. *Collectible Costume Jewelry Identification & Values.* Paducah, KY: Collectors Books, 1997.

(Definition of Bakelite)

Cockrill, Pauline. *The Teddy Bear Encyclopedia.* New York, NY: Dorling Kindersley, Inc, 199.

Page 113

Pina, Leslie. *Blenko Glass 1962-1971 Catalogs.* Atglen, PA: Schiffer Publishing Ltd., 2000.

Pages 4, 5

Baker, Stanley L. *Railroad Collectibles: An Illustrated Value Guide, 4th Edition.* Paducah, KY: Collector Books, 1990.

Pages 84, 88, 89, 90, 91, 100-105

Website References

"Legends and Legacies." *Legacy*. 4 Nov. 2010. Web. 7 Nov. 2015.

"Barbie Vintage Dolls Identified 1959-1962." *Barbie Vintage Dolls Identified 1959-1962*. Web. 7 Sept. 2015.

"The Barbie Collection." *The Barbie Collection*. Web. 7 Sept. 2015.

"Herbie's World of Kitsch & Toys: Barbie Green Ear Syndrome." *Herbie's World of Kitsch & Toys: Barbie Green Ear Syndrome*. Web. 21 Sept. 2012.

"Doll Care and Restoration Tips." *Doll Care and Restoration Tips*. Web. 7 Oct. 2015.

"Doll Cleaning Tips." *Doll Cleaning Tips*. Web. 11 Sept. 2015.

"6 Ways to Tell If Your Bakelite Is Authentic." *About.com Home*. Web. 7 Nov. 2015.

"Vintage Apple Computer Sells For $668,000." *Business Insider*. Business Insider, Inc, 25 May 2013. Web. 13 June 2015.

"Atlanta Antique Gallery - Rushton Toys." *Rushton Toys*. Web. 14 Nov. 2015.

"Bakelite First Synthetic Plastic - National Historic Chemical Landmark." *American Chemical Society*. Web. 1 Nov. 2015.

"11 Insanely Expensive Vintage Sneakers For Sale On EBay." *Total Pro Sports RSS*. Web. 7 May 2015.

"Margaret Keane - Keen Look, Inc." *Margaret Keane Gallery*. Web. 3 Mar. 2015.

"Traditional Auction Tips." *Auction Tips*. Web. 16 Sept. 2015.

"The 10 Most Ridiculously Expensive Items Ever Sold On EBay." *Complex*. Web. 7 Nov. 2015.

"Schuco Bears." *Schuco Bears*. Web. 3 Aug. 2015.

"EBay." *What Is ? A Webopedia Definition*. Web. 7 Nov. 2015.

"13 of the Most Expensive Items Ever Sold on EBay." *Refined Guy RSS*. Web. 7 Nov. 2015.

"The Richest People in Tech." *Forbes*. Forbes Magazine. Web. 17 May 2015.

McGrath, Skip. "77 Tips and Tools for Selling on the New Ebay." *SkipMcgrath.com*. Web. 9 May 2015.

"EBay Case Study - Smart Insights Digital Marketing Advice." *Smart Insights*. 24 June 2013. Web. 7 Nov. 2015.

"Difference Between Art Nouveau and Art Deco Designs." *Interior Design, Design News and Architecture Trends*. 6 Apr. 2013. Web. 7 Nov. 2015.

"15 EBay Listing Tools to Make Selling Online Easier, Faster." *15 EBay Listing Tools to Make Selling Online Easier, Faster.* Web. 15 May 2015.

"Free Background Textures Library." *Background Textures and Images Library, Free Download.* N.p., n.d. Web. 09 Nov. 2015.

"EBay Help: Community Standards: EBay Help: Rules and Safety." *EBay Help: Community Standards: EBay Help: Rules and Safety.* Web. 14 Oct. 2015.

"How to Make Money on Amazon." *How to Make Money on Amazon.* Web. 8 Nov. 2015.

"Getting Started Collecting Kitchen Items May Be Something That Happens By Mistake." *Tribunedigital-chicagotribune.* 21 May 1995. Web. 8 Nov. 2015.

"Vera." *Vintage Fashion Guild : Label Resource :.* Web. 8 Nov. 2015.

"Just Collectibles." *Holt Howard.* Web. 8 Nov. 2015.

"Antique Holt-Howard | Pottery & Porcelain Price Guide | Antiques & Collectibles Price Guide | Kovels.com."

Antique Holt-Howard | Pottery & Porcelain Price Guide | Antiques & Collectibles Price Guide | Kovels.com. Web. 8 Nov. 2015.

"Christmas Peanut Butter Glasses by Barbara E. Mauzy." *- I Antique Online.* Web. 8 Nov. 2015.

"Cathrineholm – a Norwegian Design Classic." *ThorNews.* 27 Feb. 2012. Web. 8 Nov. 2015.

Reif, Rita. "Warhol Cookie Jars Sell for $247,830." *The New York Times.* The New York Times, 24 Apr. 1988. Web. 8 Nov. 2015.

"Pyrex Vintage Pattern Guide : Pyrex Love." *Pyrex Vintage Pattern Guide : Pyrex Love.* Web. 8 Nov. 2015.

"Of Frisbees/Flying Discs - What Is Ultimate." *What Is Ultimate.* Web. 8 Nov. 2015.

"The IRTP Statement." *The IRTP Statement.* Web. 8 Nov. 2015.

"How to Date Cans." *Beer Can Info.* Web. 8 Nov. 2015.

"Dating Cans." *Dating Cans.* Web. 8 Nov. 2015.

"Antique Coffee Tins - A Beginners Guide to Collecting." *Vintage Virtue.* Web. 8 Nov. 2015.

"Jobbers." *Made in Nebraska Exhibit,.* Web. 8 Nov. 2015.

"The Lace Guild." *The Craft of Lace.* Web. 18 July 2015.

"Zsa Zsa Gabor Biography." *Bio.com*. A&E Networks Television. Web. 18 Sept. 2015.

"The Charles Hosmer - Morse Museum of American Art." *Secrets of Tiffany Glassmaking*. Web. 12 Sept. 2015.

"Antique Glass: Lalique Glass." *Collecting Rene Lalique Glass Car Mascots & Perfume Bottles*. Web. 4 May 2015.

"Glass Identification: Signatures Markings." *Glass Identification: Signatures Marks*. Web. 8 Nov. 2015.

"Discover Mid-America | The Antique Detective." *Discover Mid-America | The Antique Detective*. Web. 9 Nov. 2015.

"When Money Is No Object – 14 Of The Most Expensive Gifts Disney Has to Offer." *DisneyFanaticcom*. 29 Aug. 2014. Web. 9 Nov. 2015.

"Rare Retired Discount Swarovski Crystal Collectibles at Crystal Exchange America!" *Swarovski Star Ornaments and Swarovski Snowflake Ornaments at CrystalExchange.com!* Web. 9 Aug. 2015.
"Maxfield Parrish." *Real Or Repro ~ Identifying Fakes and Reproductions*. Web. 9 Apr. 2015.

"American Antique Crazy Quilts." Web. 2 Nov. 2015.

"Handmade Jane: All about Bark Cloth." *Handmade Jane: All about Bark Cloth*. Web. 7 July 2015.

"Matelasse Bedspreads." *LoveToKnow*. Web. 21 May 2015.

"At Home: Collectors Snuggle up to Beacon Cotton Blankets." *DeseretNews.com*. 31 Jan. 2005. Web. 9 Nov. 2015.

The Definition of steampunk" from Oxford University Press. Retrieved on 6 October 2012."Antiques Attic." *: Blow Mold Craze and Some History*. Web. 9 Nov. 2015.

"Tips for Determining When a U.S. Postcard Was Published." *Tips for Determining When a U.S. Postcard Was Published*. Web. 19 Mar. 2015.

"The Vintage Halloween Website: Noisemakers." *The Vintage Halloween Website: Noisemakers*. Web. 20 June 2015.

"Bubbledog's TREND Scratch 'n Sniff Sticker Collection." *Bubbledog's TREND Scratch 'n Sniff Sticker Collection*. Web. 5 Nov. 2015.

"Wacky Packages Wacky Ads - 1969." *Wacky Packages Wacky Ads - 1969*. Web. 10 June 2015.

"WD & HO Wills Tobacco Manufacturer - History and Timeline." *WD & HO Wills Tobacco Manufacturer - History and Timeline*. Web. 20 Oct. 2015.

"CJCA - Cracker Jack Collectors Association - History & Lore." *CJCA - Cracker Jack*

Collectors Association - History & Lore. Web. 16 July 2015.

"How Much Are Your Old Records Really Worth?" *How Much Are Your Old Records Really Worth?* Web. 9 Nov. 2015.

"Grading." *Certified Guaranty Company, LLC.* Web. 5 Apr. 2015.

"Collecting Casino Chips Isn't Just For Gamblers." *From the Cotton Patch.* 2 Aug. 2008. Web. 9 Nov. 2015.

"Vegas Casino History - Flamingo Hotel." *About.com Home.* Web. 9 Nov. 2015.

"Implosions - Las Vegas Sun News." *Implosions - Las Vegas Sun News.* Web. 19 Nov. 2015.

"Howard Hughes: A Revolutionary Recluse." *LasVegasSun.com.* 15 May 2008. Web. 23 Nov. 2015.

"Hawaiian Aloha Shirts." *Collectors Weekly.* Web. 12 Sept. 2015.

"William Leigh: Confederate States Central Government Buttons." *William Leigh: Confederate States Central Government Buttons.* Web. 9 Nov. 2015.

"History-Luftwaffle." *BBC News.* BBC. Web. 9 Nov. 2015.

Antiques Roadshow Collectibles-Antiques & Collectibles 2003 Carol Prisant, Page 316

"10 Fascinating Facts About Charles Lindbergh." *History.com.* A&E Television Networks. Web. 8 Nov. 2015.

"The History of Syracuse China." Web. 6 July 2015.

"Antique Railroad Lantern Value Guide | Antique Railroad Memorabilia." *Antique Railroad Memorabilia.* Web. 9 Nov. 2015.
"JeffPo's Railroad Locks Page." *JeffPo's Railroad Locks Page.* Web. 9 Nov. 2015.

"Cigarette Pack Covers." *Cigarette Pack Covers.* Web. 9 Nov. 2015.

"Cigarette Cases of Rich and Famous." *Tribunedigital-baltimoresun.* 18 Nov. 1990. Web. 8 Nov. 2015.

"Dunhill Lighters." - *Miller's Antiques & Collectibles Price Guide.* Web. 8 Nov. 2015.

"The History of Marx." *Information Marx History.* Web. 9 Nov. 2015.

"Tin Litho Toys - Antique Toys Today." *Antique Toys Today.* 21 June 2009. Web. 8 Nov. 2015.

"Jean Shepard Reflects on Her Life 'Down Through The Years'" *Billboard.* Web. 9 Nov. 2015.

"True West vs Wallace China." *The RWCN Forums.* 27 Jan. 2009. Web. 9 Nov. 2015.

"Roy Rogers Biography." *Roy Rogers Biography*. Web. 9 Nov. 2015.

"How to Identify Vintage Levi Jean Jackets." *InfoBarrel*. Web. 9 Nov. 2015.

"Learn the History." *Levis Vintage Clothing*. Web. 8 Apr. 2015.

"Lee." *Lee*. Web. 6 Mar. 2015.

"Our Story - DUNBAR." *Our Story - DUNBAR*. Web. 8 Nov. 2015.

"Who Is Herman Miller?" *Our Story*. Web. 13 July 2015.

"Knoll Group Inc. History." *History of Knoll Group Inc. – FundingUniverse*. Web. 9 Nov. 2015.

Walsh, Julia. "11 Midcentury Modern Furniture Brands You Should Know." Web. 8 Nov. 2015.

"Mad for Mid-Century: The History of Hairpin Legs." *Mad for Mid-Century: The History of Hairpin Legs*. Web. 9 Nov. 2015.

"Glasshouse Is Dead, Long Live Glasshouse." *Glasshouse Is Dead, Long Live Glasshouse*. Web. 9 Nov. 2015.

"History's Dumpster: Rain Lamps." *History's Dumpster: Rain Lamps*. Web. 9 Nov. 2015.

"Diamond Buying Guide - The 4 C's." *Diamond Grading and Buying Guide*. Web. 9 Nov. 2015.

"TWIGGY - THE OFFICIAL SITE." *TWIGGY - THE OFFICIAL SITE*. Web. 9 Nov. 2015.

"Jackie Kennedy's Pink Suit." *Lisas History Room*. 12 Feb. 2011. Web. 9 Nov. 2015.

"Enid Collins: An Interview with Her Son, Jeep." *The Vintage Traveler*. 18 June 2011. Web. 9 Nov. 2015.

"Purse Pursuit: Designer Embarks on a Shopping Spree to Bag Her Own Bags." *WSJ*. Web. 9 Nov. 2015.

"Schiaparelli Shocking : Vintage and Modern Perfume Review." *Bois De Jasmin*. Web. 9 Mar. 2015.

"History of Farrah Fawcett." *Bio.com*. A&E Networks Television. Web. 9 Nov. 2015.

"Basic Hallmarks Identification." *Basic Hallmarks Identification*. Web. 9 Nov. 2015.

"Enamels on Jewelry - AJU." *Enamels on Jewelry - AJU*. Web. 9 Nov. 2015.

"Antique Doorknob Identification." *LoveToKnow*. Web. 9 Nov. 2015.

About the Author

My name is Patricia Penke, and I want to welcome my readers!

Here is a little history about myself: I was born in Massachusetts to a father and mother who had a passion to search for different types of buried treasure. Whether it was searching in caves, or forests of New England in search of semi-precious gemstones; mining for gold in Alaska, digging for 18th century relics in dump sites in Virginia; or metal-detecting for Blackbeard's buried treasure off the coast of North Carolina, my childhood was always full of adventure.

As time went on, my parents introduced me to a new form of treasure hunting: The world of discovering and selling valuable antiques and collectibles. It wasn't but a few years later I learned about the wonderful "World Wide Web." Since 2002, I have been generating a substantial profit margin by selling collectibles and antiques online.

During the last 17 years of being a vintage merchandise retailer, I acquired an abundance of experience evaluating, and appraising vintage and antique merchandise. Additionally, I began studying current and up-to-date buying trends in the second-hand consumer market.

I attribute my success in selling collectibles in researching, and discovering where to find these bargained hidden gems. With endless hours of research found in resources, such as the internet, and reading antique reference books. Additionally, by observing buyers at auctions and attending countless garage-tag sales, estate sales and auctions, were all necessary to being in the "know." My research and excellent reputation in the community, as well as my experiences finding and selling second-hand merchandise, has tremendously helped to me to start my own estate sale company: Assisting Hands Estate Sales and Services, located in Omaha, NE.

Since I started this business most clients would call and state, "We have tossed away most of the JUNK before the estate sale- into a dumpster." I thought to myself, "Oh, I hope nothing valuable was thrown away by mistake." Family members or acquaintances are unfortunately tossing some unknown *cash* away- not trash.

I decided it was time to try and educate the public on how to find these hidden treasures among household castoffs, and writing a book entered my mind.

In 2013 and 2014, I wrote a successful weekly article titled "Creating Cash from Trash" in *Fuse Weekly's* Digital Entertainment Magazine. The articles were a success, which helped me make my decision to write this book with hopes of more volumes to follow.

I have hopeful expectations of educating a much larger audience about making money by finding and selling what is believed to be worthless castoffs.

My readers will be able recognize some of those "low-cost" hidden gems, and how to properly resell them for a substantial amount of CASH profit.

This all-in-one resource book is for anyone interested in making some CASH, and reading a nostalgic, educational book.

Acknowledgements

I want to share my enduring gratitude to my family and close family friends for making the quest to create this book a success.

I would like to express my sincere thanks and appreciation to Mrs. Gina Foutch for her enduring support, patience, knowledge and talents with editing and putting this book together. Without you—my dear baby girl—this book would not of been successful.

George Penke, my husband, for his endless support and having to endure the numerous late nights and days watching me write this book, gather photos and brainstorming. Additionally, for being the driver and partner to several hundred auctions, garage sales, estate sales, thrift stores, junk jaunts and antique malls.

Rachel Penke, Mary Leland, Raymond Penke, Julie Rockwood, Ben Foutch, Chris Kelley, and Gigi Rock for their enthusiasm, constructive criticism, support, knowledge and encouragement. I have been working on writing this book for over 2 years, without their encouragement I was tempted a few times to give up my vision.

A special thanks for Mr. Joshua Foo. His patience, aesthetic sense of design and professional photography skills was outstanding for creating a fabulous cover for this book.

81432651R00209

Made in the USA
Columbia, SC
30 November 2017